UNIT – I
INTRODUCTION

1.1 INTRODUCTION:

A hybrid vehicle combines any two power (energy) sources. Possible combinations include diesel/electric, gasoline/fly wheel, and fuel cell (FC)/battery. Typically, one energy source is storage, and the other is conversion of a fuel to energy. The combination of two power sources may support two separate propulsion systems. Thus to be a True hybrid, the vehicle must have at least two modes of propulsion. For example, a truck that uses a diesel to drive a generator, which in turn drives several electrical motors for all-wheel drive, is *not a hybrid.* But if the truck has electrical energy storage to provide a second mode, which is electrical assists, then it is a hybrid Vehicle. These two power sources may be paired in series, meaning that the gas engine charges the batteries of an electric motor that powers the car, or in parallel, with both mechanisms driving the car directly.

CONVENTIONAL VEHICLES:

A conventional engine-driven vehicle uses its engine to translate fuel energy into shaft power, directing most of this power through the drive train to turn the wheels. Much of the heat generated by combustion cannot be used for work and is wasted, both because heat engines have theoretical efficiency limit. Moreover, it is impossible to reach the theoretical efficiency limit because:

• Some heat is lost through cylinder walls before it can do work

• Some fuel is burned at less than the highest possible pressure

• Fuel is also burned while the engine is experiencing negative load (during braking) or when the vehicle is coasting or at a stop, with the engine idling.

1.5. 1. BASIC VEHICLE PERFORMANCE:

The performance of a vehicle is usually described by its maximum cruisingspeed, gradeability, and acceleration. The predication of vehicle performanceis based on the relationship between tractive effort and vehicle speeddiscussed in Sections 2.5 and 2.6. For on-road vehicles, it is assumed thatthe maximum tractive effort is limited by the maximum torque of thepower plant rather than the road adhesion capability.

1.5.1.1. General Description of Vehicle Movement

Figure 2.1 shows the forces acting on a vehicle moving up a grade. The tractiveeffort, F_t, in the contact area between tires of the driven wheels and theroad surface propels the vehicle forward. It is produced by the power planttorque and is transferred through transmission and final drive to the drive wheels. While the vehicle is moving, there is resistance that tries to stop itsmovement. The resistance usually includes tire rolling resistance, aerodynamicdrag, and uphill resistance. According to Newton's second law, vehicle acceleration can be written aswhere $V$is vehicle speed, ΣF_tris the total tractive effort of the vehicle, $\Sigma F_{tr}$is the total resistance, $M_v$is the total mass of the vehicle, and δ is the mass factor,which is an effect of rotating components in the power train. Equation.

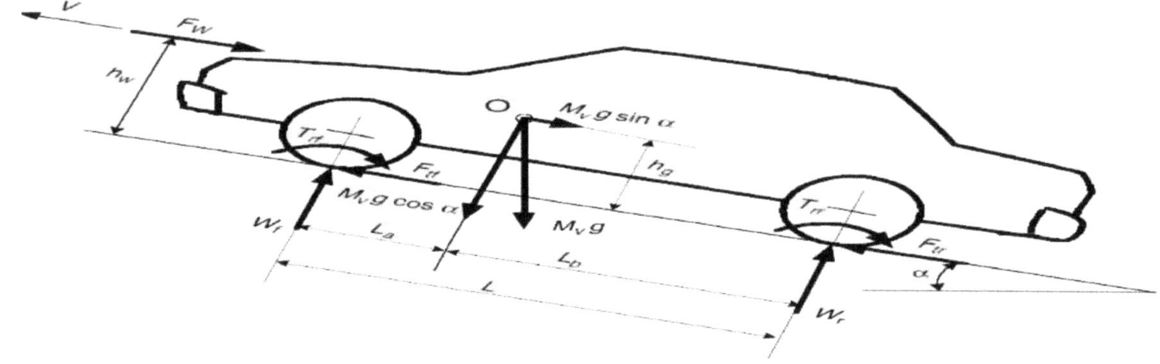

Figure 1.5.1.1. Forces acting on a vehicle

The above figindicates that speed and acceleration depend on tractive effort, resistance, And vehicle mass.

Vehicle Resistance

As shown in Figure 1.5.1.1, vehicle resistance opposing its movement includes rolling resistance of the tires, appearing in Figure 1.5..1 as rolling resistance torque *Trf*and*Trr*, aerodynamic drag, *Fw*, and grading resistance (the term*Mv g* sin α in Figure). All of the resistances will be discussed in detail inthe following sections.

Rolling Resistance

The rolling resistance of tires on hard surfaces is primarily caused by hysteresis in the tire materials. This is due to the deflection of the carcass while the tire is rolling. The hysteresis causes an asymmetric distribution of ground reaction forces. The pressure in the leading half of the contact area is larger than that in the trailing half, as shown in Figure1.5.1.1 (a).Thisphenomenonresults in the ground reaction force shifting forward. This forwardlyshifted ground reaction force, with the normal load acting on the wheel center,Creates a moment that opposes the rolling of the wheel. On soft surfaces, the rolling resistance is primarily caused by deformation of the ground surface as shown in Figure 1.5.1.1(b). The ground reaction force almost completely Shifts to the leading half.

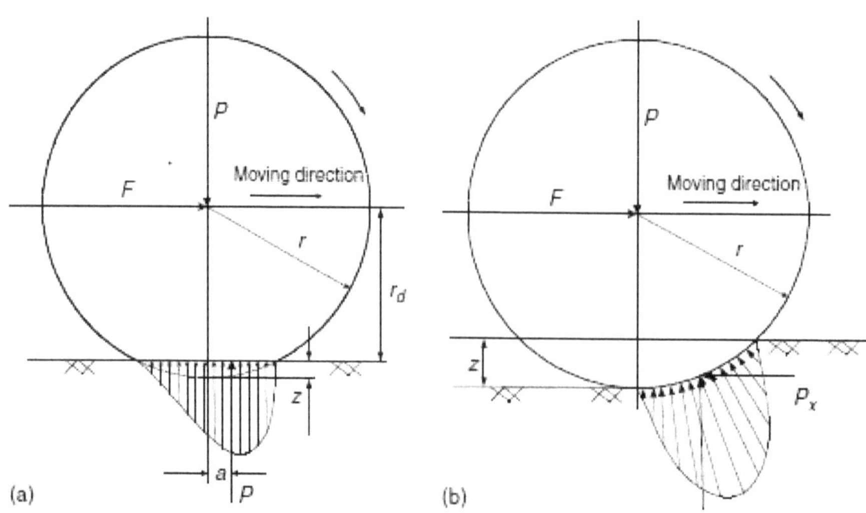

Figure 1.5.1.1(a)&(b): Tire deflection and rolling resistance on a (a) hard and (b) soft road surface

The moment produced by the forward shift of the resultant ground reaction force is called the rolling resistant moment, as shown in Figure 1.5.1.1(a),and can be expressed as

$$T_r = Pa. \quad \text{.........................eq.1}$$

To keep the wheel rolling, a force F, acting on the center of the wheels, is required to balance this rolling resistant moment. This force is expressed as

$$F = \frac{T_r}{r_d} = \frac{Pa}{r_d} = Pf_r, \quad \text{...........................eq.2}$$

Where$rd$is the effective radius of the tire and $fr= a/rd$is called the rolling resistance coefficient. In this way, the rolling resistant moment can be replaced equivalently by horizontal force acting on the wheel center in the opposite direction of the movement of the wheel. This equivalent force is called rolling resistance with a magnitude of

$$F_r = Pf_r, \quad \text{.......... eq.3}$$

Where P is the normal load, acting on the center of the rolling wheel. When a vehicle is operated on a slope road, the normal load, P, should be replaced by the component, which is perpendicular to the road surface. That is

$$F_r = Pf_r \cos\alpha. \quad \text{...................... eq.4}$$

The rolling resistance coefficient, fr, is a function of the tire material, tirestructure, tire temperature, tire inflation pressure, tread geometry, road roughness,road material, and the presence or absence.

The rolling resistance coefficient of passenger cars on concrete road may be calculated from the followingequation:

$$f_r = f_0 + f_s\left(\frac{V}{100}\right)^{2.5}, \quad \text{..................... eq.5}$$

Where$V$is vehicle speed in km/h, and $f0$ and fs depend on inflation pressureof the tire.1
In vehicle performance calculation, it is sufficient to consider the rollingresistance coefficient as a linear function of speed. For the most commonrange of inflation pressure, the following equation can be used for a passengercar on concrete road.

$$f_r = 0.01\left(1 + \frac{V}{100}\right). \quad \text{.................. eq.6}$$

This equation predicts the values of $fr$with acceptable accuracy for speeds upto128km/h.

1.5.1.2 Aerodynamic Drag:

Avehicle traveling at a particular speed in air encounters a force resisting itsmotion. This force isreferred to as aerodynamic drag. It mainly results fromtwo components: shape drag and skin friction.

Shape drag: The forward motion of the vehicle pushes the air in front of it. However, the air cannot instantaneously move out of the way and its pressures thus increased, resulting in high air pressure. In addition, the airbehind the vehicle cannot instantaneously fill the space left by the forward Motion of the vehicle. This creates a zone of low air pressure. The motion hastherefore created two zones of pressure that oppose the motion of a vehicleby pushing it forward (high pressure in front) and pulling it backward (lowpressure in the back) as shown in Figure . The resulting force on the vehicleis the shape drag.3

Skin friction: Air close to the skin of the vehicle moves almost at the speedof the vehicle while air far from the vehicle remains still.

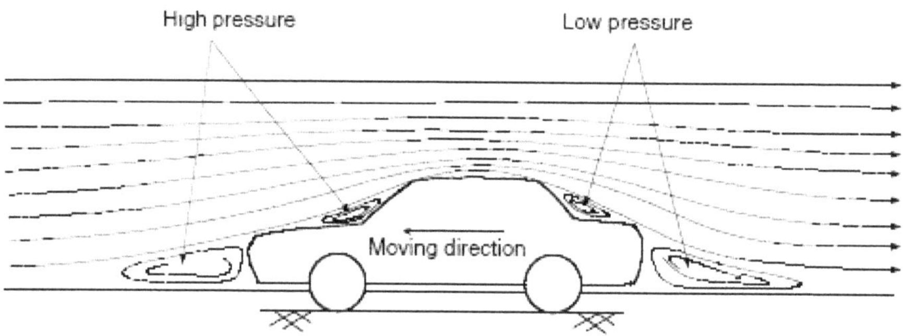

Figure 1.5.1.2. Shapedrag

molecules move at a wide range of speeds. The difference in speed betweentwo air molecules produces a friction that results in the second componentof aerodynamic drag.Aerodynamic drag is a function of vehicle speed *V*, vehicle frontal area *Af*,shape of the vehicle, and air density ρ. Aerodynamic drag is expressed as

$$F_w = \frac{1}{2}\rho A_f C_D (V+V_w)^2, \quad \text{......................................eq7}$$

where *CD* is the aerodynamic drag coefficient that characterizes the shape ofthe vehicle and *Vw*isthecomponent of wind speed on the vehicle's movingdirection, which has a positive sign when this component is opposite to thevehicle speed and a negative sign when it is in the same direction as vehiclespeed. The aerodynamic drag coefficients for a few types of vehicle bodyshapes are shown in Figure 1.5.1.3.

1.5.1.3. Grading Resistance

When a vehicle goes up or down a slope, its weight produces a component,which is always directed to the downward direction, as shown in Figure This component either opposes the forward motion (grade climbing) orhelps the forward motion (grade descending). In vehicle performance analysis,onuphill operation is considered. This grading force is usually calledgrading resistance.

Figure1.5.1.3. Indicative drag coefficients for different body shapes

Vehicle Type	Coefficient of Aerodymanic Resistance
Open convertible	0.5–0.7
Van body	0.5–0.7
Ponton body	0.4–0.55
Wedge-shaped body; headlamps and bumpers are integrated into the body, covered underbody, optimized cooling air flow	0.3–0.4
Headlamp and all wheels in body, covered underbody	0.2–0.25
K-shaped (small breakway section)	0.23
Optimum streamlined design	0.15–0.20
Trucks, road trains	0.8–1.5
Buses	0.6–0.7
Streamlined buses	0.3–0.4
Motorcycles	0.6–0.7

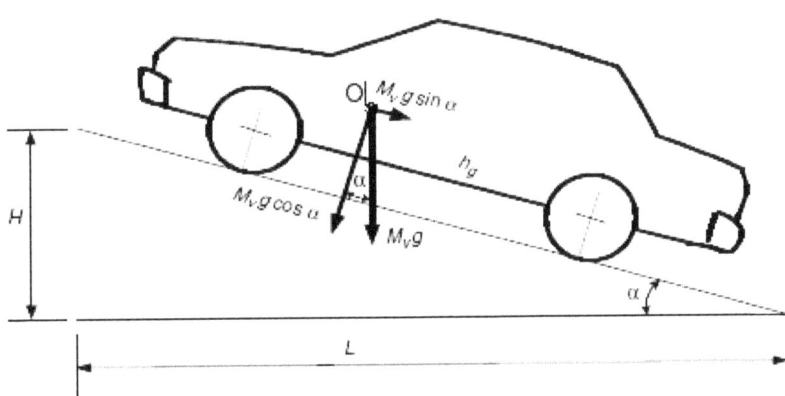

Figure 1.5.1.3. Automobile climbing a grade The grading resistance, from Figure 2.5, can be expressed as

$$F_g = M_v g \sin\alpha. \quad \text{...........eq8}$$

To simplify the calculation, the road angle, α, is usually replaced by grade valuewhen the road angle is small. As shown in Figure 1.5.1.3, the grade is defined as

$$i = \frac{H}{L} = \tan\alpha \approx \sin\alpha. \quad \text{...........eq9}$$

In some literature, the tire rolling resistance and grading resistance togetherare called road resistance, which is expressed as

$$F_{rd} = F_f + F_g = M_v g (f_r \cos\alpha + \sin\alpha). \quad \text{...............eq10}$$

When the road angle is small, the road resistance can be simplified as

$$F_{rd} = F_f + F_g = M_v g (f_r + i).$$

VEHICLE POWER SOURCE CHARACTERIZATION:

An automotive power train, as shown in Figure 2.8, consists of a power plant(engine or electric motor), a clutch in manual transmission or a torqueconverter in automatic transmission, a gearbox (transmission), final drive,

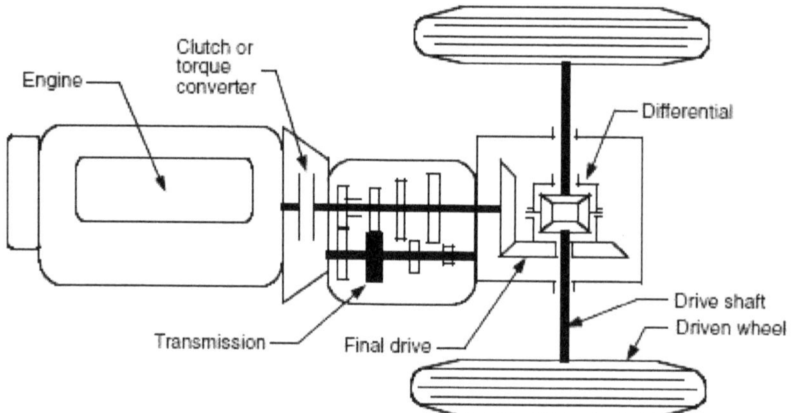

differential, drive shaft, and driven wheels. The torque and rotating speed ofthe power plant outputshaft are transmitted to the drive wheels through theclutch or torque converter, gearbox, final drive, differential, and drive shaft.

The clutch is used in manual transmission to couple the gearbox to or decoupleit from the power plant. The torque converter in automatic transmissionis a hydrodynamic device, functioning as the clutch in manual transmissionwith a continuously variable gear ratio.

Thegearbox supplies a few gear ratios from its input shaft to its output shaft forthe power plant torque–speed profile to match the requirements of the load.

The final drive is usually a pair of gears that supply a further speed reductionand distribute the torque to each wheel through the differential.

The torque on the driven wheels, transmitted from the powerplant, isexpressed as

$$T_w = i_g i_0 \eta_t T_p$$ eq1

where *ig* is the gear ratio of the transmission defined as *ig_Nin/Nout* (*Nin* —input rotating speed, *Nout* —output rotating speed), *i0* is the gear ratio of thefinal drive, η*t* is the efficiency of the driveline from the power plant to thedriven wheels, and *Tp* is the torque output from the power plant.

The tractive effort on the driven wheels, as shown in Figure 1.6, can beexpressed as

$$F_t = \frac{T_w}{r_d}$$ eq2

Substituting (eq1) into (eq2) yields the following result

$$F_t = \frac{T_p i_g i_0 \eta_t}{r_d}$$ eq3

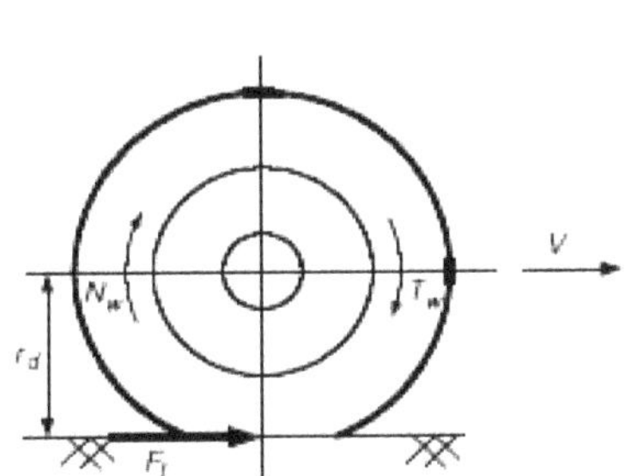

Figure 1.5.2.2: Tractive effort and torque on a driven wheel

The friction in the gear teeth and the friction in the bearings create losses inmechanical gear transmission. The following are representative values of the mechanical efficiency of various components:

Clutch: 99%

Each pair of gears: 95–97%

Bearing and joint: 98–99%

The total mechanical efficiency of the transmission between the engine outputshaft and drive wheels or sprocket is the product of the efficiencies of allthe components in the driveline. As a first approximation, the following average values of the overall mechanical efficiency of a manual gear-shift transmission may be used:

Direct gear: 90%

Other gear: 85%

Transmission with a very high reduction ratio: 75–80%

The rotating speed (rpm) of the driven wheel can be expressed as

$$N_w = \frac{N_p}{i_g i_0}, \quad \text{..........................eq4}$$

where Np is the output rotating speed (rpm). The translational speed of thewheelcenter (vehicle speed) can be expressed as

$$V = \frac{\pi N_w r_d}{30} \text{(m/s)}. \quad \text{..........................eq5}$$

Substituting (eq4) into (eq5) yields

$$V = \frac{\pi N_p r_d}{30 i_g i_0} \text{(m/s)} \quad \text{....................eq6}$$

VEHICLE POWER PLANT AND TRANSMISSION CHARACTERISTICS:

There are two limiting factors to the maximum tractive effort of a vehicle. One is the maximum tractive effort that the tire–ground contact can support and the other is the tractive effort that the power plant torque with given driveline gear ratios can provide (equation [2.29]). The smaller of these two factors will determine the performance potential of the vehicle. For on-road vehicles, the performance is usually limited by the second factor.

In order to predict the overall performance of a vehicle, its power plant and transmission characteristics must be taken into consideration.

1.5.2 .2.POWER PLANT CHARACTERISTICS:

For vehicular applications, the ideal performance characteristic of a power plant is the constant power output over the full speed range. Consequently, the torque varies with speed hyperbolically as shown in Figure 1.5.2.1.

At low speeds, the torque is constrained to be constant so as not to be over the maximaimited by the adhesion between the tire–ground contact areas. This constant power characteristic will provide the vehicle with a high tractive effortat low speed, where demands for acceleration, drawbar pull, or grade climbing capability are high.

Since the internal combustion engine and electric motor are the most commonly used power plants for automotive vehicles to date, it is appropriate to review the basic features of the characteristics that are essential to predicating vehicle performance and driveline design.

Representative characteristics of a gasoline engine in full throttle and an electric motor at full load are shown in Figure 1.5.2.2 and Figure 1.5.2.3, respectively.

The internal combustion engine usually has torque–speed characteristics far from the ideal performance characteristic required by traction. It starts operating smoothly at idle speed.

Good combustion quality and maximum engine torque are reached at an intermediate engine speed. As the speed increases further, the mean effective pressure decreases because of the growing losses in the air-induction manifold and a decline in engine torque.

Power output, however, increases to its maximum at a certain high speed. Beyond this point, the engine torque decreases more rapidly with increasing speed. This results in the decline of engine power output. In vehicular applications, the maximum permissible

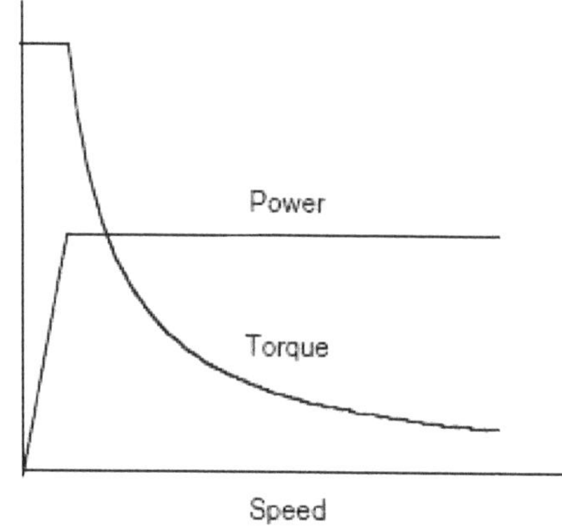

Figure1.5.2.1: Ideal performance characteristics for avehicle traction power plant

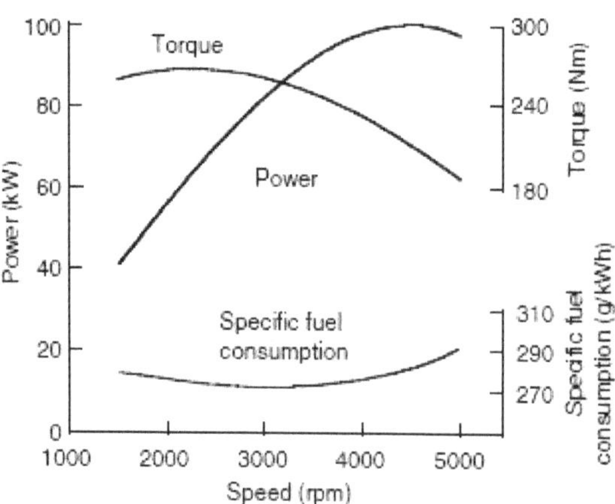

Figure1.5.2.2: Typical performance characteristics of gasoline engines

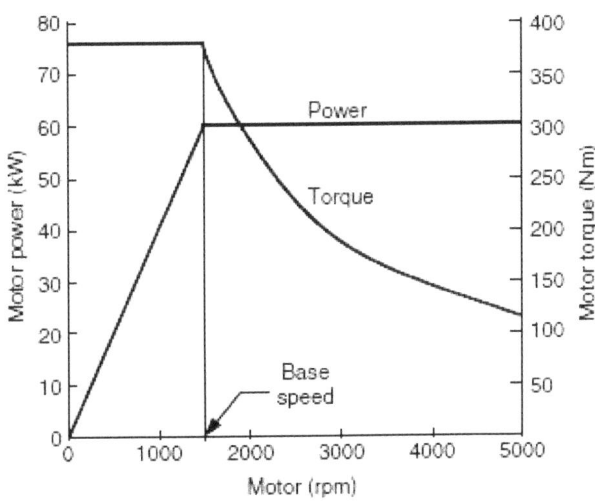

Figure1.5.2.3: Typical performance characteristics of electric motors for traction

Speed of the engine is usually set just a little above the speed of the maximum power output. The internal combustion engine has a relatively flat torque–speed profile (compared with an ideal one), as shown in Figure1.5.2.1.Consequently, a multigear transmission is usually employed to modify it, as shown in Figure 1.5.2.3.Electric motors, however, usually have a speed–torque characteristic that ismuch closer to the ideal, as shown in Figure 1.5.2.2. Generally, the electric motorstarts from zero speed.
As it increases to its base speed, the voltage increasesto its rated value while the flux remains constant. Beyond the base speed, the

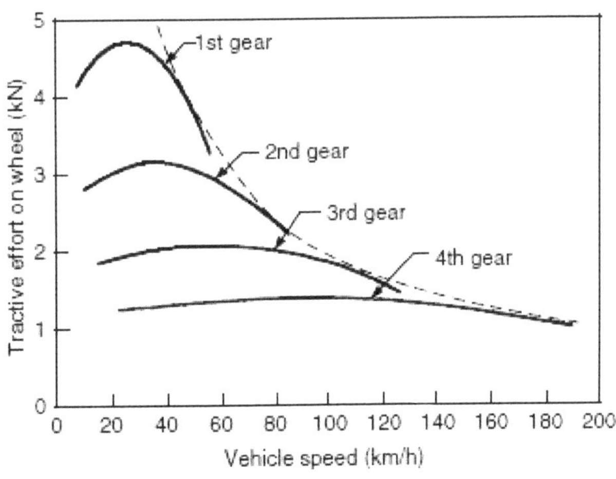

Figure 1.5.2.4: Tractive effort of internal combustion engine and a multigear transmission vehicle vs. vehiclespeed

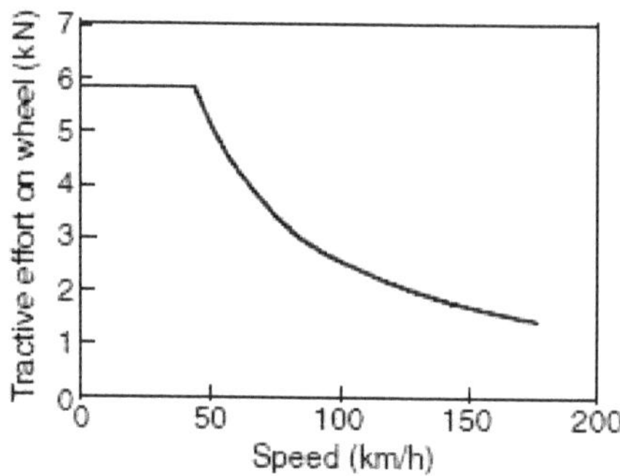

Figure1.5.2.5: Tractive effort of a single-gear electric vehicle vs. vehicle speed

Voltage remains constant and the flux is weakened. This results in constant output power while the torque declines hyperbolically with speed. Since the speed–torque profile of an electric motor is close to the ideal, a single-gear or double-gear transmission is usually employed, as shown in Figure 1.5.2.5.

TRANSMISSION CHARACTERISTICS:

The transmission requirements of a vehicle depend on the characteristics of the power plant and the performance requirements of the vehicle. As mentioned previously, a well-controlled electric machine such as the power plant of an electric vehicle will not need a multigear transmission. However, an internal combustion engine must have a multigear or continuously varying transmission to multiply its torque at low speed. The term transmission here includes all those systems employed for transmitting engine power to the drive wheels.

For automobile applications, there are usually two basic types of transmissions: manual gear transmission and hydrodynamic transmission.

1.5.3.1 Manual Gear Transmission

Manual gear transmission consists of a clutch, gearbox, final drive, and driveshaft. The final drive has a constant gear reduction ratio or a differential gear ratio. The common practice of requiring direct drive (non-reducing) in the gearbox to be in the highest gear determines this ratio.

The gearbox provides a number of gear reduction ratios ranging from three to five for passenger cars and more for heavy commercial vehicles that are powered with gasoline or diesel engines. The maximum speed requirement of the vehicle determines the gear ratio of the highest gear (i.e., the smallest ratio). On the other hand, the gear ratio of the lowest gear (i.e., the maximum ratio) is determined by the requirement of the maximum tractive effort or the grade ability. Ratios between them should be spaced in such a way that they will provide the tractive effort–speed characteristics as close to the ideal as possible, as shown in Figure

In the first iteration, gear ratios between the highest and the lowest gear may be selected in such a way that the engine can operate in the same speed range for all the gears. This approach would benefit the fuel economy and performance of the vehicle. For instance, in normal driving, the proper gear can be selected according to vehicle speed to operate the engine in its optimum speed range for fuel-saving purposes. In fast acceleration, the engine can be operated in its speed range with high power output. This approach is depicted in Figure 1.5.3.2.For a four-speed gear box, the following relationship can be established.

$$\frac{i_{g1}}{i_{g2}} = \frac{i_{g2}}{i_{g3}} = \frac{i_{g3}}{i_{g4}} = K_g$$

……….eq1

and

$$K_g = \sqrt[3]{\frac{i_{g1}}{i_{gg4}}}, \quad \ldots\ldots\ldots\ldots\text{eq2}$$

where *ig*1, *ig*2, *ig*3, and *ig*4 are the gear ratios for the first, second, third, and fourth gear, respectively. In a more general case, if the ratio of the highest

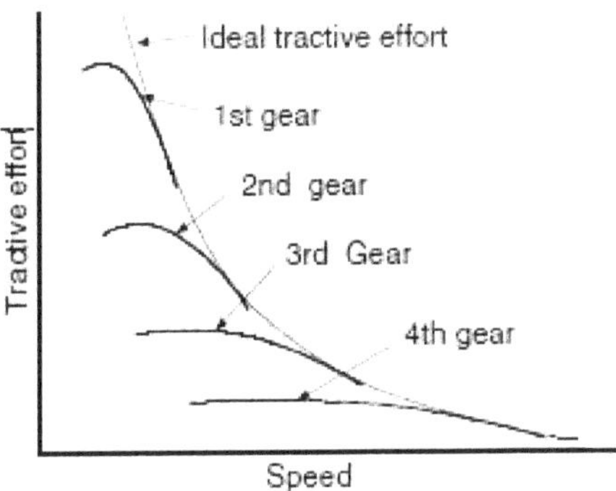

Figure1.5.3.1: Tractive effort characteristics of a gasoline engine-powered vehicle

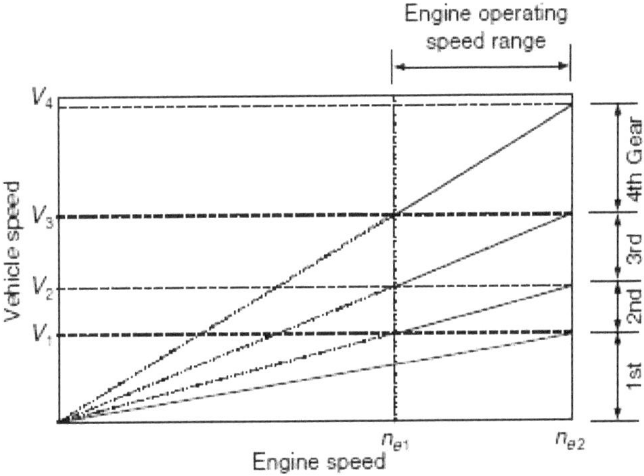

Figure1.5.3.2: Demonstration of vehicle speed range and engine speed range for each gear

gear, *ign*(smaller gear ratio), and the ratio of the lowest gear, *ig*1 (largest gearratio), have been determined and the number of the gear *ng* is known, thefactor*Kg* can be determined as

$$K_g = \left(\frac{i_{g1}}{i_{gn}}\right)^{(n_g - 1)}, \quad \ldots\ldots\ldots\ldots\text{eq3}$$

and each gear ratio can be obtained by

$$i_{gn-1} = K_g i_{gn}$$
$$i_{gn-2} = K_g^2 i_{gn}$$
$$\vdots$$
$$i_{g2} = K_g^{n_t-1} i_{gn}.$$

............eq4

For passenger cars, to suit changing traffic conditions, the step between the ratios of the upper two gears is often a little closer than that based on (eq4).That is,

$$\frac{i_{g1}}{i_{g2}} > \frac{i_{g2}}{i_{g3}} > \frac{i_{g3}}{i_{g4}}.$$

........eq5

This, in turn, affects the selection of the ratios of the lower gears. For commercialvehicles, however, the gear ratios in the gearbox are often arrangedbased on (eq5).
Figure 1.5.3.3 shows the tractive effort of a gasoline engine vehicle with fourgeartransmission and that of an electric vehicle with single-gear transmission. It is clear that electric machines with favorable torque–speed characteristicscan satisfy tractive effort with simple single-gear transmission.

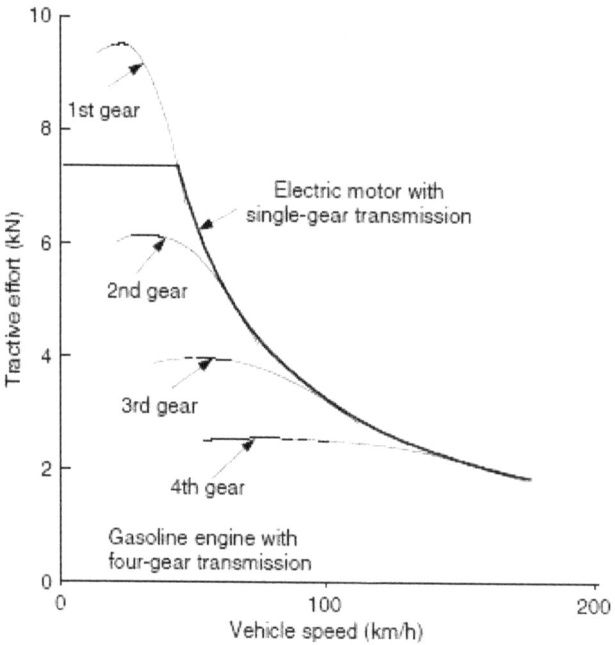

Figure1.5.3.3: Tractive efforts of a gasoline engine vehicle with four-gear transmission and an electric vehiclewith single-gear transmission

UNIT – II
INTRODUCTION TO HYBRID ELECTRIC VEHICLES

Hybrid electric vehicle (HEV):

The hybrid electric vehicle combines a gasoline engine with an electric motor. An alternate is a diesel engine and an electric motor.

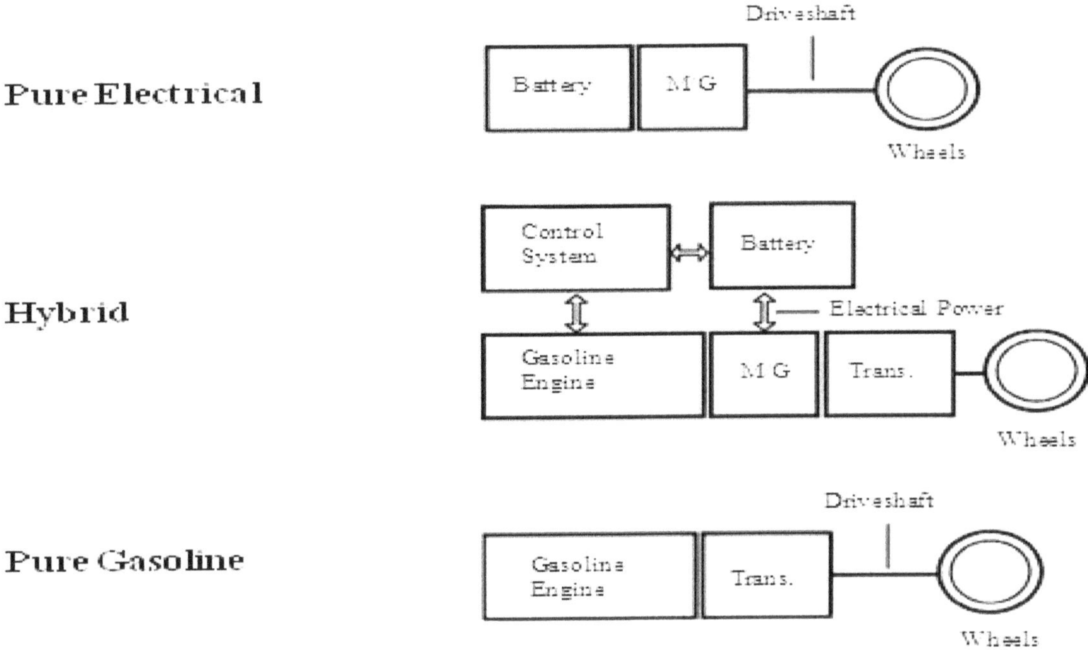

Figure 1: Components of a hybrid Vehicle that combines a pure gasoline with a pure EV.

As shown in **Figure 1**, a HEV is formed by merging components from a pure electrical vehicle and a pure gasoline vehicle. The Electric Vehicle (EV) has an M/G which allows regenerative braking for an EV; the M/G installed in the HEV enables regenerative braking. For the HEV, the M/G is tucked directly behind the engine. In Honda hybrids, the M/G is connected directly to the engine.

The transmission appears next in line. This arrangement has two torque producers; the M/G in motor mode, M-mode, and the gasoline engine. The battery and M/G are connected electrically. HEVs are a combination of electrical and mechanical components. Three main sources of electricity for hybrids are batteries, FCs, and capacitors. Each device has a low cell voltage, and, hence, requires many cells in series to obtain the voltage demanded by an HEV. Difference in the source of Energy can be explained as:

- The FC provides high energy but low power.
- The battery supplies both modest power and energy.
- The capacitor supplies very large power but low energy.

The components of an electrochemical cell include anode, cathode, and electrolyte (shown in fig2). The current flow both internal and external to the cell is used to describe the current loop.

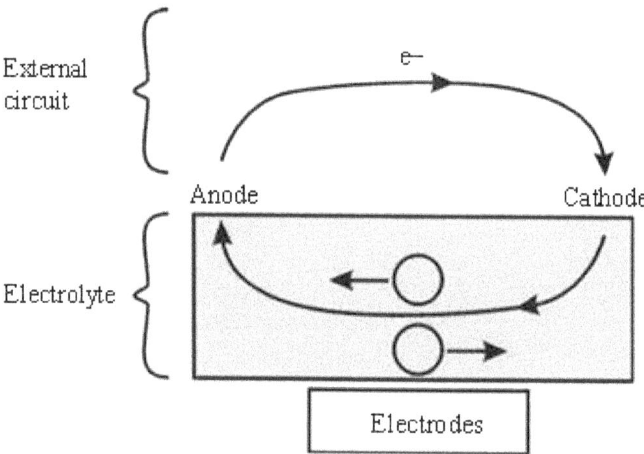

Figure 2: An electrode, a circuit for a cell which is converting chemical energy to electrical energy. The motion of negative charges is clockwise and forms a closed loop through external wires and load and the electrolyte in the cell.

A critical issue for both battery life and safety is the precision control of the Charge/Discharge cycle. Overcharging can be traced as a cause of fire and failure. Applications impose two boundaries or limitations on batteries. The first limit, which is dictated by battery life, is the minimum allowed State of Charge. As a result, not all the installed battery energy can be used. The battery feeds energy to other electrical equipment, which is usually the inverter. This equipment can use a broad range of input voltage, but cannot accept a low voltage. The second limit is the minimum voltage allowed from the battery.

HISTORY OF ELECTRIC VEHICLES:

In 1900, steam technology was advanced. The advantages of ***steam-powered cars*** included high performance in terms of power and speed. However, the disadvantages of steam-powered cars included poor fuel economy and the need to —fire up the boiler‖ before driving. Feed water was a necessary input for steam engine, therefore could not tolerate the loss of fresh water. Later, Steam condensers were applied to the steam car to solve the feed water problem. However, by that time Gasoline cars had won the marketing battle.

Gasoline cars of 1900 were noisy, dirty, smelly, cantankerous, and unreliable. In comparison, electric cars were comfortable, quiet, clean, and fashionable. Ease of control was also a desirable feature. Lead acid batteries were used in 1900 and are still used in modern cars. Hence lead acid batteries have a long history (since 1881) of use as a viable energy storage device. Golden age of ***Electrical vehicle*** marked from 1890 to 1924 with peak production of electric vehicles in 1912. However, the range was limited by energy storage in the battery. After every trip, the battery required recharging. At the 1924 automobile show, no electric cars were on display. This announced the end of the Golden Age of electric-powered cars.

The range of a ***gasoline car*** was far superior to that of either a steam or an electric car and dominated the automobile market from 1924 to 1960. The gasoline car had one dominant feature; it used gasoline as a fuel. The modern period starts with the oil embargoes and the gasoline shortages during the 1970s which created long lines at gas stations. Engineers recognized that the good features of the gasoline engine could be combined with those of the electric motor to produce a superior car. A marriage of the two yields the hybrid automobile.

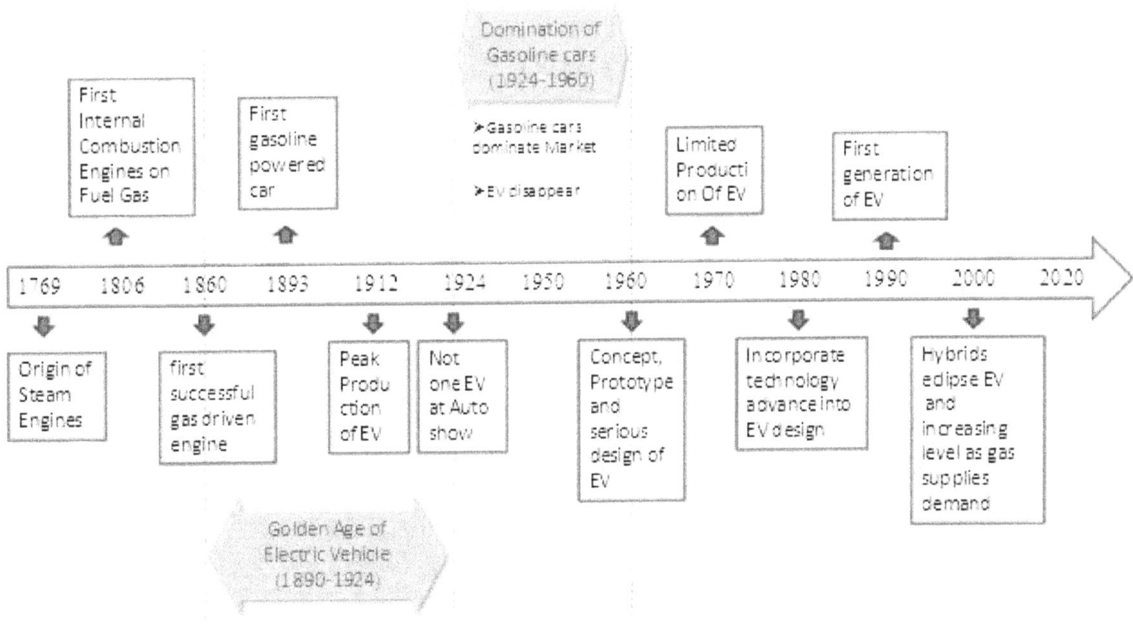

Figure 3: Historical development of automobile and development of interest and activity in the EV from 1890 to present day. Electric Vchicle merged into hybrid electric vehicle.

1769:

The first steam-powered vehicle was designed by Nicolas-Joseph Cugnot and constructed by M. Brezin that could attain speeds of up to 6 km/hour. These early steam-powered vehicles were so heavy that they were only practical on a perfectly flat surface as strong as iron.

1807:

The next step towards the development of the car was the invention of the internal combustion engine. Francois Isaac de Rivaz designed the first internal combustion engine in, using a mixture of hydrogen and oxygen to generate energy.

1825:

British inventor Goldsworthy Gurney built a steam car that successfully completed an 85 mile round-trip journey in ten hours' time.

1839:

Robert Anderson of Aberdeen, Scotland built the first electric vehicle.

1860:

In, Jean Joseph Etienne Lenoir, a Frenchman, built the first successful two-stroke gas driven engine.

1886:

Historical records indicate that an electric-powered taxicab, using a battery with 28 cells and a small electric motor, was introduced in England.

1888:

Immisch& Company built a four-passenger carriage, powered by a one-horsepower motor and 24-cell battery, for the Sultan of the Ottoman Empire. In the same year, Magnus Volk in Brighton, England made a three-wheeled electric car. *1890 – 1910 (*Period of significant improvements in battery technology)

INVENTION OF HYBRID VEHICLES:

1890:

Jacob Lohner, a coach builder in Vienna, Austria, foresaw the need for an electric vehicle that would be less noisy than the new gas-powered cars. He commissioned a design for an electric vehicle from Austro-Hungarian engineer Ferdinand Porsche, who had recently graduated from the Vienna Technical College. Porsche's first version of the electric car used a pair of electric motors mounted in the front wheel hubs of a conventional car. The car could travel up to 38 miles. To extend the vehicle's range, Porsche added a gasoline engine that could recharge the batteries, thus giving birth to the first hybrid, the ***Lohner-Porsche Elektromobil.***

EARLY HYBRID VEHICLES:

1900:

Porsche showed his hybrid car at the Paris Exposition of 1900. A gasoline engine was used to power a generator which, in turn, drove a small series of motors. The electric engine was used to give the car a little bit of extra power. This method of ***series hybrid engine*** is still in use today, although obviously with further scope of performance improvement and greater fuel savings.

1915:

Woods Motor Vehicle manufacturers created the Dual Power hybrid vehicle, second hybrid car in market. Rather than combining the two power sources to give a single output of power, the Dual Power used an electric battery motor to power the engine at low speeds (below 25km/h) and used the gasoline engine to carry the vehicle from these low speeds up to its 55km/h maximum speed. While Porsche had invented the series hybrid, Woods invented the parallel hybrid.

1918:

The Woods Dual Power was the firsthybrid to go into mass production.In all, some 600 models were built by. However, the evolution of the internal combustion engine left electric power a marginal technology

1960:

Victor Wouk worked in helping create numerous hybrid designs earned him the nickname of the —Godfather of the Hybrid‖. In 1976 he even converted a Buick Skylark from gasoline to hybrid.

1978:

Modern hybrid cars rely on the regenerative braking system. When a standard combustion engine car brakes, a lot of power is lost because it dissipates into the atmosphere as heat. Regenerative braking means that the electric motor is used for slowing the car and it essentially collects this power and uses it to help recharge the electric batteries within the car. This development alone is believed to have progressed hybrid vehicle manufacture significantly. The Regenerative Braking System, was first designed and developed in 1978 by David Arthurs. Using standard car components he converted an Opel GT to offer 75 miles to the gallon and many home conversions are done using the plans for this system that are still widely available on the Interne

MODERN PERIOD OF HYBRID HISTORY:

The history of hybrid cars is much longer and more involved than many first imagine. It is, however, in the last ten years or so that we, as consumers, have begun to pay more attention to the hybrid vehicle as a viable alternative to ICE driven cars. Whether looking for a way to save money on spiralling gas costs or in an attempt to help reduce the negative effects on the environment we are buying hybrid cars much more frequently.

1990:

Automakers took a renewed interest in the hybrid, seeking a solution to dwindling energy supplies and environmental concerns and created modern history of hybrid car

1993:

In USA, Bill Clinton's administration recognized the urgency for the mass production of cars powered by means other than gasoline. Numerous government agencies, as well as Chrysler, Ford, GM, and USCAR combined forces in the PNGV (Partnership for a New Generation of Vehicles), to create cars using alternative power sources, including the development and improvement of hybrid electric vehicles.

1997:

The Audi Duo was the first European hybrid car put into mass production and hybrid production and consumer take up has continued to go from strength to strength over the decades.

2000:

Toyota Prius and Honda Insight became the first mass market hybrids to go on sale in the United States, with dozens of models following in the next decade. The Honda Insight and Toyota Prius were two of the first mainstream Hybrid Electric Vehicles and both models remain a popular line.

2005:

A hybrid Ford Escape, the SUV, was released in 2005. Toyota and Ford essentially swapped patents with one another, Ford gaining a number of Toyota patents relating to hybrid technology and Toyota, in return, gaining access to Diesel engine patents from Ford.

PRESENT OF HYBRID ELECTRIC VEHICLES:

Toyota is the most prominent of all manufacturers when it comes to hybrid cars. As well as the specialist hybrid range they have produced hybrid versions of many of their existing model lines, including several Lexus (now owned and manufactured by Toyota) vehicles. They have also stated that it is their intention to release a hybrid version of every single model they release in the coming decade. As well as cars and SUVs, there are a select number of hybrid motorcycles, pickups, vans, and other road going vehicles available to the consumer and the list is continually increasing.

FUTURE OF HYBRID ELECTRICAL VEHICLE:

Since petroleum is limited and will someday run out of supply. In the arbitrary year 2037, an estimated one billion petroleum-fuelled vehicles will be on the world's roads. Gasoline will become prohibitively expensive. The world need to have solutions for the —400 million otherwise useless cars". So year 2037 —gasoline runs out year‖ means, petroleum will no longer be used for personal mobility. A market may develop for solar-powered EVs of the size of a scooter or golf cart. Since hybrid technology applies to heavy vehicles, hybrid buses and hybrid trains will be more significant.

SOCIAL AND ENVIRONMENTAL IMPORTANCE OF HYBRID EECTRIC VEHICLES:

As modern culture and technology continue to develop, the growing presence of global warming and irreversible climate change draws increasing amounts of concern from the world's population. It has only been recently, when modern society has actually taken notice of these changes and decided that something needs to change if the global warming process is to be stopped.

Countries around the world are working to drastically reduce CO_2 emissions as well as other harmful environmental pollutants. Amongst the most notable producers of these pollutants are automobiles, which are almost exclusively powered by internal combustion engines and spew out unhealthy emissions.

According to various reports, cars and trucks are responsible for almost 25% of CO_2 emission and other major transportation methods account for another 12%. With immense quantities of cars on the road today, pure combustion engines are quickly becoming a target of global warming blame. One potential alternative to the world's dependence on standard combustion engine vehicles are hybrid cars. Cost-effectiveness is also an important factor contributing to the development of an environment friendly transportation sector.

ENVIRONMENTAL IMPACT ANALYSIS:

All stages of the life cycle were considered, starting from

a. The extraction of natural resources to produce materials and

b. Ending with conversion of the energy stored on board the vehicle into mechanical energy for vehicle displacement and

c. Other purposes (heating, cooling, lighting, etc.).

In addition, vehicle production stages and end-of-life disposal contribute substantially when quantifying the life cycle environmental impact of fuel-propulsion alternatives.

The analysis were conducted on six vehicles, each was representative of one of the above discussed categories. The specific vehicles were:

1. Toyota Corolla (conventional vehicle),
2. Toyota Prius (hybrid vehicle),
3. Toyota RAV4EV (electric vehicle),
4. Honda FCX (hydrogen fuel cell vehicle),
5. Ford Focus H_2 -ICE (hydrogen ICE vehicle),
6. Ford Focus H_2 -ICE adapted to use ammonia as source of hydrogen (ammonia-fuelled ICE vehicle).

Two environmental impact elements were accounted for in the:

a. Air pollution (AP) and
b. Greenhouse gas (GHG) emissions

The main GHGs were CO_2,CH_4, N_2O, and SF_6 (sulphur hexafluoride), which have GHG impact weighting coefficients relative to CO_2 of 1, 21, 310, and 24,900, respectively.

For AP, the airborne pollutants CO, NO_x,SO_x, and VOCs are assigned the following weighting coefficients: 0.017, 1, 1.3, and 0.64, respectively.

The vehicle production stage contributes to the total life cycle environmental impact through the pollution associated with

a. The extraction and processing of material resources,

b. Manufacturing and

c. The vehicle disposal stage.

Additional sources of GHG and AP emissions were associated with the fuel production and utilization stages. The environmental impacts of these stages have been evaluated in numerous life cycle assessments of fuel cycles.

Regarding electricity production for the electric car case, three case scenarios were considered here:

1. When electricity is produced from renewable energy sources and nuclear energy;
2. When 50% of the electricity is produced from renewable energy sources and 50% from natural gas at an efficiency of 40%;
3. When electricity is produced from natural gas at an efficiency of 40%.

AP emissions were calculated assuming that GHG emissions for plant manufacturing correspond entirely to natural gas combustion. GHG and AP emissions embedded in manufacturing a natural gas power generation plant were negligible compared to the direct emissions during its utilization. Taking those factors into account, GHG and AP emissions for the three scenarios of electricity generation were presented in Table 2.

Electricity-generation scenario	Description of Electricity generation Scenario	GHG emission (g)	AP emission (g)
1	Electricity produced = 100% (Renewable Energy + Nuclear Energy)	5.11	0.195
2	Electricity produced = (50% Renewable Energy + 50% Natural gas)	77.5	0.296
3	Electricity produced = 100% Natural Gas	149.9	0.573

Table2: GHG and air pollution emissions per MJ of electricity produced

Hydrogen charging of fuel tanks on vehicles requires compression. Therefore, presented case considered the energy for hydrogen compression to be provided by electricity.

Fuel	GHG emissions, g	AP emissions, g
Hydrogen from natural gas		
Scenario 1	78.5	0.0994
Scenario 2	82.1	0.113
Scenario 3	85.7	0.127

Table 3: GHG and air pollution emissions per MJ fuel of Hydrogen from natural gas produced

GHG and AP emissions were reported for hydrogen vehicles for the three electricity-generation scenarios considered (see table 3), accounting for the environmental effects of hydrogen compression.

	Fuel utilization stage		Overall life cycle	
Vehicle type	GHG emissions	AP emissions	GHG emissions	AP emissions
	(kg/100 km)	(kg/100 km)	(kg/100 km)	(kg/100 km)
Conventional	19.9	0.0564	21.4	0.06
Hybrid	11.6	0.0328	13.3	0.037
Electric-S1	0.343	0.00131	2.31	0.00756
Electric-S2	5.21	0.0199	7.18	0.0262
Electric-S3	10.1	0.0385	12	0.0448
Fuel Cell -S1	10.2	0.0129	14.2	0.0306
Fuel Cell -S2	10.6	0.0147	14.7	0.0324
Fuel Cell -S3	11.1	0.0165	15.2	0.0342
H2-ICE	10	0.014	11.5	0.018
NH3–H2-ICE	0	0.014	1.4	0.017

Table 4. Environmental impact associated with vehicle Overall Life cycle and Fuel Utilization State.

The environmental impact of the fuel utilization stage, as well as the overall life cycle is presented in Table 4. The H2-ICE vehicle results were based on the assumption that the only GHG emissions during the utilization stage were associated with the compression work, needed to fill the fuel tank of the vehicle. The GHG effect of water vapor emissions was neglected in this analysis due its little value,. For the ammonia fuel vehicle, a very small amount of pump work was needed therefore, ammonia fuel was considered to emit no GHGs during fuel utilization.

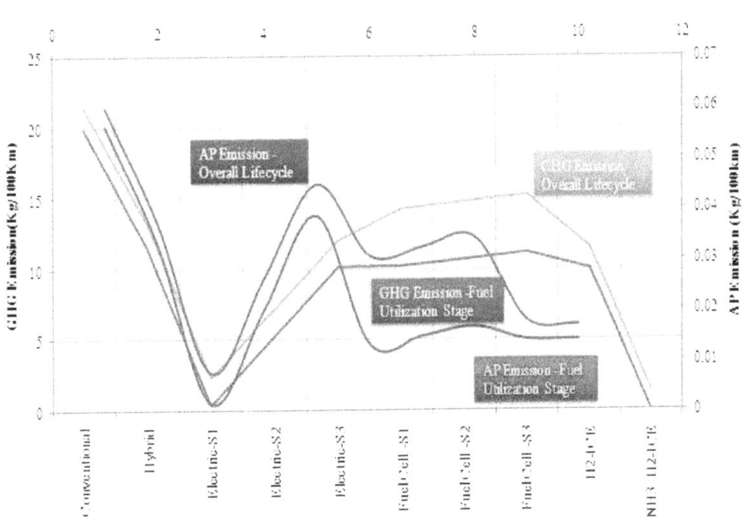

ECONOMICAL ANALYSIS

A number of key economic parameters that characterize vehicles were:

a. Vehicle price,

b. Fuel cost, and

c. Driving range.

This case neglected maintenance costs; however, for the hybrid and electric vehicles, the cost of battery replacement during the lifetime was accounted for. The driving range determines the frequency (number and separation distance) of fuelling stations for each vehicle type. The total fuel cost and the total number of kilometres driven were related to the vehicle life (see Table 1).

Vehicle type	Fuel Type	Initial Price (USk$)	Specific fuel Price (US$/100 km)	Driving Range (Km)	Price of battery Changes During Vehicle Life cycle (USk$)
Conventional *(Toyota Corolla)*	Gasoline	15.3	2.94	540	1 x 0.1
Hybrid *(Toyota Prius)*	Gasoline	20	1.71	930	1 x 1.02
Electric *(Toyota RAV4EV)*	Electricity	42	0.901	164	2 x 15.4
Fuel cell *(Honda FCX)*	Hydrogen	100	1.69	355	1 x 0.1
H2-ICE *(Ford Focus H_2-ICE)*	Hydrogen	60	8.4	300	1 x 0.1
NH3–H2-ICE *(Ford Focus H_2-ICE and ammonia Adaptive)*	Ammonia	40	6.4	430	1 x 0.1

Table1: Technical and economical values for selected vehicle types

For the Honda FCX the listed initial price for a prototype leased in 2002 was USk$2,000, which is estimated to drop below USk$100 in regular production. Currently, a Honda FCX can be leased for 3 years with a total price of USk$21.6. In order to render the comparative study reasonable, the initial price of the hydrogen fuel cell vehicle is assumed here to be USk$100. For e electric vehicle, the specific cost was estimated to be US$569/kWh with nickel metal hydride (NiMeH) batteries which are typically used in hybrid and electric cars. Historical prices of typical fuels were used to calculate annual average price.

RESULTS OF TECHNICAL–ECONOMICAL–ENVIRONMENTAL ANALYSIS:

In present situation this case study provides a general approach for assessing the combined technical–economical–environmental benefits of transportation options.

This analysis showed that the hybrid and electric cars have advantages over the others. The economics and environmental impact associated with use of an electric car depends significantly on the source of the electricity:

a. If electricity is generated from renewable energy sources, the electric car is advantageous to the hybrid vehicle.

b. If the electricity is generated from fossil fuels, the electric car remains competitive only if the electricity is generated on-board.

c. If the electricity is generated with an efficiency of 50–60% by a gas turbine engine connected to a high-capacity battery and electric motor, the electric car is superior in many respects.

d. For electricity-generation scenarios 2 and 3, using ammonia as a means to store hydrogen onboard a vehicle is the best option among those analysed (as shown in figure 2).

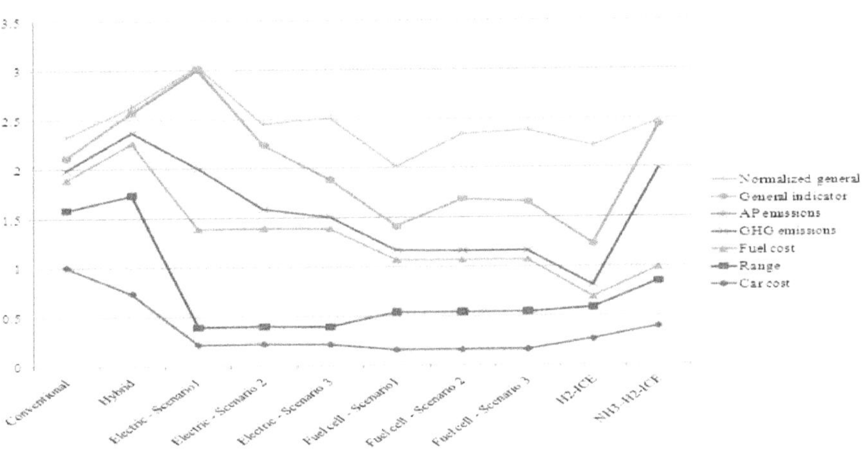

Figure2: Normalized economic and environmental indicators for six vehicle types

The electric car with capability for on-board electricity generation represents a beneficial option and is worthy of further investigation, as part of efforts to develop energy efficient and ecologically benign vehicles.

The main limitations of this study were as follows:

(i) The use of data which may be of limited accuracy in some instances;

(ii) The subjectiveness of the indicators chosen; and

(iii) The simplicity of the procedure used for developing the general indicator without using unique weighting coefficients.

Despite these limitations, the study reflects relatively accurately and realistically the present situation and provides a general approach for assessing the combined technical–economical–environmental benefits of transportation options.

IMPACT OF MODERN DRIVE TRAINS ON ENERGY SUPPLIES:

In terms of overall energy efficiency, the conceptual advantages of a hybrid over a conventional vehicle are:

• **Regenerative braking.** A hybrid can capture some of the energy normally lost as heat to the mechanical brakes by using its electric drive motor(s) in generator mode to break the vehicle

• **More efficient operation of the ICE, including reduction of idle.** A hybrid can avoid some of the energy losses associated with engine operation at speed and load combinations where the engine is inefficient by using the energy storage device to either absorb part of the ICE's output or augment it or even substitute for it. This allows the ICE to operate only at speeds and loads where it is most efficient. When an HEV is stopped, rather than running the engine at idle, where it is extremely inefficient, the control system may either shut off the engine, with the storage device providing auxiliary power (for heating or cooling the vehicle interior, powering headlights, etc.), or run the engine at a higher-than-idle (more efficient) power setting and use the excess power (over auxiliary loads) to recharge the storage device. When the vehicle control system can shut the engine off at idle, the drivetrain can be designed so that the drive motor also serves as the starter motor, allowing extremely rapid restart due to the motor's high starting torque.

• **Smaller ICE:** Since the storage device can take up a part of the load, the HEV's ICE can be down sized. The ICE may be sized for the continuous load and not for the very high short term acceleration load. This enables the ICE to operate at a higher fraction of its rated power, generally at higher fuel efficiency, during most of the driving.

There are counterbalancing factors reducing hybrids' energy advantage, including:

• **Potential for higher weight.** Although the fuel-driven energy source on a hybrid generally will be of lower power and weight than the engine in a conventional vehicle of similar performance, total hybrid weight is likely to be higher than the conventional vehicle it replaces because of the added weight of the storage device, electric motor(s), and other components. This depends, of course, on the storage mechanism chosen, the vehicle performance requirements, and so forth.

• **Electrical losses.** Although individual electric drive train components tend to be quite efficient for one-way energy flows, in many hybrid configurations, electricity flows back and forth through components in a way that leads to cascading losses. Further, some of the components may be forced to operate under conditions where they have reduced efficiency. For example, like ICEs, most electric motors have lower efficiency at the low-speed, low-load conditions often encountered in city driving. Without careful component selection and a control strategy that minimizes electric losses, much of the theoretical efficiency advantage often associated with an electric drive train can be lost.

HYDRODYNAMIC TRANSMISSION

Hydrodynamic transmissions use fluid to transmit power in the form oftorque and speed and arewidely used in passenger cars. They consist of atorque converter and an automatic gearbox. The torque converter consists ofat least three rotary elements known as the impeller (pump), the turbine, andthe reactor, as shown in Figure 2.18.

The impeller is connected to the engineshaft and the turbine is connected to the output shaft of the converter, whichin turn is coupled to the input shaft of the multispeed gearbox. The reactor iscoupled to external housing to provide a reaction on the fluid circulating in theconverter. The function of the reactor is to enable the turbine to develop anoutputtorque higher than the input torque of the converter, thus producingtorque multiplication. The reactor is usually mounted on a free wheel (one-wayclutch) so that when the starting period has been completed and the turbinespeed is approaching that of the pump, the reactor is in free rotation. Atthis point, the converter operates as a fluid coupled with a ratio of output torque to input torque that is equal to 1.0.

The major advantages of hydrodynamic transmission may be summarizedas follows:

- When properly matched, the engine will not stall.
- It provides flexible coupling between the engine and the drivenwheels.
- Together with a suitably selected multispeed gearbox, it providestorque–speed characteristics that approach the ideal.

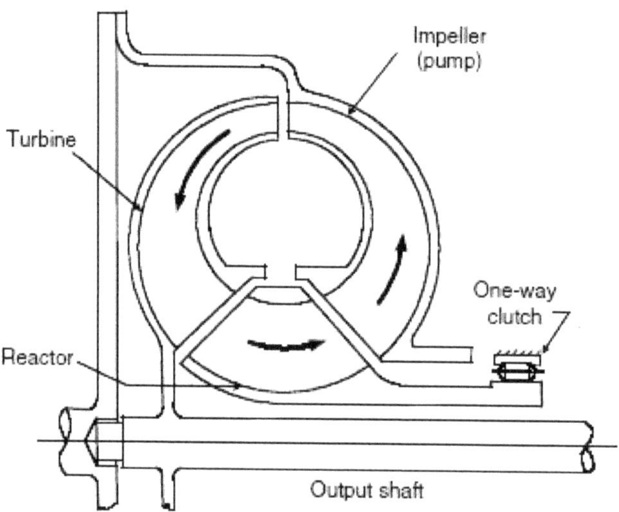

Figure1.5.3.2.1. Schematic view of a torque converter

The major disadvantages of hydrodynamic transmission are its low efficiencyin a stop–go driving pattern and its complex construction.

The performance characteristics of a torque converter are described interms of the following four parameters:

1. *Speed ratio*:

$$C_{sr} = \frac{output\_speed}{input\_speed},$$ eq1

Which is the reciprocal of the gear ratio mentioned before.

2. Torque ratio:

$$C_{tr} = \frac{output\_torque}{input\_torque}.$$ eq2

3. Efficiency:

$$\eta_c = \frac{output\_speed \times output\_torque}{input\_speed \times input\_torque} = C_{sr}C_{tr}.$$ eq3

4. Capacity factor (size factor):

$$K_{tc} = \frac{speed}{\sqrt{torque}}.$$ eq4

The capacity factor, *Kc*, is an indicator of the ability of the converter to absorber transmit torque, which is proportional to the square of the rotary speed. Typical performance characteristics of the torque converter are shown inFigure 1.5.3.2.2, in which torque ratio, efficiency, and input capacity factor — thatis the ratio of input speed to the square root of input torque — are plottedagainst speed ratio. The torque ratio has the maximum value at stall condition, where the output speed is zero. The torque ratio decreases as the speedratio increases (gear ratio decreases) and the converter eventually acts as ahydraulic coupling with a torque ratio of 1.0. At this point, a small difference between the input and output speed exists because of the slip between theimpeller (pump) and the turbine. The efficiency of the torque converter iszero at stall condition and increases with increasing speed ratio (decrease inthe gear ratio). It reaches the maximum when the converter acts as a fluid
coupling (torque ratio equal to 1.0).

To determine the actual operating condition of the torque converter, theengine operating point has to be specified because the engine drives thetorque converter.

To characterize the engine operating condition for the purposeof determining the combined performance of the engine and the converter, an engine capacity factor, *Ke*, is introduced and defined as

$$K_e = \frac{n_e}{\sqrt{T_e}},$$ eq5

Where*ne*and *Te*are engine speed and torque, respectively.

The variation ofthe capacity factor with speed for a typical engine is shown in Figure 1.5.3.2.3.

To achieve proper matching, the engine and the torque converter shouldhave a similar range in the capacity factor.

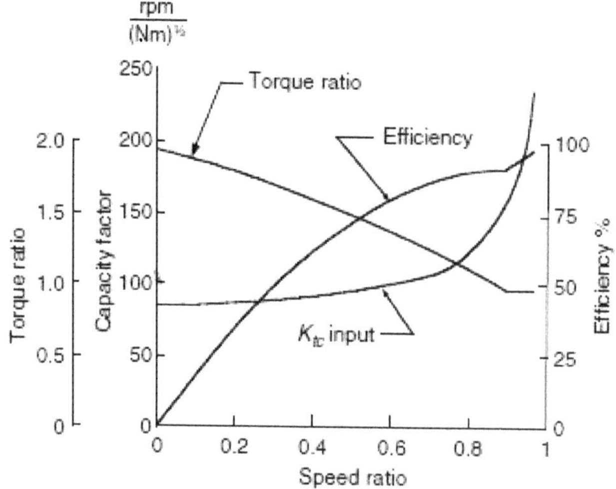

Figure 1.5.3.2.3.: Performance characteristics of a torque converter

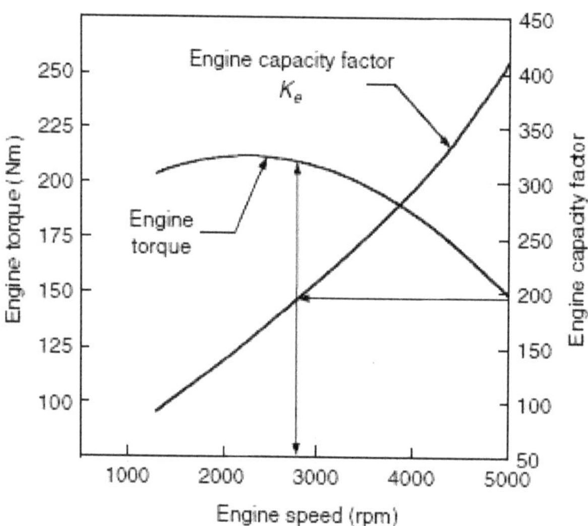

Figure 1.5.3.2.4: Capacity factor of a typical engine

The engine shaft is usually connected to the input shaft of the torque converter,as mentioned above. That is,

$$K_e = K_c. \qquad \text{..........eq6}$$

The matching procedure begins with specifying the engine speed andengine torque. Knowing the engine operating point, one can determine theengine capacity factor, *Ke*(see Figure 1.5.3.2.5). Since *Ke*_ *Kc*, the input capacityfactor of the torque converter corresponding to the specific engine operatingpoint is then known. As shown in Figure 1.5.3.2.4, for a particular value ofthe input capacity factor of the torque converter, *Ktc*, the converter speedratio, *Csr*, and torque ratio, *Ctr*, can be determined from the torque converterperformance characteristics. The output torque and output speed of theconverter are then given by

$$T_{tc} = T_e C_{tr} \quad \text{.........................eq7}$$

and

$$n_{tc} = n_e C_{sr} \quad \text{................eq8}$$

Where T_{tc} and n_{tc} are the output torque and output speed of the converter, Respectively.
Since the torque converter has a limited torque ratio range (usually less than 2), a multispeed gearbox is usually connected to it. The gearbox comprises several planetary gear sets and is automatically shifted. With the gear

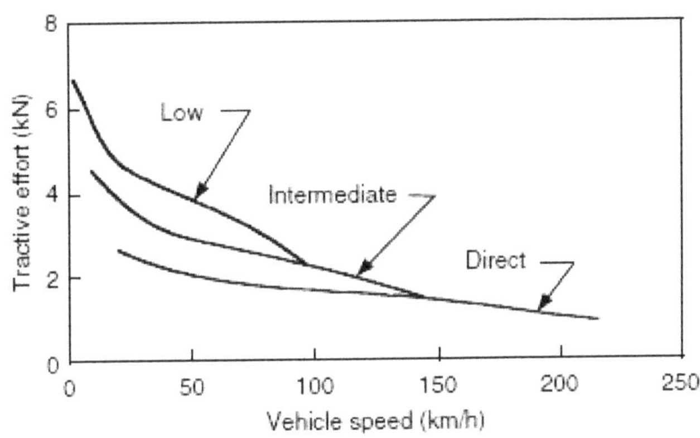

Figure 1.5.3.2.5.: Tractive effort–speed characteristics of a passenger car with automatic transmission

Ratios of the gearbox, the tractive effort and speed of the vehicle can be calculated by

$$F_t = \frac{T_e C_{tr} i_g i_0 \eta_t}{r} \quad \text{.........eq9}$$

and

$$V = \frac{\pi n_e C_{sr} r}{30 i_g i_0} (\mathrm{m/s}) = 0.377 \frac{n_e C_{sr} r}{i_t} (\mathrm{km/h}). \quad \text{............eq10}$$

Above fig shows the variation of the tractive effort with speed for a passenger car equipped with a torque converter and a three-speed gearbox.

UNIT –III
ELECTRIC TRAINS

HYBRID ELECTRIC DRIVE TRAINS:

The term hybrid vehicle refers to a vehicle with at least two sources of power. Hybrid-electric vehicle indicates that one source of power is provided by an electric motor. The other source of motive power can come from a number of different technologies, but is typically provided by an internal combustion engine designed to run on either gasoline or diesel fuel. As proposed by Technical Committee (Electric Road Vehicles) of the International Electro technical Commission, an HEV is a vehicle in which propulsion energy is available from two or more types of energy sources and at least one of them can deliver electrical energy. Based on this general definition, there are many types of HEVs, such as:

- the gasoline ICE and battery
- diesel ICE and battery
- battery and FC
- battery and capacitor
- battery and flywheel
- Battery and battery hybrids.

Most commonly, the propulsion force in HEV is provided by a combination of electric motor and an ICE. The electric motor is used to improve the energy efficiency (improves fuel consumption) and vehicular emissions while the ICE provides extended range capability.

Energy Savings Potential of Hybrid Drive trains

In terms of overall energy efficiency, the conceptual advantages of a hybrid over a conventional vehicle are:

- **Regenerative braking.**

  A hybrid can capture some of the energy normally lost as heat to the mechanical brakes by using its electric drive motor(s) in generator mode to brake thevehicle

- **More efficient operation of the ICE, including reduction of idle:**

  A hybrid can avoid some of the energy losses associated with engine operation at speed and load combinations where the engine is inefficient by using the energy storage device to either absorb part of the ICE's output or augment it or even substitute for it. This allows the ICE to operate only at speeds and loads where it is most efficient. When an HEV is stopped, rather than running the engine at idle, where it is extremely inefficient, the control system may either shut off the engine, with the storage device providing auxiliary power (for heating or cooling the vehicle interior, powering headlights, etc.), or run the engine at a higher-than-idle (more efficient) power setting and use the excess power (over auxiliary loads) to recharge the storage device. When the vehicle control system can shut the engine off at idle, the drivetrain can be designed so that the drive motor also serves as the starter motor, allowing extremely rapid restart due to the motor's high startingtorque.

- **Smaller ICE:** Since the storage device can take up a part of the load, the HEV's ICE can be down sized. The ICE may be sized for the continuous load and not for the very high short-term acceleration load. This enables the ICE to operate at a higher fraction of its rated power, generally at higher fuel efficiency, during most of thedriving.

There are counterbalancing factors reducing hybrids' energy advantage, including:

- **Potential for higher weight.**

  Although the fuel-driven energy source on a hybrid generally will be of lower power and weight than the engine in a conventional vehicle of similar performance, total hybrid weight is likely to be higher than the conventional vehicle it replaces because of the added weight of the storage device, electric motor(s), and other components.

Electrical losses.

Although individual electric drivetrain components tend to be quite efficient for one-way energy flows, in many hybrid configurations, electricity flows back and forth through components in a way that leads to cascading losses. Further, some of the components may be forced to operate under conditions where they have reduced efficiency. For example, like ICEs, most electric motors have lower efficiency at the low-speed, low-load conditions often encountered in city driving. Without careful component selection and a control strategy that minimizes electric losses, much of the theoretical efficiency advantage often associated with an electric drivetrain canbelost.

HEV Configurations

In **Figure 2** the generic concept of a hybrid drivetrain and possible energy flow route is shown. The various possible ways of combining the power flow to meet the driving requirements are:

i. power train 1 alone deliverspower

ii. power train 2 alone deliverspower

iii. both power train 1 and 2 deliver power to load at the sametime
iv. power train 2 obtains power from load (regenerativebraking)
v. power train 2 obtains power from power train1
vi. power train 2 obtains power from power train 1 and load at the sametime
vii. power train 1 delivers power simultaneously to load and to power train2
viii. power train 1 delivers power to power train 2 and power train 2 delivers power aton load
ix. power train 1 delivers power to load and load delivers power to power train 2.

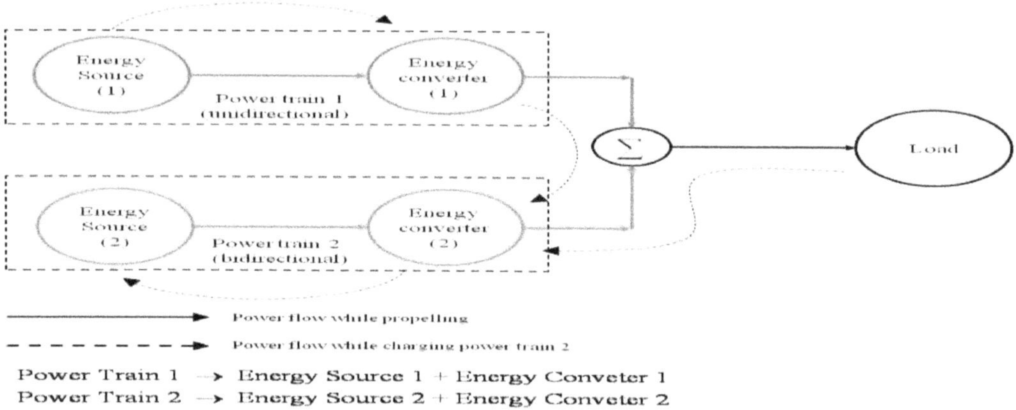

Figure 2: Generic Hybrid Drivetrain [1]

The load power of a vehicle varies randomly in actual operation due to frequent acceleration, deceleration and climbing up and down the grades. The power requirement for a typical driving scenario is shown in **Figure 3**. The load power can be decomposed into two parts:

i. steady power, i.e. the power with a constant value
ii. dynamic power, i.e. the power whose average value is zero

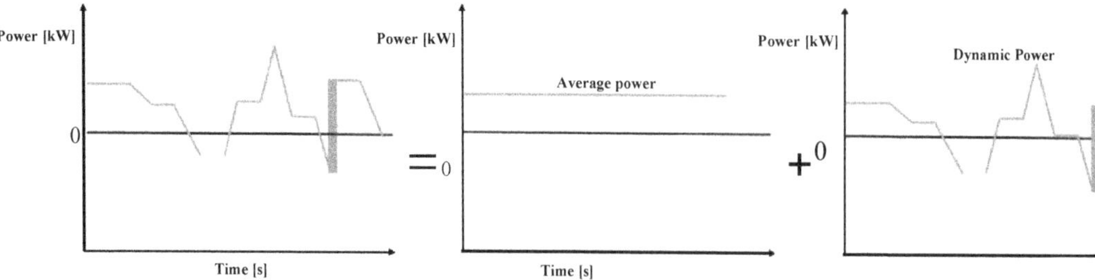

Figure3: Loadpower decomposition

In HEV one powertrain favours steady state operation, such as an ICE or fuel cell. The other powertrain in the HEV is used to supply the dynamic power. The total energy output from the dynamic powertrain will be zero in the whole driving cycle. Generally, electric motors are used to meet the dynamic power demand. This hybrid drivetrain concept can be implemented by different configurations asfollows:

- Seriesconfiguration
- Parallelconfiguration
- Series-parallelconfiguration
- Complexconfiguration

In **Figure 4** the functional block diagrams of the various HEV configurations is shown. From **Figure 4** it can be observed that the key feature of:

- series hybrid is to couple the ICE with the generator to produce electricity for pure electricpropulsion.
- parallel hybrid is to couple both the ICE and electric motor with the transmission via the same drive shaft to propel thevehicle

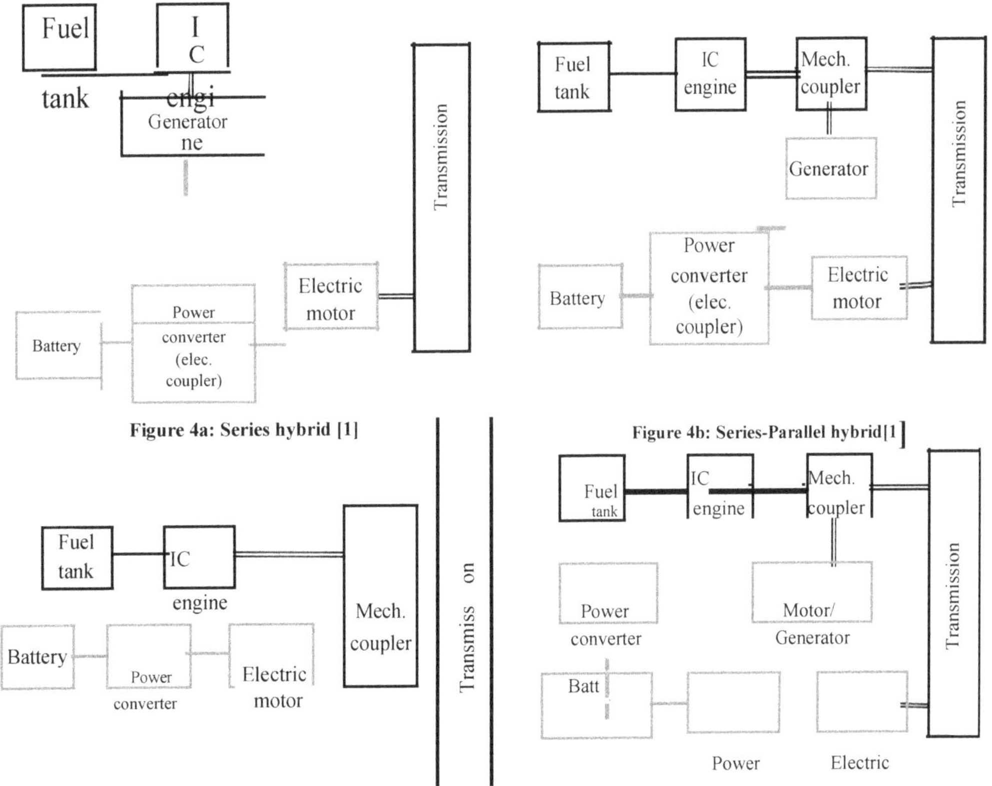

Figure 4a: Series hybrid [1]

Figure 4b: Series-Parallel hybrid[1]

Series Hybrid System:

In case of series hybrid system (**Figure 4a**) the mechanical output is first converted into electricity using a generator. The converted electricity either charges the battery or can bypass the battery to propel the wheels via the motor and mechanical transmission. Conceptually, it is an ICE assisted Electric Vehicle (EV). The advantages of series hybrid drivetrainsare:

- mechanical decoupling between the ICE and driven wheels allows the IC engine operating at its very narrow optimal region as shown in **Figure5**.
- nearly ideal torque-speed characteristics of electric motor make multigeartransmissionunnecessary.

However, a series hybrid drivetrain has the following disadvantages:

- the energy is converted twice (mechanical to electrical and then to mechanical) and this reduces the overallefficiency.
- Two electric machines are needed and a big traction motor is required because it is the only torque source of the drivenwheels.

The series hybrid drivetrain is used in heavy commercial vehicles, military vehicles and buses. The reason is that large vehicles have enough space for the bulky engine/generator system.

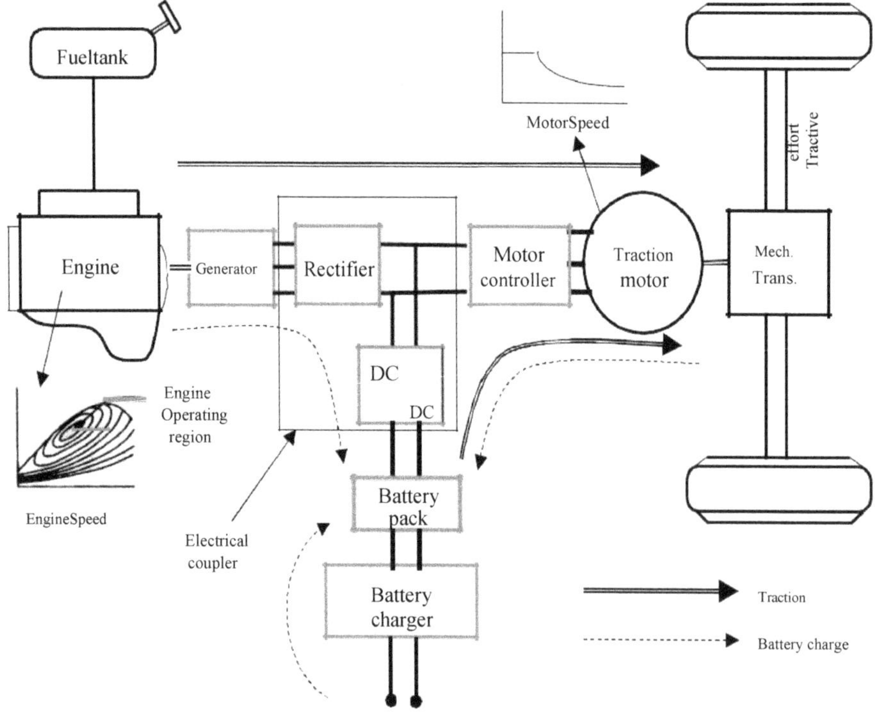

Figure 5: Detailed Configuration of Series Hybrid Vehicle [1]

Parallel Hybrid System:

The parallel HEV (**Figure 4b**) allows both ICE and electric motor (EM) to deliver power to drive the wheels. Since both the ICE and EM are coupled to the drive shaft of the wheels via two clutches, the propulsion power may be supplied by ICE alone, by EM only or by both ICE and EM. The EM can be used as a generator to charge the battery by regenerative braking or absorbing power from the ICE when its output is greater than that required to drive the wheels. The advantages of the parallel hybrid drivetrainare:

- both engine and electric motor directly supply torques to the driven wheels and no energy form conversion occurs, hence energy loss isless
- compactness due to no need of the generator and smaller traction motor.

- mechanical coupling between the engines and the driven wheels, thus the engine operating points cannot be fixed in a narrow speedregion.
- The mechanical configuration and the control strategy are complex compared to series hybriddrivetrain.

Due to its compact characteristics, small vehicles use parallel configuration. Most passenger cars employ this configuration.

Series-Parallel System:

In the series-parallel hybrid (**Figure 4c**), the configuration incorporates the features of both the series and parallel HEVs. However, this configuration needs an additional electric machine and a planetary gear unit making the control complex.

Complex Hybrid System:

The complex hybrid system (**Figure 4d**) involves a complex configuration which cannot be classified into the above three kinds. The complex hybrid is similar to the series-parallel hybrid since the generator and electric motor is both electric machines. However, the key difference is due to the bi-directional power flow of the electric motor in complex hybrid and the unidirectional power flow of the generator in the series-parallel hybrid. The major disadvantage of complex hybrid is higher complexity.

POWER FLOW CONTROL:

Due to the variations in HEV configurations, different power control strategies are necessary to regulate the power flow to or from different components. All the control strategies aim satisfy the following goals:

- maximum fuelefficiency
- minimumemissions
- minimum systemcosts
- good drivingperformance

The design of power control strategies for HEVs involves different considerations such as:

- ***Optimal ICE operating point:*** The optimal operating point on the torque-speed plane of the ICE can be based on maximization of fuel economy, the minimization of emissions or a compromise between fuel economy and emissions.
- ***Optimal ICE operating line:*** In case the ICE needs to deliver different power demands, the corresponding optimal operating points constitute an optimal operatingline.
- ***Safe battery voltage:*** The battery voltage may be significantly altered during discharging, generator charging or regenerative charging. This battery voltage should not exceed the maximum voltage limit nor should it fall below the minimum voltagelimit.

POWER FLOW CONTROL IN SERIES HYBRID:

In the series hybrid system there are four operating modes based on the power flow:

- **Mode 1:** During startup (**Figure 1a**), normal driving or acceleration of the series HEV, both the ICE and battery deliver electric energy to the power converter which then drives the electric motor and hence the wheels via transmission.
- **Mode 2:** At light load (**Figure 1b**), the ICE output is greater than that required to drive the wheels. Hence, a fraction of the generated electrical energy is used to charge the battery. The charging of the batter takes place till the battery capacity reaches a properlevel.
- **Mode 3:** During braking or deceleration (**Figure 1c**), the electric motor acts as a generator, which converts the kinetic energy of the wheels into electricity and this, is used to charge thebattery.

Mode 4: The battery can also be charged by the ICE via the generator even when the vehicle omes to a complete stop (**Figure)**

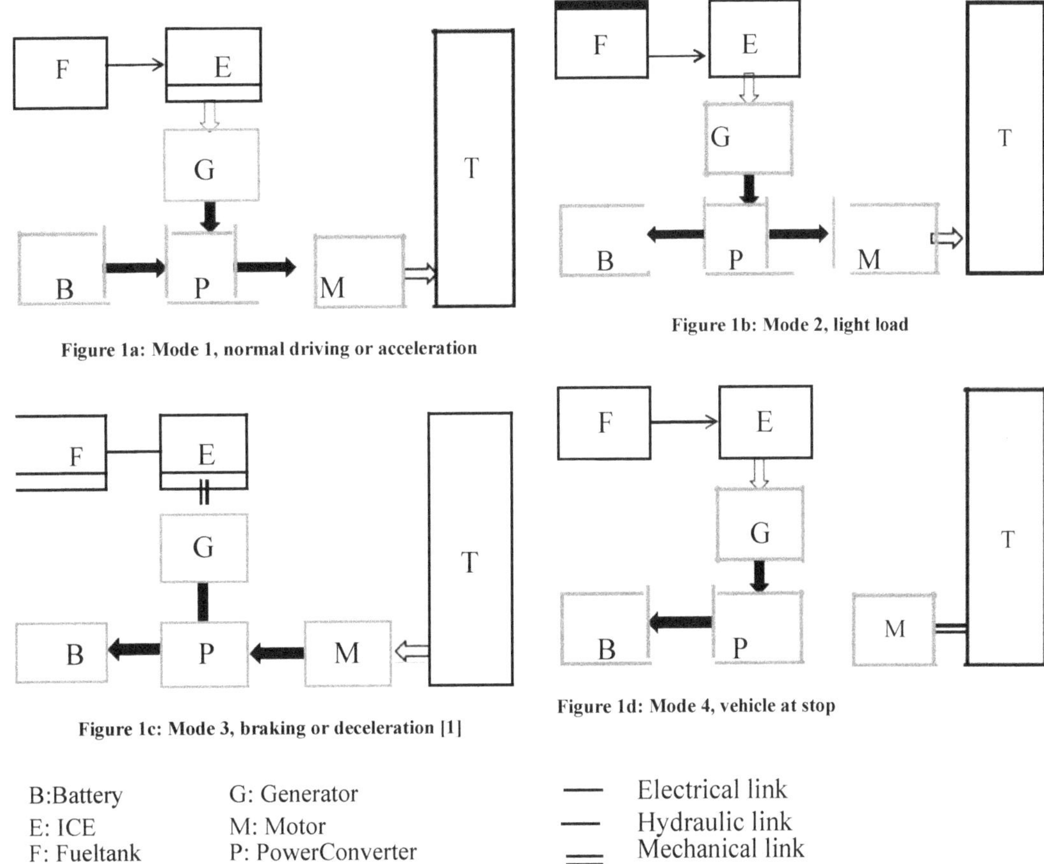

Figure 1a: Mode 1, normal driving or acceleration

Figure 1b: Mode 2, light load

Figure 1c: Mode 3, braking or deceleration [1]

Figure 1d: Mode 4, vehicle at stop

B:Battery
E: ICE
F: Fueltank
G: Generator
M: Motor
P: PowerConverter

— Electrical link
— Hydraulic link
═ Mechanical link

T: Transmission (including brakes, clutches and gears)

Power Flow Control in Parallel Hybrid

The parallel hybrid system has four modes of operation. These four modes of operation are

- **Mode 1:** During start up or full throttle acceleration (**Figure 2a**); both the ICE and the EM share the required power to propel the vehicle. Typically, the relative distribution between the ICE and electric motor is80-20%.
- **Mode 2:** During normal driving (**Figure 2b**), the required traction power is supplied by the ICE only and the EM remains in offmode.
- **Mode 3:** During braking or deceleration (**Figure 2c**), the EM acts as a generator to charge the battery via the powerconverter.
- **Mode 4:** Under light load condition (**Figure 2d**), the traction power is delivered by the ICE and the ICE also charges the battery via theEM.

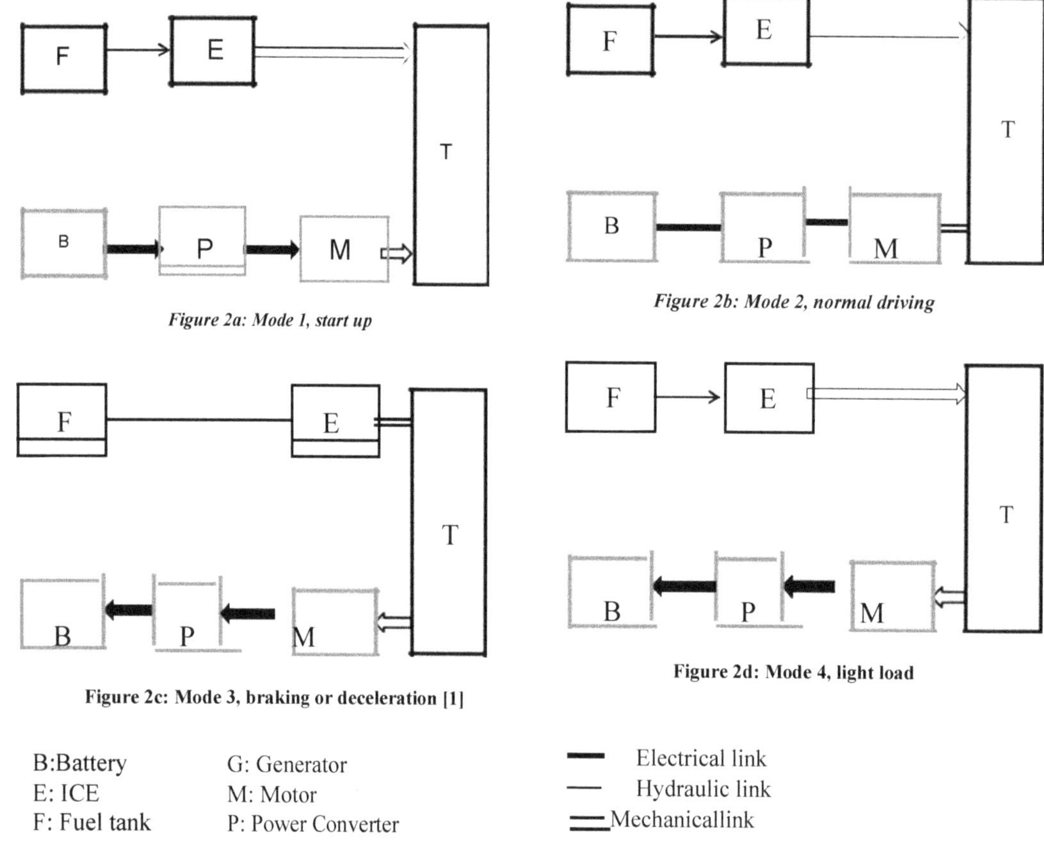

Figure 2a: Mode 1, start up

Figure 2b: Mode 2, normal driving

Figure 2c: Mode 3, braking or deceleration [1]

Figure 2d: Mode 4, light load

Power Flow Control Series-Parallel Hybrid

The series-parallel hybrid system involves the features of series and parallel hybrid systems. Hence, a number of operation modes are feasible. Therefore, these hybrid systems are classified into two categories: **the ICE dominated** and the **EM dominated**.

The various operating modes of **ICE dominated** system are:

- **Mode 1:** At startup (**Figure 3a**), the battery solely provides the necessary power to propel the vehicle and the ICE remains in offmode.
- **Mode 2:** During full throttle acceleration (**Figure 3b**), both the ICE and the EM share the required tractionpower.
- **Mode 3:** During normal driving (**Figure 3c**), the required traction power is provided by the ICE only and the EM remains in the offstate.
- **Mode 4:** During normal braking or deceleration (**Figure 3d**), the EM acts as a generator to charge thebattery.

- **Mode 5:** To charge the battery during driving (**Figure 3e**), the ICE delivers the required traction power and also charges the battery. In this mode the EM acts as a generator.
- **Mode 6:** When the vehicle is at standstill (**Figure 3f**), the ICE can deliver power to charge the battery via theEM

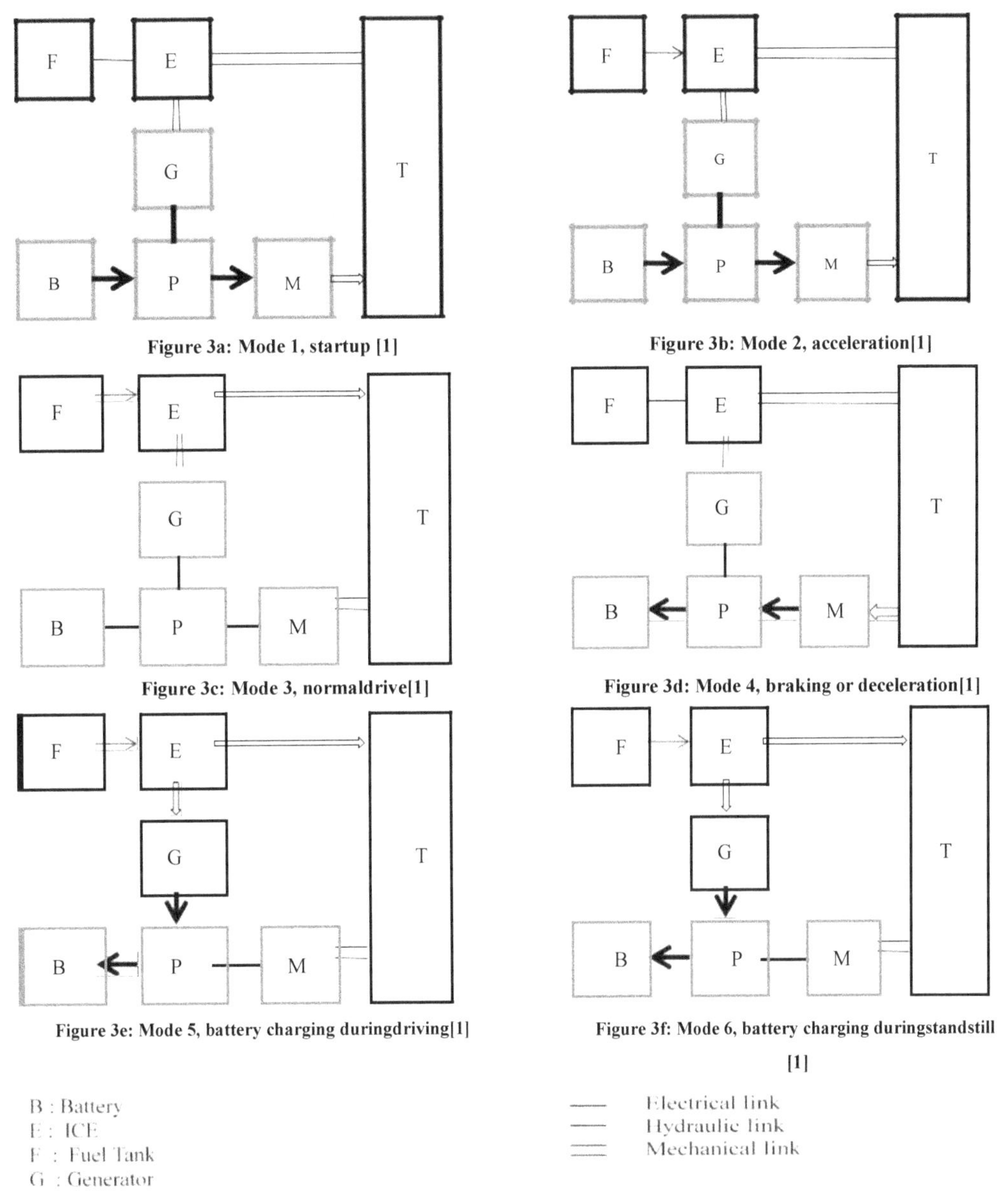

Figure 3a: Mode 1, startup [1]

Figure 3b: Mode 2, acceleration[1]

Figure 3c: Mode 3, normaldrive[1]

Figure 3d: Mode 4, braking or deceleration[1]

Figure 3e: Mode 5, battery charging duringdriving[1]

Figure 3f: Mode 6, battery charging duringstandstill [1]

The operating modes of **EM dominated** system are:

- **Mode 1:** During startup (**Figure 4a**), the EM provides the traction power and the ICE remains in the offstate.
- **Mode 2:** During full throttle (**Figure 4b**), both the ICE and EM provide the tractionpower.
- **Mode 3:** During normal driving (**Figure 4c**), both the ICE and EM provide the tractionpower.
- **Mode 4:** During braking or deceleration (**Figure 4d**), the EM acts as a generator to charge thebattery.
- **Mode 5:** To charge the battery during driving (**Figure 4e**), the ICE delivers the required traction power and also charges the battery. The EM acts as a generator.
- **Mode 6:** When the vehicle is at standstill (**Figure 4f**), the ICE can deliver power to charge the battery via theEM

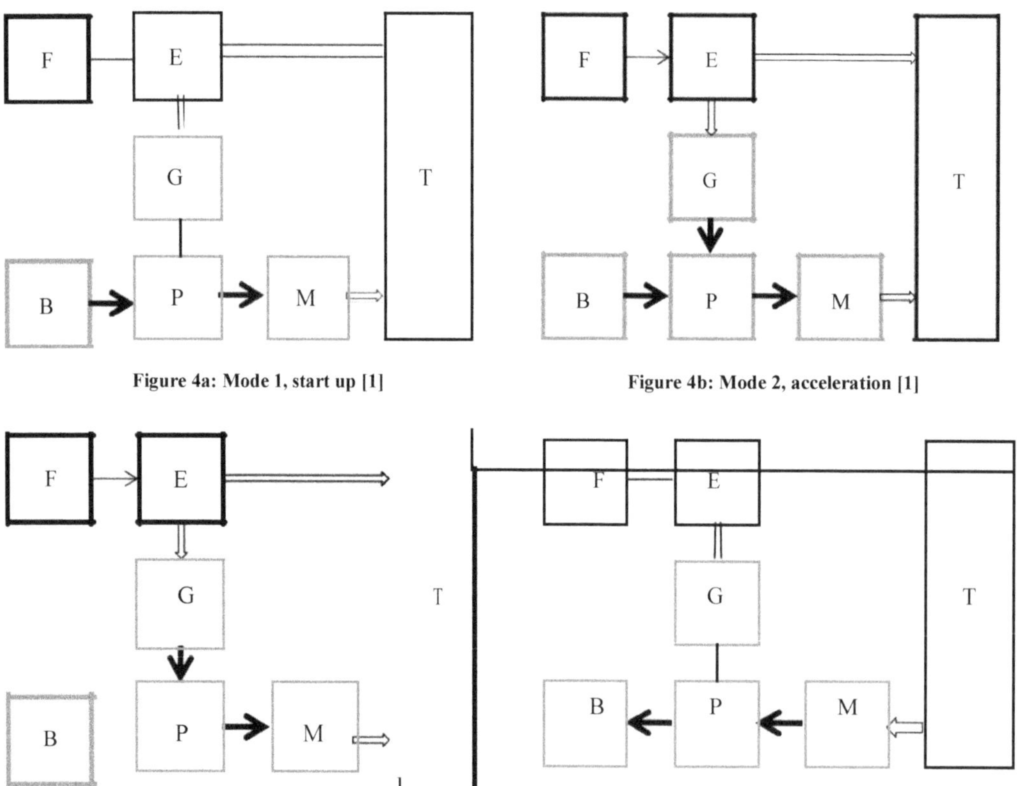

Figure 4a: Mode 1, start up [1]

Figure 4b: Mode 2, acceleration [1]

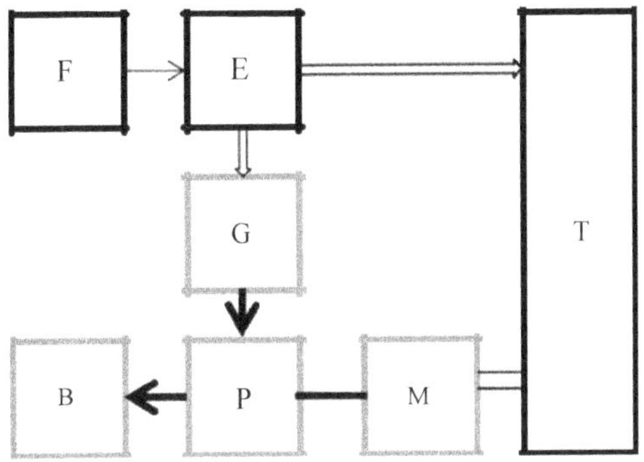

Figure 4e: Mode 5, battery charging during driving [1]

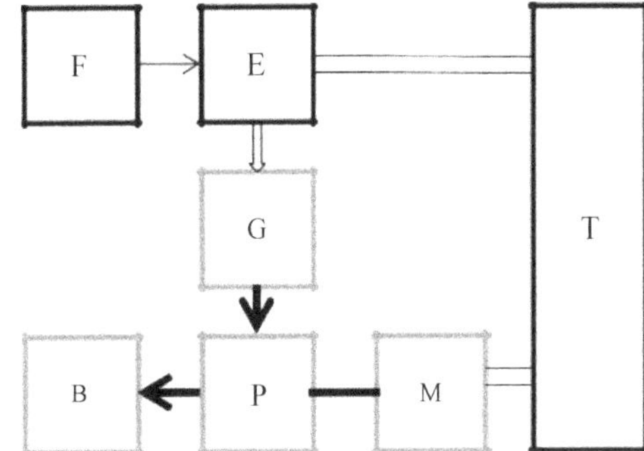

Figure 4f: Mode 6, battery charging during standstill [1]

B : Battery
E : ICE
F : Fuel Tank
G : Generator
M : Motor
P : Power Converter
T : Transmission(including brakes, clutches and gears)

Electrical link
Hydraulic link
Mechanical link

Power Flow Control Complex Hybrid Control

The complex hybrid vehicle configurations are of two types:

- Front hybrid rear electric
- Front electric and rearhybrid

Both the configurations have six modes of operation:

- **Mode 1:** During startup (**Figure 5a**), the required traction power is delivered by the EMs and the engine is in offmode.
- **Mode 2:** During full throttle acceleration (**Figure 5b**), both the ICE and the front wheel EM deliver the power to the front wheel and the second EM delivers power to the rearwheel.
- **Mode 3:** During normal driving (**Figure 5c**), the ICE delivers power to propel the front wheel and to drive the first EM as a generator to charge thebattery.
- **Mode 4:** During driving at light load (**Figure 5d**) first EM delivers the required traction power to the front wheel. The second EM and the ICE are in offsate.
- **Mode 5:** During braking or deceleration (**Figure 5e**), both the front and rear wheel EMs act as generators to simultaneously charge thebattery.

- **Mode 6:** A unique operating mode of complex hybrid system is **axial balancing**. In this mode (**Figure 5f**) if the front wheel slips, the front EM works as a generator to absorb the change of ICE power. Through the battery, this power difference is then used to drive the rear wheels to achieve the axle balancing.

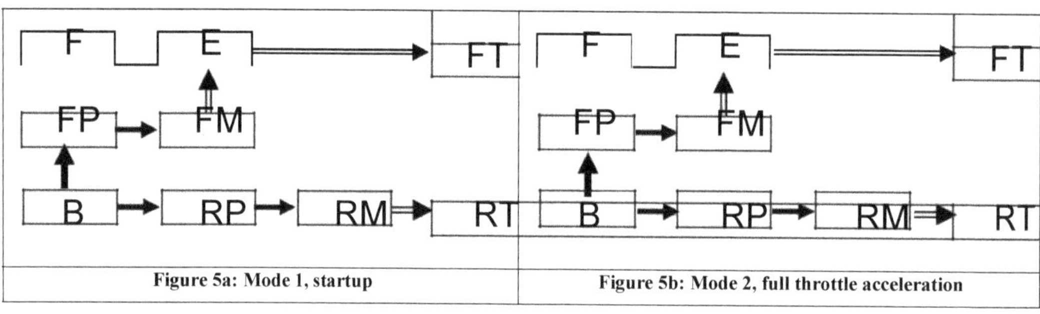

Figure 5a: Mode 1, startup | **Figure 5b: Mode 2, full throttle acceleration**

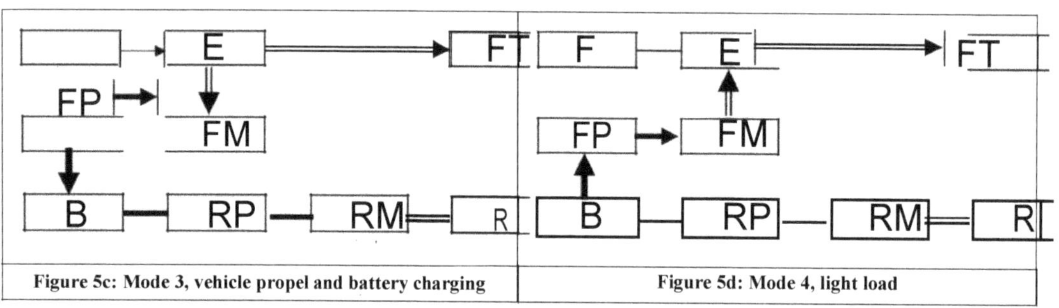

Figure 5c: Mode 3, vehicle propel and battery charging | **Figure 5d: Mode 4, light load**

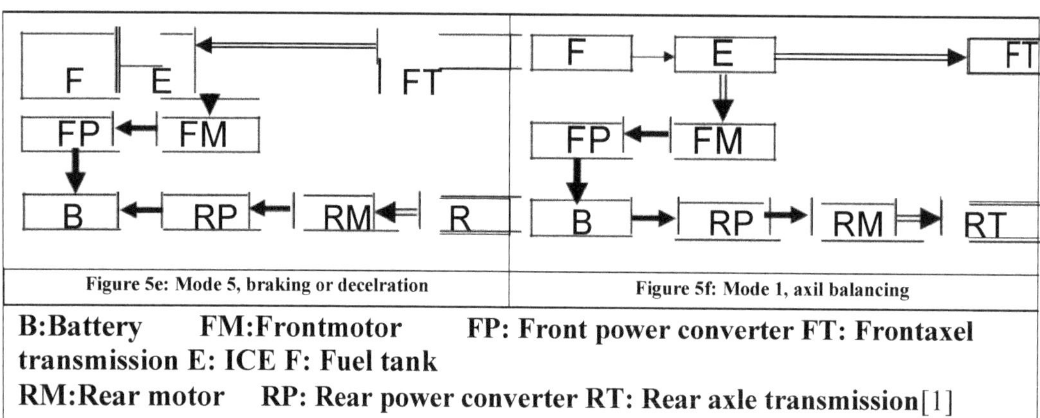

Figure 5e: Mode 5, braking or decelration | **Figure 5f: Mode 1, axil balancing**

B:Battery FM:Frontmotor FP: Front power converter FT: Frontaxel transmission E: ICE F: Fuel tank
RM:Rear motor RP: Rear power converter RT: Rear axle transmission[1]

Electricallink
Hydraulic link
Mechanicallink

In **Figures 6a-f** all the six modes of operation of front electric and rear hybrid is shown.

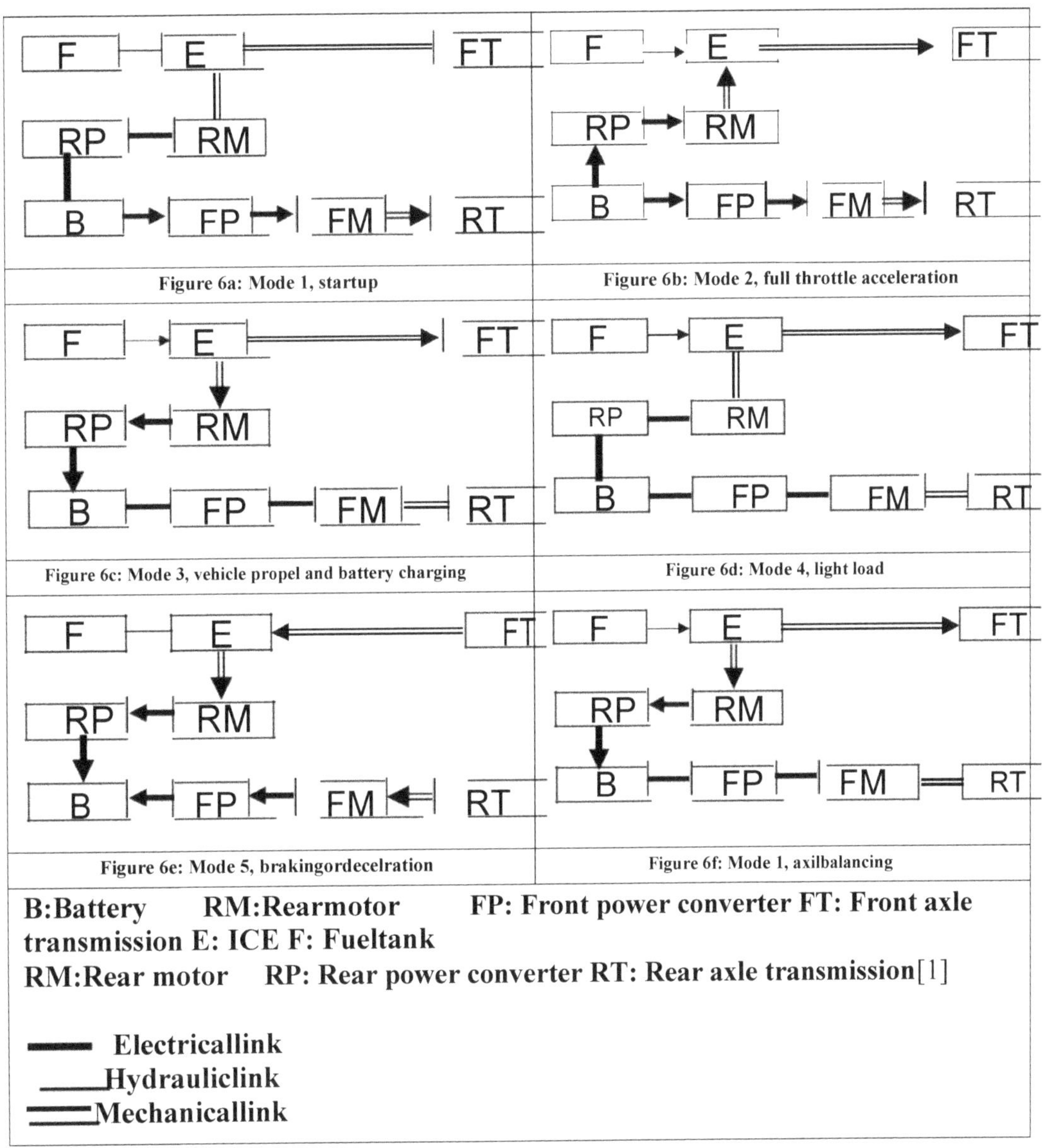

Figure 6a: Mode 1, startup

Figure 6b: Mode 2, full throttle acceleration

Figure 6c: Mode 3, vehicle propel and battery charging

Figure 6d: Mode 4, light load

Figure 6e: Mode 5, brakingordecelration

Figure 6f: Mode 1, axilbalancing

B:Battery RM:Rearmotor FP: Front power converter FT: Front axle transmission E: ICE F: Fueltank
RM:Rear motor RP: Rear power converter RT: Rear axle transmission[1]

Electricallink
Hydrauliclink
Mechanicallink

ELECTRIC DRIVE TRAINS:

Electric Vehicle (EV) Configurations

Compared to HEV, the configuration of EV is flexible. The reasons for this flexibility are:

- The energy flow in EV is mainly via flexible electrical wires rather than bolted flanges or rigid shafts. Hence, distributed subsystems in the EV are really achievable.
- The EVs allow different propulsion arrangements such as independent four wheels and in wheel drives.

In **Figure 1** the general configuration of the EV is shown. The EV has three major subsystems:

- Electric propulsion
- Energy source
- Auxiliary system

The electric propulsion subsystem comprises of:

- The electronic controller
- Power converter
- Electric Motor(EM)
- Mechanical transmission
- Driving wheels

The energy source subsystem consists of

- The energy source (battery, fuel cell, ultracapacitor)
- Energy management unit
- Energy refueling unit

- Power steering unit
- Temperature control unit
- Auxiliary power supply

In **Figure 1** the black line represents the mechanical link, the green line represents the electrical link and the blue line represents the control information communication. Based on the control inputs from the brake and accelerator pedals, the electronic controller provides proper control signals to switch on or off the power converter which in turn regulates the power flow between the electric motor and the energy source. The backward power flow is due to regenerative braking of the EV and this regenerative energy can be stored provided the energy source is receptive.

The energy management unit cooperates with the electronic controller to control regenerative braking and its energy recovery. It also works with the energy-refueling unit to control refueling and to monitor usability of the energy source.

The auxiliary power supply provides the necessary power with different voltage levels for all EV auxiliaries, especially the temperature control and power steering units.

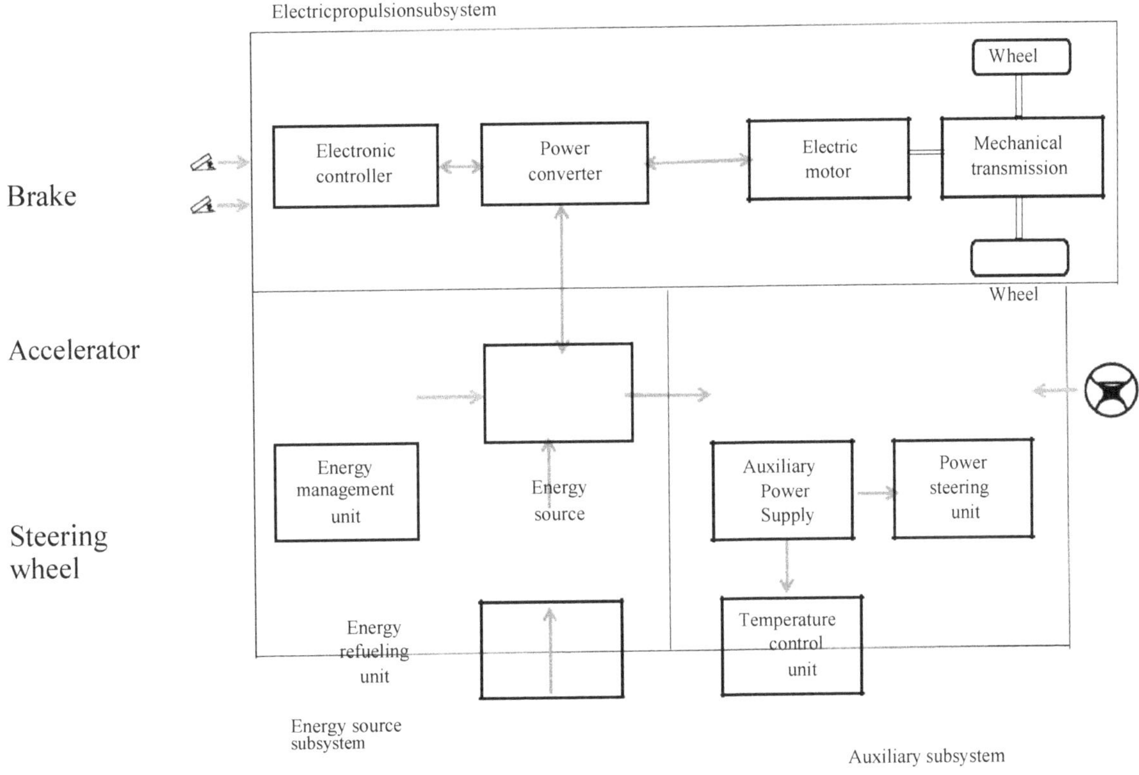

Figure 1:General Configuration of a Electric Vehicle [1]

In modern EV's configuration:

- Three phase motors are generally used to provide the tractionforce
- The power converter is a three-phase PWMinverter
- Mechanical transmission is based on fixed gearing and adifferential
- Li-ion battery is typically selected as the energy source

The typical setup of the EV is shown in **Figure2**.

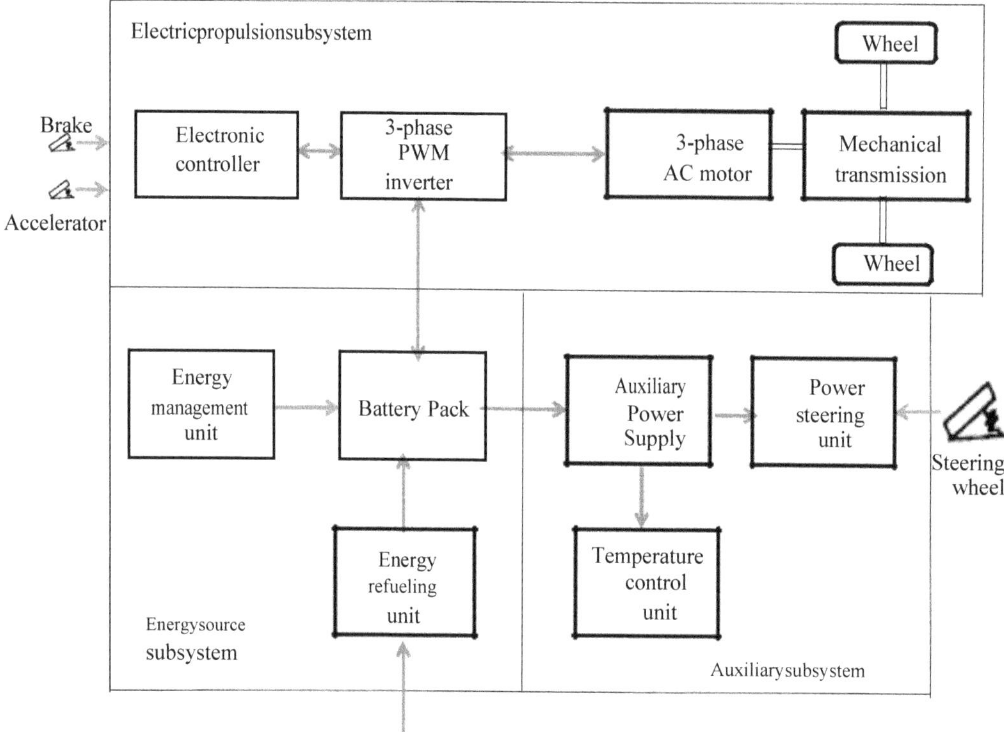

Figure 2:Typical Configuration of a Electric Vehicle [1]

Electric Vehicle (EV) Drive train Alternatives Based on Drive train Configuration There are many possible EV configurations due the variations in electric propulsion and energy sources. Based on these variations, six alternatives are possible as shown in **Figure 3**. These six alternativesare

- In **Figure 3a** a single EM configuration with gearbox (GB) and a clutch is shown. It consists of an EM, a clutch (C), a gearbox, and a differential (D). The clutch enables the connection or disconnection of power flow from EM to the wheels. The gear consists of a set of gears with different gear ratios. With the use of clutch and gearbox, the driver can shift the gear ratios and hence the torque going to the wheels can be changed. The wheels have high torque low speed in the lower gears and high-speed low torque in the highergears.

- In **Figure 3b** a single EM configuration without the gearbox and the clutch is shown. The advantage of this configuration is that the weight of the transmission is reduced. However, this configuration demands a more complex control of the EM to provide the necessary torque to thewheels.
- **Figure 3c** shows a configuration of EV using one EM. It is a transverse front EM front wheel drive configuration. It has a fixed gearing and differential and they are integrated into a singleassembly.
- In **Figure 3d** a dual motor configuration is shown. In this configuration the differential action of an EV when cornering can be electronically provided by two electricmotors.
- In order to shorten the mechanical transmission path from the EM to the driving wheel, the EM can be placed inside a wheel. This configuration is called in-wheel drive. **Figure 3e** shows this configuration in which fixed planetary gearing is employed to reduce the motor speed to the desired wheel speed.
- In **Figure 3f** an EV configuration without any mechanical gearing is shown. By fully abandoning any mechanical gearing, the in-wheel drive can be realized by installing a low speed outer-rotor electric motor inside awheel.

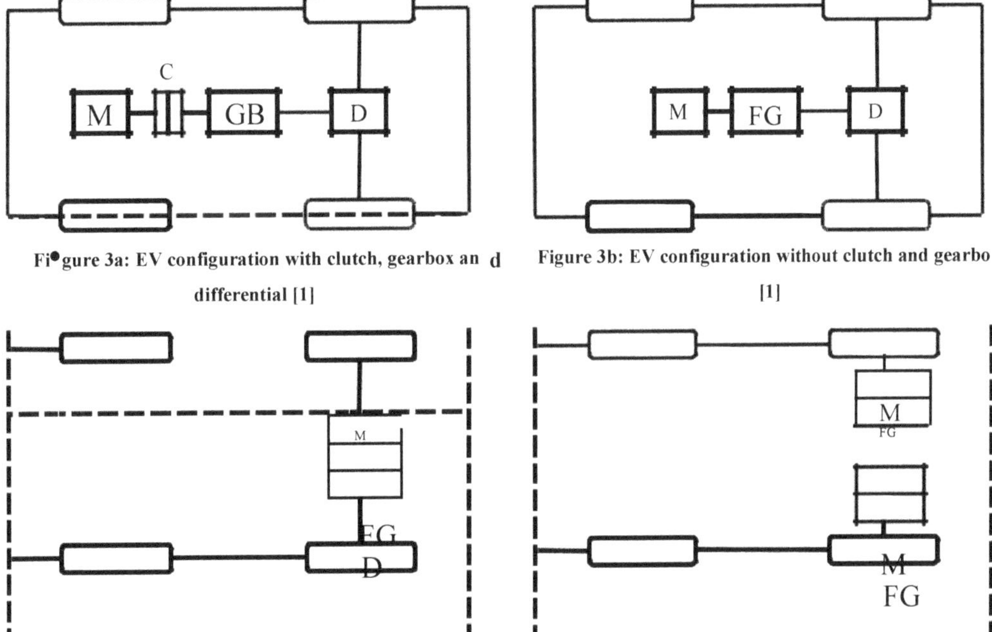

Fi●gure 3a: EV configuration with clutch, gearbox an d differential [1]

Figure 3b: EV configuration without clutch and gearbo [1]

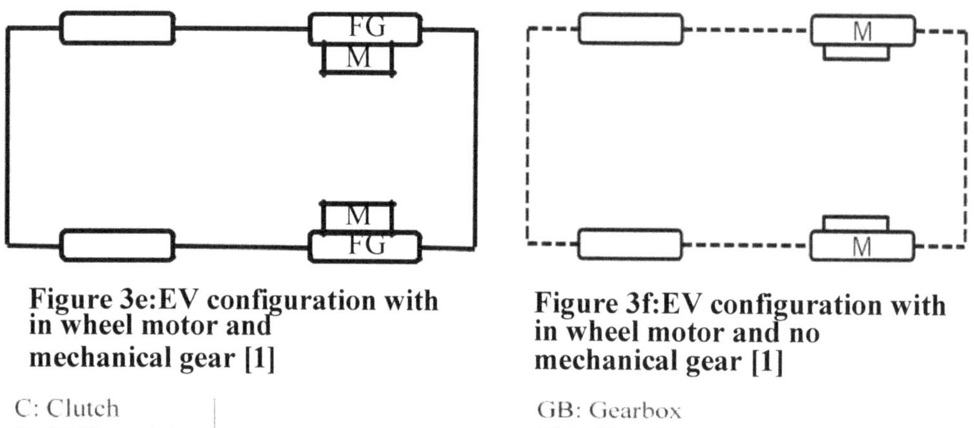

Figure 3e:EV configuration with in wheel motor and mechanical gear [1]

C: Clutch
D: Differential
FG: Fixed gearing

Figure 3f:EV configuration with in wheel motor and no mechanical gear [1]

GB: Gearbox
EM: Electric motor

Electric Vehicle (EV) Drive train Alternatives Based on Power Source Configuration

Besides the variations in electric propulsion, there are other EV configurations due to variations in energy sources. There are five configurations possible and they are:

- **Configuration 1:** It is a simple battery powered configuration, **Figure 4a**. The battery may be distributed around the vehicle, packed together at the vehicle back or located beneath the vehicle chassis. The battery in this case should have reasonable specific energy and specific power and should be able to accept regenerative energy during braking. In case of EVs, the battery should have both high specific energy and specific power because high specific power governs the driving range while the high power density governs the acceleration rate and hill climbingcapability.
- **Configuration 2:** Instead of two batteries, this design uses two different batteries, **Figure 4b**. One battery is optimized for high specific energy and the other for high specificpower.
- **Configuration 3:** In this arrangement fuel cell is used, **Figure 4c**. The battery is an energy storage device, whereas the fuel cell is an energy generation device. The operation principle of fuel cells is a reverse process of electrolysis. In reverse and electrolysis, hydrogen and oxygen gases combine to form electricity and water. The hydrogen gas used by the fuel cell can be stored in an on-board tank whereas oxygen gas is extracted from air. Since fuel cell can offer high specific energy but cannot accept regenerative energy, it is preferable to combine it with battery with high specific power and high-energy receptivity.

- **Configuration 4:** Rather than storing it as a compressed gas, a liquid or a metal hydride, hydrogen can be can be generated on-board using liquid fuels such as methanol, **Figure 4d.** In this case a mini reformer is installed in the EV to produce necessary hydrogen gas for the fuelcell.
- **Configuration 5:** In fuel cell and battery combination, the battery is selected to provide high specific power and high-energy receptivity. In this configuration a battery and supercapacitor combination is used as an energy source, **Figure 4e**. The battery used in this configuration is a high energy density device whereas the supercapacitor provides high specific power and energy receptivity. Usually, the supercapacitors are of relatively low voltage levels, an additional dc-dc power converter is needed to interface between the battery and capacitorterminals.

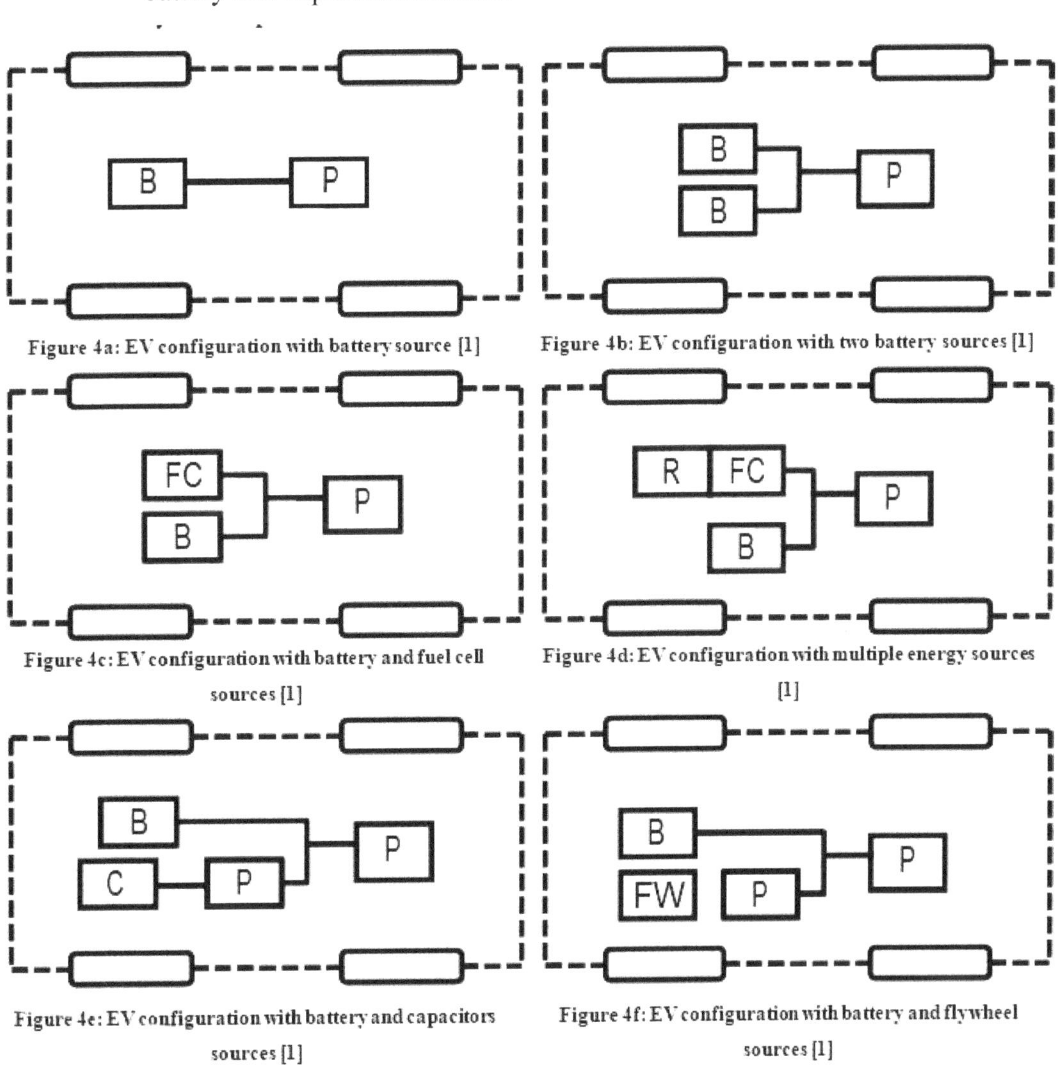

Figure 4a: EV configuration with battery source [1]

Figure 4b: EV configuration with two battery sources [1]

Figure 4c: EV configuration with battery and fuel cell sources [1]

Figure 4d: EV configuration with multiple energy sources [1]

Figure 4e: EV configuration with battery and capacitors sources [1]

Figure 4f: EV configuration with battery and flywheel sources [1]

B: Battery
C: Capacitor
FC: Fuel cell

FW: Flywheel
P: Power converter
R: Reformer

Single and Multi-motor Drives

A differential is a standard component for conventional vehicles. When a vehicle is rounding a curved road, the outer wheel needs to travel on a larger radius than the inner wheel. Thus, the differential adjusts the relative speeds of the wheels. If relative speeds of the wheels are not adjusted, then the wheels will slip and result in tire wear, steering difficulties and poor road holding. In case of EVs, it is possible to dispense the mechanical differential by using two or even four EMs. With the use of multiple EMs, each wheel can be coupled to an EM and this will enable independent control of speed of each wheel in such a way that the differential action can be electronically achieved. In **Figure 5**, a typical dual motor drive with an electronic differential is shown.

Wheel

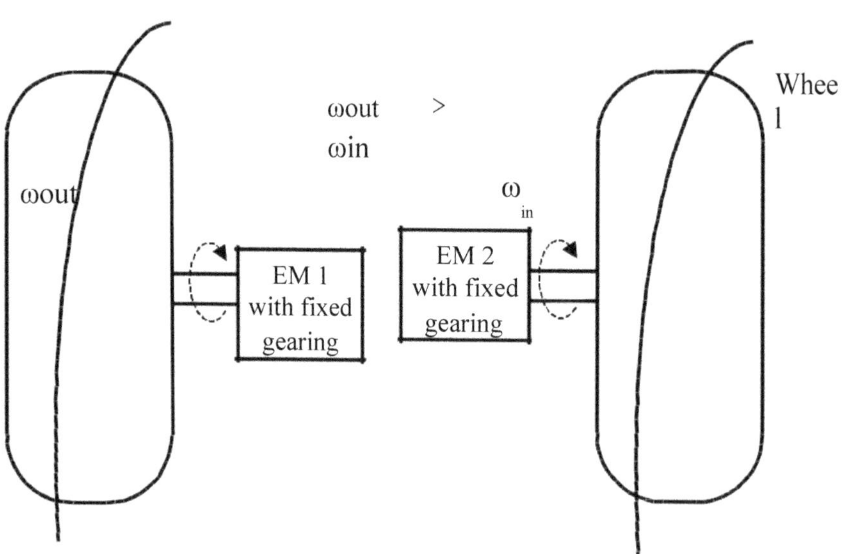

Figure 5: Differential action [1]

In Wheel Drives

By placing an electric motor inside the wheel, the in wheel motor has the advantage that the mechanical transmission path between the electric motor and the wheel can be minimized. Two possible configurations for in wheel drives are:

- When a high-speed inner-rotor motor is used (**Figure 6a**) then a fixed speed-reduction gear becomes necessary to attain a realistic wheel speed. In general, speed reduction is achieved using a planetary gear set. This planetary gear is mounted between the motor shaft and the wheel rim. Usually this motor is designed to operate up to 1000 rpm so as to give high powerdensity.
- In case outer rotor motor is used (**Figure 6b**), then the transmission can be totally removed and the outer rotor acts as the wheel rim and the motor speed is equivalent to the wheel speed and no gears arerequired.

- It has the advantage of smaller size, lighter weight and lowercost
- Needs additional planetary gearset

- Low speed and hence does not need additional gears
- The drawbacks are larger size, weight and cost because of the low speed design.

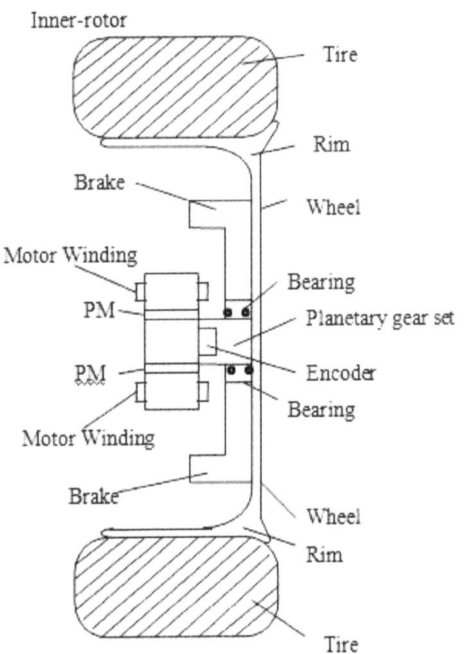

Figure 6a: Inner rotor *In Wheel* drive [1]

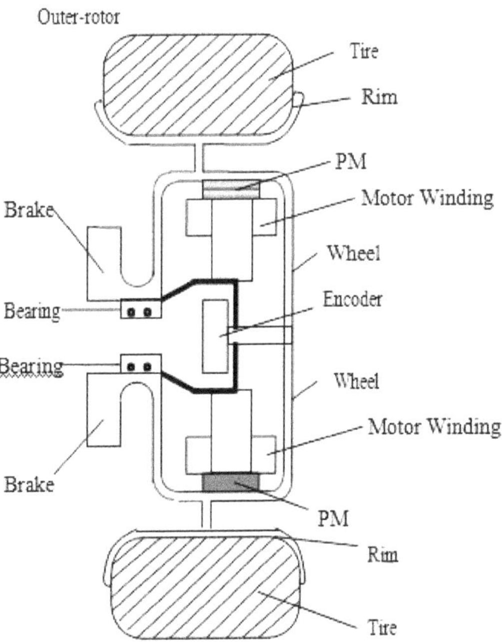

Figure 6b: Outer rotor *In Wheel* drive [1]

Considerations of EMs used in EVs

The requirements of EMs used in EVs are:

- Frequent start/stop
- High rate of acceleration and deceleration
- High torque low speed hill climbing
- Low torque cruising
- Very wide speed range of operation

The EMs for EVs are unique and their major differences with respect to industrial motors in load requirement, performance specification and operating environment are as follows:

- EV motors need to produce the maximum torque that is four to five times of the rated torque for acceleration and hill climbing, while industrial motors generally offer the maximum torque that is twice of the rated torque for overload operation
- EV motors need to achieve four to five times the base speed for highway cruising, while industrial motors generally achieve up to twice the base speed for constant power operation
- EV motors require high power density as well as good efficiency map (high efficiency over wide speed and torque ranges), while industrial motors are generally optimized to give high efficiency at a rated point.
- EV motors need to be installed in mobile vehicles with harsh operating conditions such as high temperature, bad weather and frequent vibration, while industrial motors are generally located in fixed places.

UNIT –III

ELECTRIC TRAINS

ELECTRICAL MACHINES IN EVS AND HEVS:

Vehicle propulsion has specific requirements that distinguish stationary and onboard motors. Every kilogram onboard the vehicle represents an increase in structural load. This increase structural load results in lower efficiency due to increase in the friction that the vehicle has to overcome. Higher efficiency is equivalent to a reduction in energy demand and hence, reduced battery weight. The fundamental requirement for traction motors used in EVs is to generate propulsion torque over a wide speed range. These motors have intrinsically neither nominal speed nor nominal power. The power rating mentioned in the catalog and on the name plate of the motor corresponds to the maximum power that the drive can deliver. Two most commonly used motors in EV propulsion are Permanent Magnet (PM) Motors and Induction Motors (IM). These two motors will be investigated in detail in the coming lectures. However, before going into the details of these machines some basic fundamentals of electrical machines, such as torque production, are discussed in this chapter.

DC MOTOR DRIVES

DC motor drives have been widely used in applications requiring adjustable speed, good speed regulation, and frequent starting, braking and reversing. Various DC motor drives have been widely applied to different electric traction.

principle of operation:

The operation principle of a DC motor is straightforward. When a wire carrying electric current is placed in a magnetic field, a magnetic force acting on the wire is produced. The force is perpendicular to the wire and the magnetic field as shown in Figure 6.3. The magnetic force is proportional to the wire length, magnitude of the electric current, and the density of the magnetic field, that is,

$$F = BIL. \qquad \text{............. eq1}$$

When the wire is shaped into a coil, as shown in Figure 6.3, the magnetic forces acting on both sides produce a torque, which is expressed as

$$T = BIL \cos \alpha, \qquad \text{.................eq2}$$

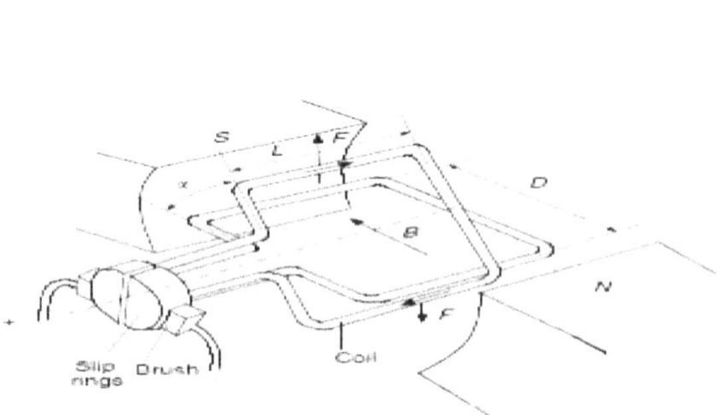

Figure 3.1: Operation principle of a DC motor

where α is the angle between the coil plane and magnetic field as shown in Figure 3.1. The magnetic field may be produced by a set of windings or permanent magnets. The former is called wound-field DC motor and the latteris called the PM DC motor.

The coil carrying the electric current is called thearmature. In practice, the armature consists of a number of coils. In order to obtain continuous and maximum torque, slip rings and brushes are used toconduct each coil at the position of $\alpha=0$.

Practically, the performance of DC motors can be described by the armaturevoltage, back electromotive force (EMF), and field flux.Typically, there are four types of wound-field DC motors, depending onthe mutual interconnection between the field and armature windings. Theyare separately excited, shunt excited, series excited, and compound excitedas shown in Figure 3.2.

In the case of a separately excited motor, the field and armature voltage can be controlled independently of one another.

In a shunt motor, the field and armature are connected in parallel to a common source. Therefore, an independent control of field current and armature or armature voltage can be achieved by inserting a resistance into the appropriate circuit.

This is an inefficient method of control. The efficient method is to use power electronics-based DC– DC converters in the appropriate circuit to replace the resistance.

The DC–DC converters can be actively controlled to produce proper armature and field voltage. In the case of a series motor, the field current is the same as the armature current; therefore, field flux is a function of
armature current.

In a cumulative compound motor, the magnetomotive force (mmf) of a series field is a function of the armature current and is in thesame direction as the mmf of the shunt field.

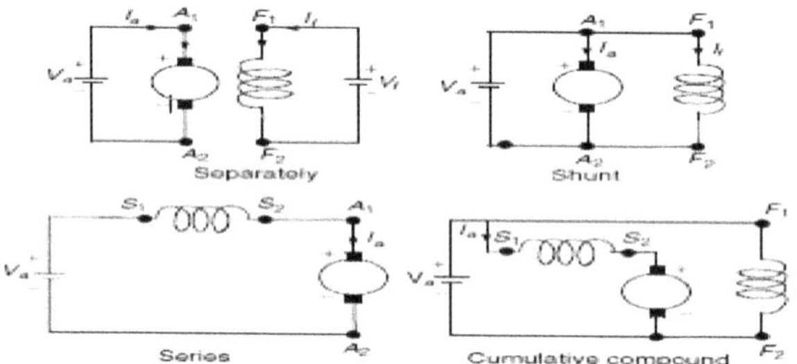

Figure 3.2: Wound-field DC motors

The steady-state equivalent circuit of the armature of a DC motor is shownin Figure 3.3. The resistor *Ra* is the resistance of the armature circuit. For separatelyexcited and shunt DC motors, it is equal to the resistance of the armaturewindings; for the series and compound motors, it is the sum of armatureand series field winding resistances.

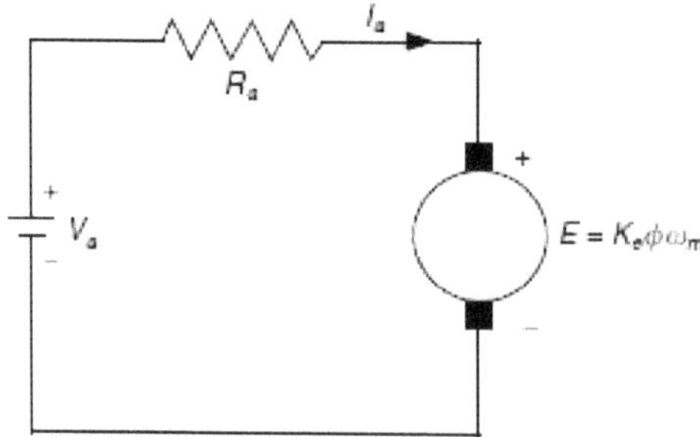

Figure 3.3: Steady-state equivalent circuit of the armature circuit of a DC motor

$$V_a = E + R_a I_a,\ E = K_e \phi \omega_m,$$

$$T = K_e \phi I_a, \qquad \text{.........eq3}$$

where φ is the flux per pole in Webers, *Ia*is the armature current in *A*, *Va* is the armature voltage in volt, *Ra* is the resistance of the armature circuit in ohms, ω*m*is the speed of the armature in rad/sec, *T* is the torque developed by the motor in Nm, and *Ke*is constant.
From equations 3 one can obtain

$$T = \frac{K_e \phi}{R_a} V - \frac{(K_e \phi)^2}{R_a} \omega_m. \qquad \text{................ eq4}$$

Equations 3 are applicable to all the DC motors, namely, separately (or shunt) excited, series, and compound motors. In the case of separately excited motors, if the field voltage is maintained as constant, one can assume the flux to be practically constant as the torque changes. In this case, the speed–torque characteristic of a separately excited motor is a straight line, as shown in Figure 3.4.

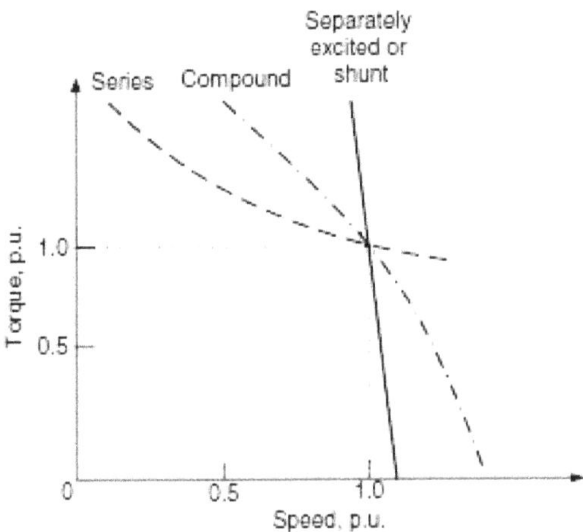

Figure 3.4 Speed characteristics of DC motors

The nonload speed ω*m*0 is determined by the values of the armature voltage and the field excitation. Speed decreases as torque increases, and speed regulation depends on the armature circuit resistance. Separately excited motors are used in applications requiring good speed regulation and proper adjustable speed.
In the case of series motors, the flux is a function of armature current. Inan unsaturated region of the magnetization characteristic, φ can be assumed to be proportional to *Ia*. Thus

$$\phi = K_f I_a. \qquad \text{...........eq5}$$

By equations 3&5, the torque for series excited DC motors can obtained as

$$T = \frac{K_e K_f V_a^2}{(R_a + K_e K_f \omega_m)^2}, \qquad \text{..................eq6}$$

A speed–torque characteristic of a series DC motor is shown in Figure 3.4.In the case of series, any in magnetic flux. Because flux increases with the torque, the speed drops to maintain a balance between the induced voltage and the supply voltage. The characteristic, therefore, shows a dramatic drop. A motor of standard design works at the knee point of the magnetization curve at the rated torque. At heavy torque (large current) overload, the magnetic circuit saturates and the speed–torque curve approaches a straight line.

Series DC motors are suitable for applications requiring high starting torqueand heavy torque overload, such as traction. This was just the case for electrictraction before the power electronics and micro control era. However, series DC motors for traction application have some disadvantages. They are notallowed to operate without load torque with full supply voltage. Otherwise,
their speed will quickly increase up to a very high value . Another disadvantage is the difficulty in regenerative braking. Performance equations for cumulative compound DC motors can be derived from equations (3).

The speed–torque characteristics arebetween series and separately excited (shunt) motors, as shown in Figure 3.4.

COMBINED ARMATURE VOLTAGE AND FIELD CONTROL

The independence of armature voltage and field provides more flexible control of the speed and torque than other types of DC motors. In EV and HEVapplications, the most desirable speed–torque characteristic is to have a constant torque below a certain speed (base speed), with the torque dropping parabolically with the increase of speed (constant power) in the range abovethe base speed, as shown in Figure 6.7. In the range of lower than base speed, the armature current and field are set at their rated values, producing the rated torque. From equations (3), it is clear that the armature voltage must be increased proportionally with the increase of the speed. At thebase speed, the armature voltage reaches its rated value (equal to the source voltage) and cannot be increased further. In order to further increase thespeed, the field must be weakened with the increase of the speed, and then the back EMF *E* and armature current must be maintained constant. The torque produced drops parabolically with the increase in the speed and the output power remains constant, as shown in Figure 3.5.

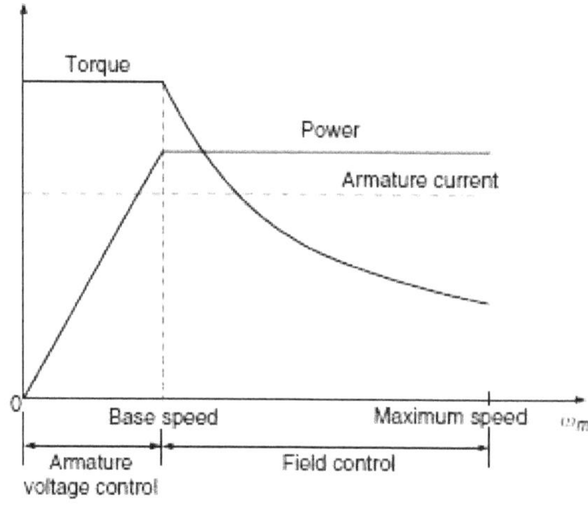

Figure3.5: Torque and power limitations in combined armature voltage and field control

CHOPPER CONTROL OF DC MOTORS

Choppers are used for the control of DC motors because of a number of advantages such as high efficiency, flexibility in control, light weight, small size, quick response, and regeneration down to very low speeds. Presently, the separately excited DC motors are usually used in traction, due to the control flexibility of armature voltage and field.

For a DC motor control in open-loop and closed-loop configurations, the chopper offers a number of advantages due to its high operation frequency. High operation frequency results in high-frequency output voltage ripple and, therefore, less ripple in the motor armature current and a smaller region

of discontinuous conduction in the speed–torque plane. A reduction in the armature current ripple reduces the armature losses. A reduction or elimination of the discontinuous conduction region improves speed regulation and the transient response of the drive.
The power electronic circuit and the steady-state waveform of a DC chopper drive are shown in Figure 3.6

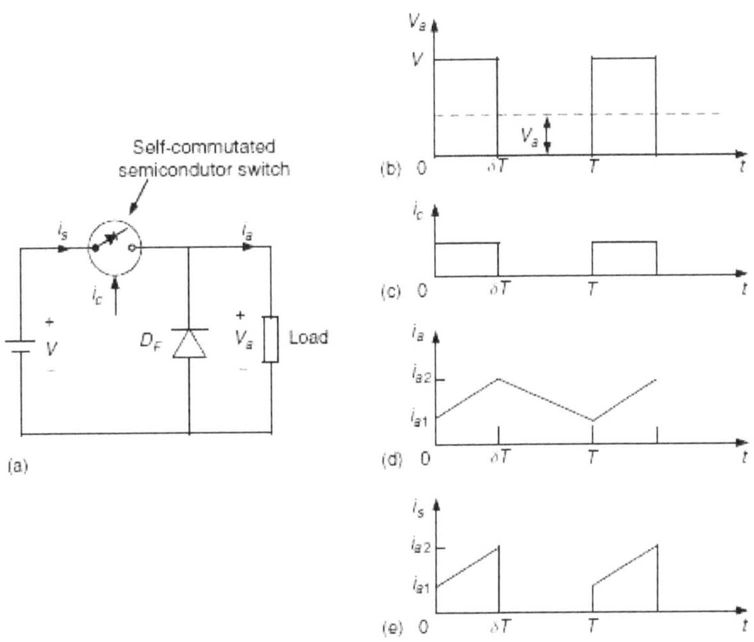

Figure3.6: Principle of operation of a step down (or class A) chopper: (a) basic chopper circuit; (b) to (e)waveforms

ADC voltage source, V, supplies an inductive load through a self-commutated semiconductor switch S. The symbol of a self-commutated semiconductor switch has been used because a chopper can be built using any device among thyristors with a forced commutation circuit: GTO, power transistor, MOSFET, and IGBT. The diode shows the direction in which the device can carry current. A diode DF is connected in parallel with the load. The semiconductor switch S is operated periodically over a period T and remains closed for a time$ton=\delta T$with $0\leq\delta\leq1$. The variable$\delta=ton/T$ is called the duty ratio or duty cycle of a chopper. Figure 6.8also shows the waveform of control signal ic. Control signal icwill be the base current for a transistor chopper, and a gate current for the GTO of a GTO

chopper or the main thyristor of a thyristor chopper. If a power MOSFET isused, it will be a gate to the source voltage. When the control signal is present, the semiconductor switch S will conduct, if forward biased. It is assumed that the circuit operation has been arranged such that the removaloficwill turn off the switch.
During the on interval of the switch ($0\leq t\leq\delta T$), the load is subjected to a voltage$V$and the load current increases from $ia1$ to $ia2$. The switch is opened at$t=\delta T$. During the off period of the switch ($\delta T\leq t\leq1$), the load inductance maintains the flow of current through diode DF. The load terminal voltage remains zero (if the voltage drop on the diode is ignored in comparison to V)and the current decreases from $ia2$ to $ia1$. The internal $0\leq t\leq\delta T$ is called the duty interval and the interval $\delta T\leq t\leq T$ is known as the freewheeling interval.
Diode DF provides a path for the load current to flow when switch S isoff, and thus improves the load current waveform. Furthermore, by maintaining the continuity of the load current at turn off, it prevents transient voltage from appearing across switch S, due to the sudden change of the load current.

The source current waveform is also shown in Figure 6.8e. The source current flows only during the duty interval and is equal to the load current. The direct component or average value of the load voltage *Va* is given by

$$V_a = \frac{1}{T}\int_0^T v_a\,dt = \frac{1}{T}\int_0^{\delta T} V\,dt = \delta t.$$

..........eq7

By controlling δ between 0 and 1, the load voltage can be varied from 0 to *V*;thus, a chopper allows a variable DC voltage to be obtained from a fixed voltage DC source. The switch *S* can be controlled in various ways for varying the duty ratioδ.

The control technologies can be divided into the following categories:

1. Time ratio control (TRC).
2. Current limit control (CLC).

In TRC, also known as pulse width control, the ratio of on time to chopper period is controlled. The TRC can be further divided as follows:

1. Constant frequency TRC:
2. The chopper period *T* is kept fixed and

the on period of the switch is varied to control the duty ratio δ.

3. Varied frequency TRC:
4. Here, δ is varied either by keeping *ton* constantand varying *T* or by varying both *ton* and *T*.

In variable frequency control with constant on-time, low-output voltage is obtained at very low values of chopper frequencies. The operation of a chopper at low frequencies adversely affects the motor performance. Furthermore, the operation of a chopper with variable frequencies makes the design of an input filter very difficult. Thus, variable frequency control israrely used.

In current limit control, also known as point-by-point control, δ is controlled indirectly by controlling the load current between certain specified maximum and minimum values. When the load current reaches a specified maximum value, the switch disconnects the load from the source and reconnectsItwhen the current reaches a specified minimum value. For a DC motor load, this type of control is, in effect, a variable frequency variable on time control.

The following important points can be noted from the waveform ofFigure3.5:

1. The source current is not continuous but flows in pulses. The pulsed current makes the peak input power demand high and may cause fluctuation in the source voltage. The source current waveform can be resolved into DC and AC harmonics. The fundamental AC harmonic frequency is the same as the chopper frequency. The AC harmonics are undesirable because they interfere with other loads connected to the DC source and cause radio frequency interference through conduction and electromagnetic radiation. Therefore, anL-C filter is usually incorporated between the chopper and the DC source. At higher chopper frequencies, harmonics can be reduced toa tolerable level by a cheaper filter. From this point, a chopper should be operated at the highest possible frequency.
2. The load terminal voltage is not a perfect direct voltage. In addition to a direct component, it has harmonics of the chopping frequency and its multiples. The load current also has an AC ripple.

The chopper of Figure 3.6 is called a class A chopper. It is one of a numberof chopper circuits that are used for the control of DC motors. This chopperis capable of providing only a positive voltage and a positive current. It istherefore called a single-quadrant chopper, capable of providing DCseparatelyexcited motor control in the first quadrant, positive speed, and positivetorque. Since it can vary the output voltage from *V* to 0, it is also a step-downchopper or a DC to DC buck converter. The basic principle involved can alsobe used to realize a step-up chopper or DC to DCboostconverter. The circuit diagram and steady-state waveforms of a step-up chopper areshown in Figure 3.6. This chopper is known as a class B chopper. The presence of control signal *ic*indicates the duration for which the switch can conduct if forward-biased. During a chopping period T, it remains closed for aninterval $0 \leq t \leq \delta T$ and remains open for an interval $\delta T \leq t \leq T$. During the on period, $i_S$increases from i_{S1} to i_{S2}, thus increasing the magnitude of energystored in inductance L. When the switch is opened, current flows through the parallel combination of the load and capacitor C. Since the current isforced against the higher voltage,the rate of change of the current is negative. It decreases from i_{S2} to i_{S1} in the switch's off period. The energy storedin the inductance L and the energy supplied by the low-voltage source aregiven to the load. The capacitor C serves two purposes. At the instant ofopening of switch S, the source current, i_S, and load current, i_a, are not the same. In the absence of C, the turn off of S will force the two currents to have the same values. This will cause high induced voltage in the inductance $L$and the load inductance. Another reason for using capacitor C is to reduce the load voltage ripple. The purpose of the diode D is to prevent any flow ofcurrent from the load into switch S or source V.

For understanding the step-up operation, capacitor C is assumed to be large enough to maintain a constant voltage V_a across the load. The averagevoltage across the terminal a, b is given as

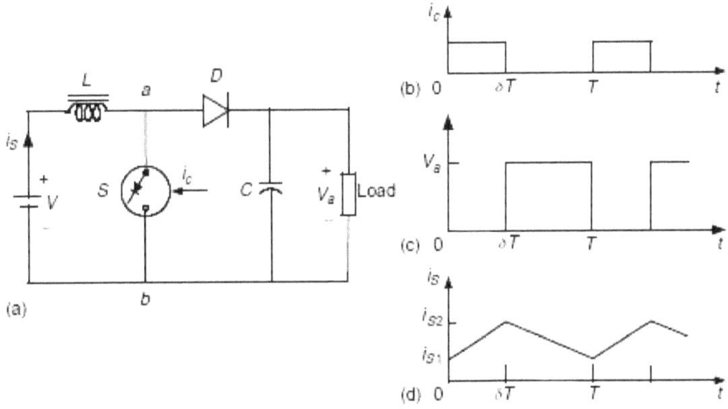

Figure3.7: Principle of operation of a step-up (or class B) chopper: (a) basic chopper circuit; (b) to (d)waveforms

$$V_{ab} = \frac{1}{T}\int_0^T v_{ab}\, dt = V_a(1-\delta \quad \text{................eq8}$$

The average voltage across the inductance L is

$$V_L = \frac{1}{T}\int_0^T \left(L\frac{di}{dt}\right) dt = \frac{1}{T}\int_{i_{s1}}^{i_{s2}} L\, di = 0. \quad \text{.....................eq9}$$

The source voltage is

$$V = V_L + V_{ab} \quad \text{......................eq10}$$

Substituting from equations (8) and (9) into (10) gives

$$V = V_a(1-\delta) \text{ or } V_a = \frac{V}{1-\delta} \quad \text{.............eq11}$$

According to (11), theoretically the output voltage Va can be changed from V to ∞ by controlling δ from 0 to 1. In practice, Va can be controlled from V to a higher voltage, which depends on the capacitor C, and the parametersof the load and chopper.

The main advantage of a step-up chopper is the low ripple in the source current. While most applications require a step-down chopper, the step-up chopper finds application in low-power battery-driven vehicles. The principle of the step-up chopper is also used in the regenerative braking ofDC motor drives.

MULTIQUADRANT CONTROL OF CHOPPER-FED DC MOTOR DRIVES:

The application of DC motors on EVs and HEVs requires the motors to operate in Multiquadarant, including forward motoring, forward braking, backward motoring, and backward braking, as shown in Figure 3.8. For vehicles with reverse mechanical gears, two-quadrant operation (forward motoring and forward braking, or quadrant I and quadrant IV) is required. However, for vehicles without reverse mechanical gears, four-quadrant operation is needed. Multiquadarant operation of a separately excited DC motor is implemented by controlling the voltage poles and magnitude through power electronics-based choppers.

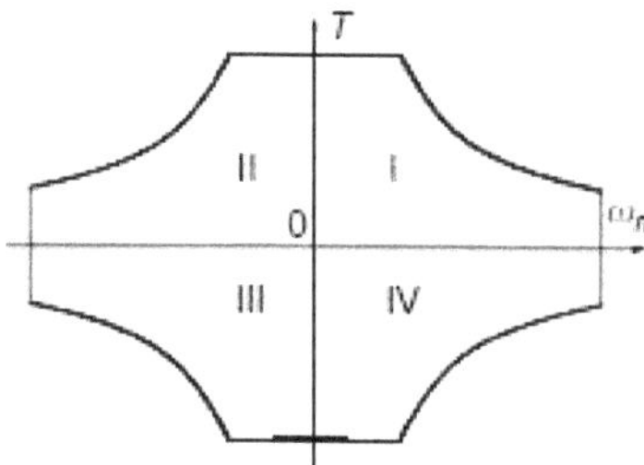

Figure 3.8: Speed–torque profiles of Multiquadarantoperation

TWO-QUADRANT CONTROL OF FORWARD MOTORING AND REGENERATIVE BRAKING:

A two-quadrant operation consisting of forward motoring and forward regenerative braking requires a chopper capable of giving a positive voltage and current in either direction. This two-quadrant operation can be realizedin the following two schemes.

Single Chopper with a Reverse Switch:

The chopper circuit used for forward motoring and forward regenerative braking is shown in Figure 3.9, where S is a self-commutated semiconductorswitch, operated periodically such that it remains closed for aduration of $\delta T$and remains open for a duration of (1-δ) T.C is the manual switch.

When C is closed and S is in operation, the circuit is similar to that of+

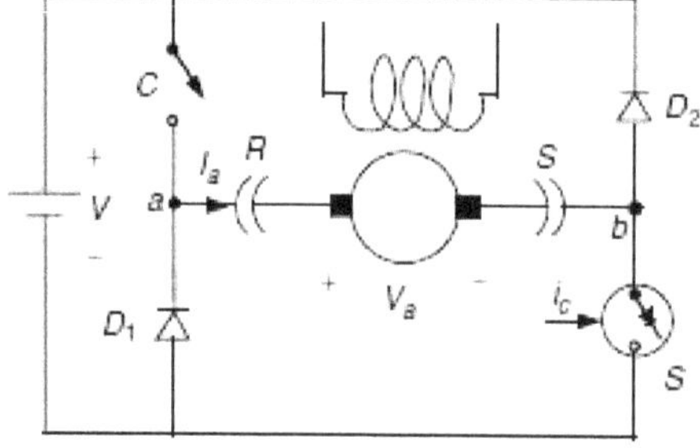

Figure3.9: Forward motoring and regenerative braking control with a single chopper

Under these conditions, terminal *a* is positive and terminal *b* is negative. Regenerative braking in the forward direction is obtained when *C* is opened and the armature connection is reversed with the help of the reversing switch *RS*, making terminal *b* positive and terminal *a* negative. During the on-period of the switch *S*, the motor current flows through a path consisting of the motor armature, switch *S*, and diode *D*1, and increases the energy stored in the armature circuit inductance. When *S* is opened, the current flows through the armature diode *D*2, source *V*, diode *D*1 and back to the armature, thus feeding energy into the source. During motoring, the changeover to regeneration is done in the following steps. Switch *S* is deactivated and switch *C* is opened. This forces the armature current to flow through diode *D*2, source *V*, and diode *D*1. The energy stored in the armature circuit is fed back to the source and the armature current falls to zero. After an adequate delay to ensure that the current has indeed become zero, the armature connection is reversed and switch *S* isreactivated with a suitable value of *d* to start regeneration.

Class C Two-Quadrant Chopper:

In some applications, a smooth transition from motoring to braking and vice versa is required. For such applications, the class C chopper is used as shown in Figure 3.10.

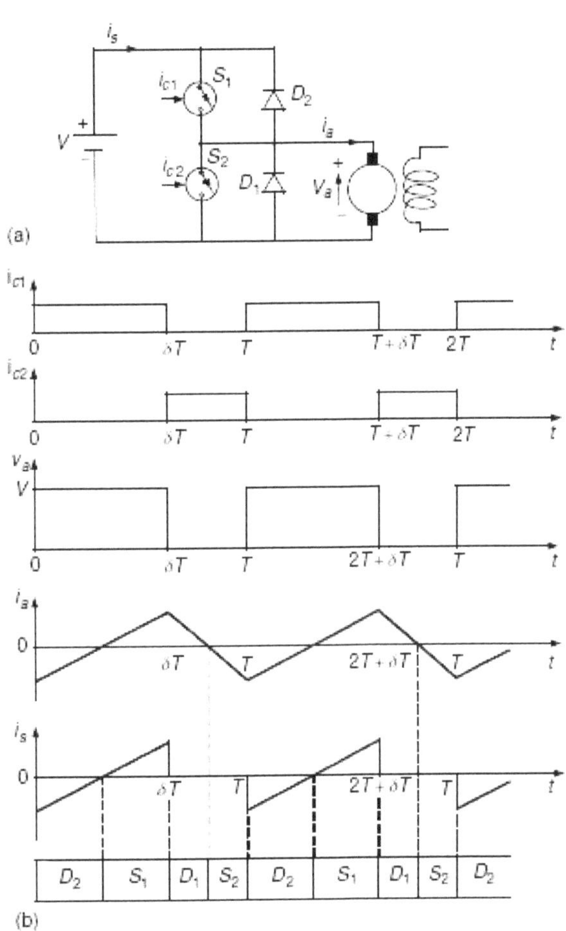

Figure3.10: Forward motoring and regenerative braking control using class C two-quadrant chopper:(a) chopper circuit and (b) waveforms

The self-commutated semiconductor switch *S*1 and diode*D*1 constitute one chopper and the self-commutator switch *S*2 and diode*D*2 form another chopper. Both the choppers are controlled simultaneously, both for motoring and regenerative braking. The switches *S*1 and *S*2are closed alternately. In the chopping period *T*, *S*1 is kept on for a durationδT, and *S*2 is kept on from $\delta T$to$T$. To avoid a direct, short-circuit across the source, care is taken to ensure that *S*1 and *S*2 do not conduct at the same time. This is generally achieved by providing some delay between the turn off of one switch and the turn on of another switch. The waveforms of the control signals *vaia*, and *is*

inFigure3.10(b). In drawing these waveforms, the delay between the turn off of one switch and the turn on of another switch has been ignored because itis usually very small. The control signals for the switches *S*1 and *S*2 are denoted by *ic*1 and *ic*2, respectively. It is assumed that a switch conducts only when the control signal is present and the switch is forward biased.
The following points are helpful in understanding the operation of this two-quadrant circuit:

1. In this circuit, discontinuous conduction does not occur, irrespective of its frequency of operation. Discontinuous conduction occurs interval of time. The current may become zero either during the freewheeling interval or in the energy transfer interval. In this circuit, freewheeling willoccur when *S*1 is off and the current is flowing through *D*1. This will happen in interval $\delta T \leq t \leq T$, which is also the interval for which *S*2 receives the control signal. If *ia*falls to zero in the freewheeling interval, the back EMF will immediately drive a current through *S*2 in the reverse direction, thus preventing the armature current from remaining zero for a finite interval of time. Similarly, energy transfer will be present when *S*2 is off and *D*2is conducting — that is, during the interval 0_*t*_δ*T*. If the current falls to zero during this interval, *S*1 will conductimmediatelybecause*ic*is present and *V*_*E*. The armature current will flow, preventing discontinuous conduction.
2. Since discontinuous conditions are absent, the motor current will be flowing all the time. Thus, during the interval $0 \leq t \leq \delta T$, the motor armature will be connected either through *S*1 or *D*2. Consequently, the motor terminal voltage will be *V* and the rate of change of *ia*will be positive because $V>E$. Similarly, during the interval $\delta T \leq t \leq T$, the motor armature will be shorted either through *D*1 or *S*2. Consequently, the motor voltage will be zero and the rate of change of *ia*will be negative.
3. During the interval $0 \leq t \leq \delta T$, the positive armature current is carried by*S*1 and the negative armature current is carried by *D*2. The source current flows only during this interval and it is equal to *ia*. During the interval $\delta T \leq t \leq T$, the positive current is carried by *D*1and the negative current is carried by *S*2.
4. From the motor terminal voltage waveform of Figure 3.10 $V_a = \delta V$. Hence,

$$I_a = \frac{\delta V - E}{R_a}. \quad \text{..............eq12}$$

Equation (12) suggests that the motoring operation takes place whenδ=*E*/*V*, and that regenerative braking occurs when δ =*E*/*V*. The no-loadoperation is obtained when δ =*E*/*V*.

FOUR-QUADRANT OPERATION:

The four-quadrant operation can be obtained by combining two class C choppers (Figure 3.10) as shown in Figure 3.11,

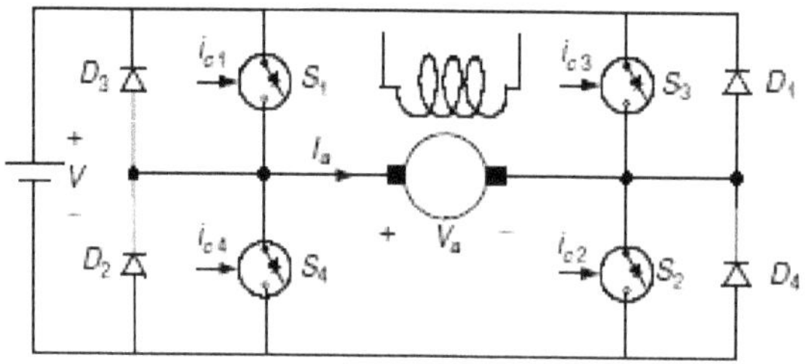

Figure3.11: Class E four-quadrant chopper

which is referred to as a class Echopper. In this chopper, if *S*2 is kept closed continuously and *S*1 and *S*4 are controlled, a two-quadrant chopper is obtained, which provides positive terminal voltage (positive speed) and the armature current in either direction (positive or negative torque), giving a motor control in quadrants I and IV. Now if *S*3 is kept closed continuously and *S*1 and *S*4 are controlled, one obtains a two-quadrant chopper, which can supply a variable negative terminal

voltage (negative speed) and the armature current can be in either direction (positive or negative torque), giving a motor control in quadrants II and III.This control method has the following features: the utilization factor of the switches is low due to the asymmetry in the circuit operation. Switches $S3$ and$S2$ should remain on for a long period. This can create commutation problems when the switches use thyristors. The minimum output voltage depends directly on the minimum time for which the switch can be closed, since there is always a restriction on the minimum time for which the switch can be closed, particularly in thyristor choppers.47 The minimum available output voltage, and therefore the minimum available motor speed, is restricted. To ensure that switches $S1$ and $S4$, or $S2$ and $S3$ are not on at the same time, some fixed time interval must elapse between the turn off for one switch and the turn on of another switch. This restricts the maximum permissible frequency of operation. It also requires two switching operations during a cycle of the output voltage.

INDUCTION MOTOR DRIVES:

Commutator fewer motor drives offer a number of advantages over conventional DC commutator motor drives for the electric propulsion of EVs andHEVs. At present, induction motor drives are the mature technology among commutator less motor drives. Compared with DC motor drives, theACinduction motor drive has additional advantages such as lightweight nature, small volume, low-cost, and high efficiency. These advantages are particularly important for EV and HEVapplications. There are two types of induction motors, namely, wound-rotor and squirrel cage motors. Because of the high cost, need for maintenance, and lack of sturdiness, wound-rotor induction motors are less attractive than their squirrel-cage counterparts, especially for electric propulsion in EVs and HEVs.Hence, squirrel-cage induction motors are loosely termed as induction motors.

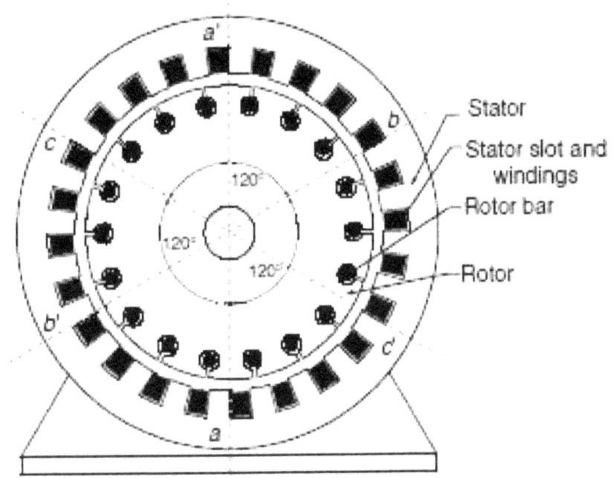

Figure1: Cross-section of an induction motor

A cross section of a two-pole induction motor is shown in Figure 1. Slots in the inner periphery of the stator are inserted with three phase windings, $a–a'$, $b–b'$, and $c–c'$. The turns of each winding are distributed such that the current in the winding produces an approximate sinusoidally distributed flux density around the periphery of the air gap.

The three windings are spatially arranged by 120° as shown in Figure 1. The most common types of induction motor rotors are the squirrel cage inwhich aluminium bars are cast into slots in the outer periphery of the rotor. Thealuminium bars are short-circuited together at both ends of the rotor by cast aluminium end rings, which can also be shaped into fans.

PRINCIPLES OF OPERATION OF INDUCTION MOTOR (MATHEMATICAL TREATMENT):

In **Figure 1** a cross section of the stator of a three phase, two pole induction motor is shown.

energized from a three-phase system. When the stator windings are energized from a three-phase system, the currents in the coils reach their maximum values at different instants. Since the three currents are displaced from each other by 120° electrical, their respective flux contributions will also be displaced by 120° electrical. Let a balanced three phase current be applied to the stator with the phase sequence ***A-B-C***

$$I_A = I_m \cos \omega t$$
$$I_B = I_m \cos\left(\omega t - \frac{2\pi}{3}\right)$$
$$I_C = I_m \cos\left(\omega t - \frac{4\pi}{3}\right)$$

...............eq1

The instantaneous flux produced by the stator will hence be

$$\phi_A = \phi_m \cos \omega t$$
$$\phi_B = \phi_m \cos\left(\omega t - \frac{2\pi}{3}\right)$$
$$\phi_C = \phi_m \cos\left(\omega t - \frac{4\pi}{3}\right)$$

..............eq2

The resultant flux at an angle θ from the axis of phase ***A*** is

$$\phi_T = \phi_A \cos(\theta) + \phi_B \cos(\theta - \frac{2\pi}{3}) + \phi_C \cos(\theta - \frac{4\pi}{3})$$

..................eq3

Substituting **equation 2** into **equation 3** gives

$$\phi_T = \phi_A \cos(\theta)\cos(\omega t) + \phi_B \cos(\theta - \frac{2\pi}{3})\cos(\omega t - \frac{2\pi}{3}) + \phi_C \cos(\theta - \frac{4\pi}{3})\cos(\omega t - \frac{4\pi}{3})$$

$$\Rightarrow \phi_T = \frac{3}{2}\phi_m \cos(\theta - \omega t)$$

.... eq4

From **equation** 4 it can be seen that the resultant flux has amplitude of 1.5∅ , is a sinusoidal function of angle and rotates in synchronism with the supply frequency. Hence, it is called a ***rotating field***.

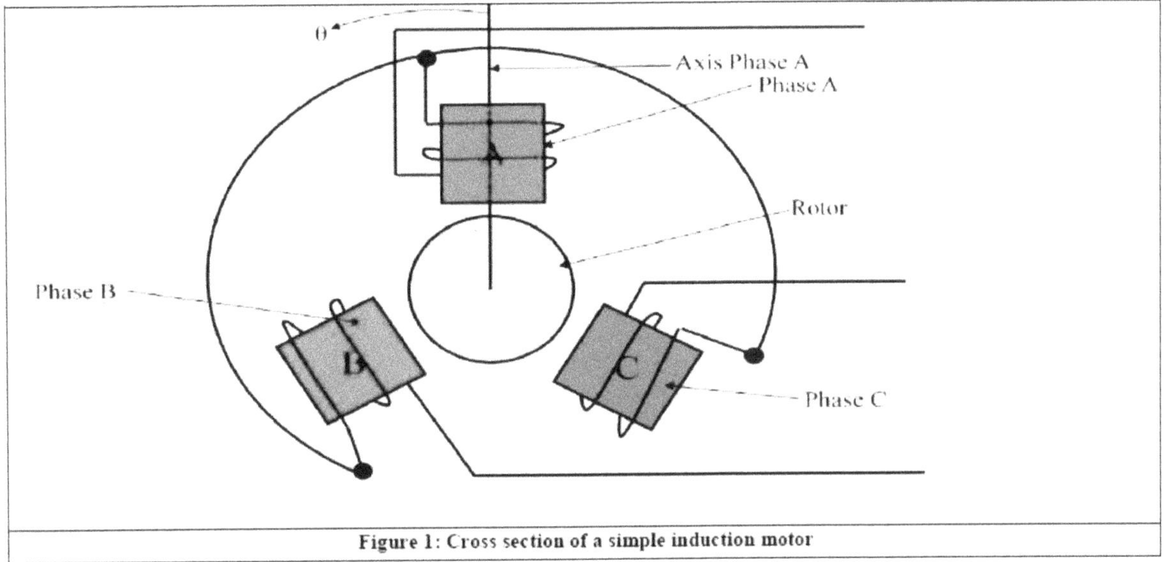

Figure 1: Cross section of a simple induction motor

PRINCIPLES OF OPERATION OF INDUCTION MOTOR (GRAPHICAL TREATMENT):

Let the synchronous frequency be 1rad/sec. Hence, the spatial distribution of resultant flux at t=0sec, t=60sec, t=120sec, t=180 sec, t=240sec and t=300sec and are shown in **Figure 2**. The explanation of the flux creation is as follows

- At t=0, phase **A** is a maximum north pole, while phase **B** and phase **C** are weak south poles, **Figure (2a)**.
- At t=60, phase **C** is a strong south pole, while phase **B** and phase **A** are weak north poles **Figure (2b)**.
- At t=120, phase **B** is a strong north pole, while phase **A** and phase **C** are weak south poles **Figure (2c)**.
- At t=180, phase **A** is a strong south pole, while phase **B** and phase **C** are weak north poles **Figure (2a)**.
- At t=240, phase **C** is a strong north pole, while phase **A** and phase **B** are weak south poles **Figure (2e)**.
- At t=300, phase **B** is s strong south pole, while phase **C** and phase **A** are weak north poles **Figure (2f)**.

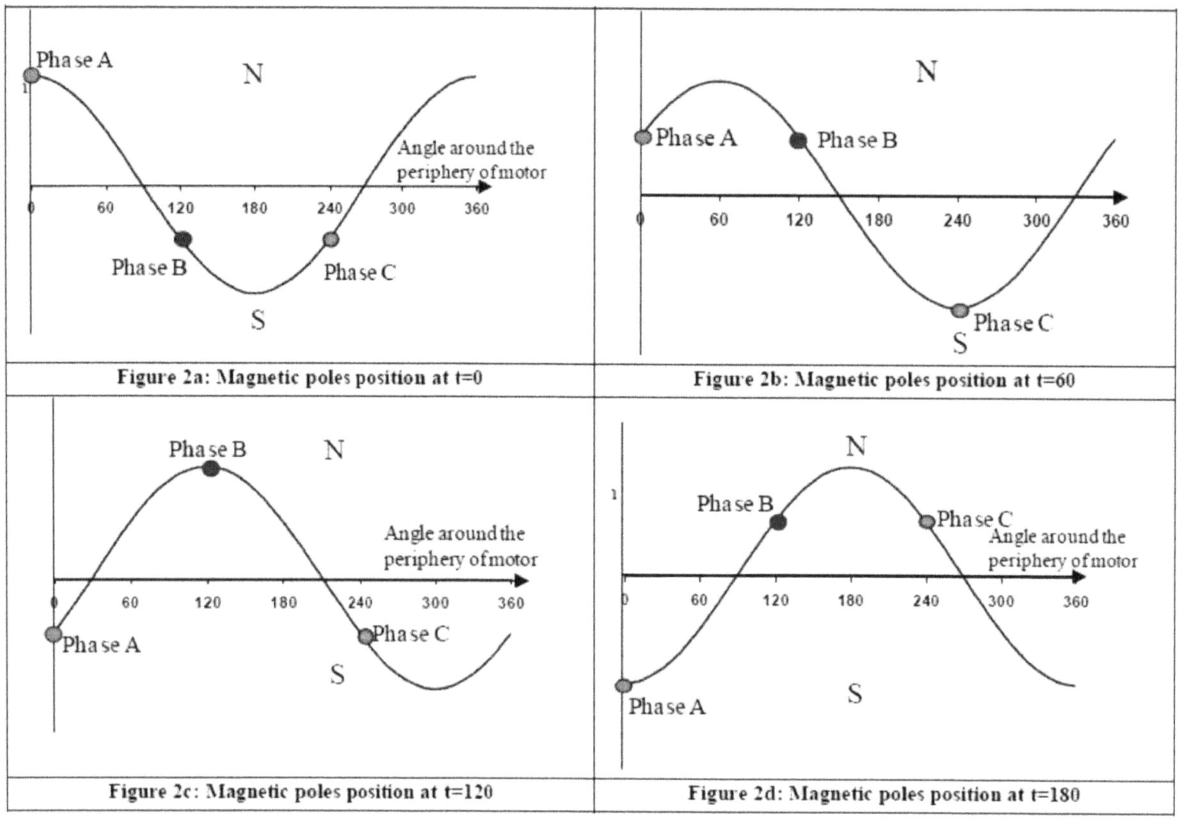

Figure 2a: Magnetic poles position at t=0

Figure 2b: Magnetic poles position at t=60

Figure 2c: Magnetic poles position at t=120

Figure 2d: Magnetic poles position at t=180

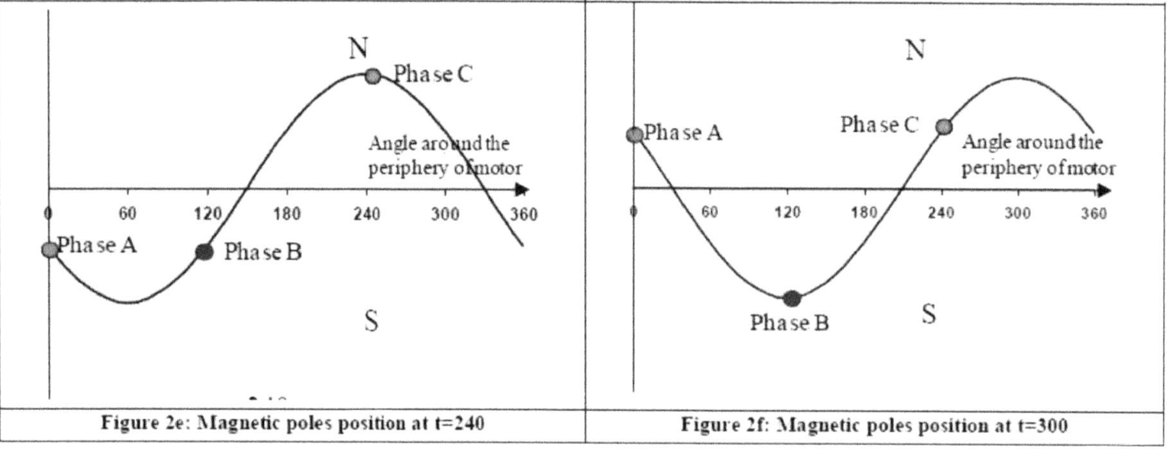

Figure 2e: Magnetic poles position at t=240

Figure 2f: Magnetic poles position at t=300

FLUXES AND MMF IN INDUCTION MOTOR:

Although the flux generated by each coil is only alternating flux, the combined flux contributions of the three coils, carrying current at appropriate sequential phase angles, produces a two pole rotating flux.

The rotating flux produced by three phase currents in the stationary coils, may be linked to the rotating field produced by a magnet sweeping around the rotor (**Figure 3a**). The rotating field cuts the rotor bars in its anti-clockwisesweep around the rotor. According to Lenz's law, the voltage, current and flux generated by the relative motion between a conductor and a magnetic field will be in a direction to oppose the relative motion. From **Figure 3a** it can be seen that the bars **a** and **b** are just under the pole centres and have maximum electromotive force (e.m.f) generated in them and this is indicated by large cross and dots. The bars away from the pole centreshave reduced magnitude of generated e.m.fs and these are indicated by varying sizes of dots and crosses. If the rotor circuit is assumed purely resistive, then current in any bar is in phase with the e.m.f generated

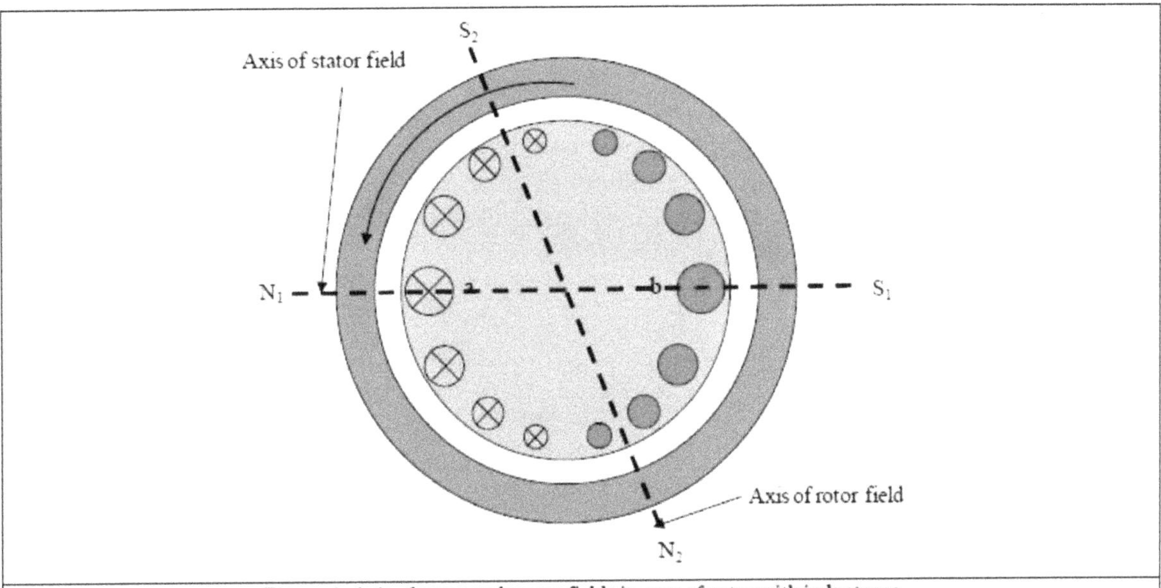

Figure 4: Axis of rotor and stator fields in case of rotor with inductance

ROTOR ACTION:

At standstill, rotor conductors are being cut by rotating flux wave at synchronous speed . Hence, the frequency of 2the rotor e.m.f and current is equal to the input voltage frequency 1.When the rotor rotates at a speed of rotations per second (r.p.s) in the direction of rotating flux wave, the relative speed between synchronously rotating flux and rotor conductors becomes(-)r.p.s.

$$f_2 = \frac{P(n_s - n_r)}{2} \qquad \text{......................eq4}$$

Where P is the no of poles of a machine
Hence, the slip of the machine is definedas

$$s = \frac{n_s - n_r}{n_s} \qquad \text{............................eq5}$$

Thus, the rotor frequency is defined as

$$f_2 = \frac{P \times s \times n_s}{2} = sf_1$$

—

..................................eq6

At standstill the rotor frequency is 1and the field produced by rotor currents revolves at a speed equal to w.r.t. rotor structure. When the rotor rotates at a speed of nr, the rotor frequency is 1 and the rotor produced field revolves at a speed of /**P**= w.r.t. rotor structure. The rotor is already rotating at a speed of w.r.t. stator. Hence, the speed of rotor field w.r.t. to stator is equal to the sum of mechanical rotor speed nr and rotor field speed w.r.t. rotor. Hence, the speed of the rotor field with respect to stator is given by

$$n_r + sn_s = n_s(1-s) + sn_s = n_s \text{ r.p.s}$$ eq7

The stator and rotor fields are stationary with respect to each other at all possible rotor speeds. Hence, a steady torque is produced by their interaction. The rotor of an induction motor can never attain synchronous speed. If does so then the rotor conductors will be stationary w.r.t. the synchronously rotating rotor conductors and hence, rotor m.m.f. would be zero.

ROTOR E.M.F AND EQUIVALENT CIRCUIT:

Let the rotor e.m.f. at standstill be 2 . When the rotor speed is0.4 , the slip is 0.6 and the relative speed between rotating field and rotor conductors is0.6 . Hence, the induced e.m.f. , per phase, in the rotor is

$$0.6n_s \frac{E_2}{n_s} = 0.6E_2$$ eq8

In general, for any value of slipS , the per phase induced e.m.f in the rotor conductors is equal to . The other quantities of the rotor are given as 2

The rotor leakage reactance at standstill is

$$x_2 = 2\pi f_1 L_2$$ eq9

The rotor leakage reactance at any slip s is

$$2\pi s f_1 L_2 = s x_2 \Omega$$ eq10

The rotor leakage impedance at standstill is

$$\sqrt{r_2^2 + x_2^2}$$ eq11

At any slip s rotor leakage impedance is

$$\sqrt{r_2^2 + (sx_2)^2}$$ eq12

The per phase rotor current at standstill is

$$\frac{E_2}{\sqrt{r_2^2 + x_2^2}}$$ eq13

The per phase rotor current at any slip s is

$$\frac{sE_2}{\sqrt{r_2^2 + (sx_2)^2}} = \frac{E_2}{\sqrt{\left(\frac{r_2}{s}\right)^2 + (x_2)^2}}$$ eq14

Based on **equation 13f** the equivalent circuit of the rotor is shown in **Figure 5**.

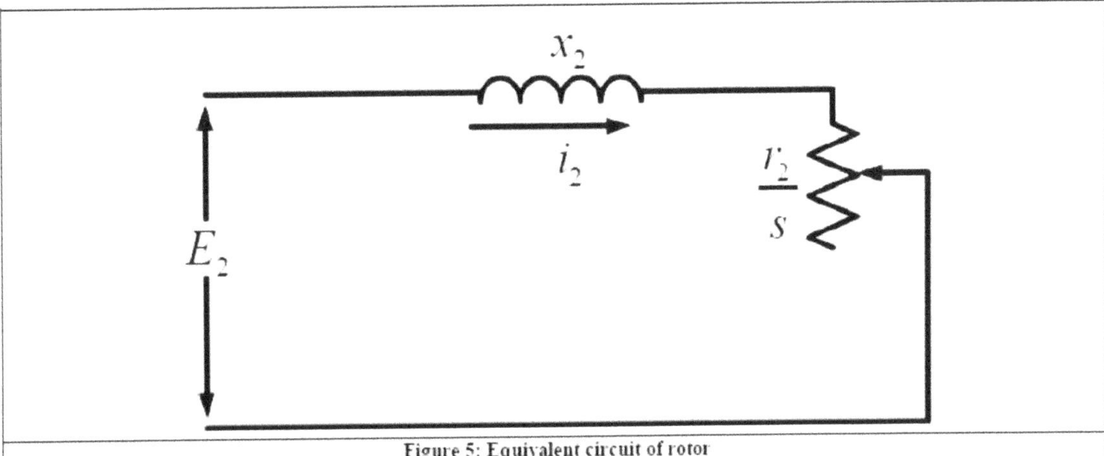

Figure 5: Equivalent circuit of rotor

COMPLETE EQUIVALENT CIRCUIT

The rotating air gap flux generates back e.m.f. ($_2$) in all the three phases of the stator. The stator applied terminal voltage $_1$has to overcome back e.m.f. $_1$and the stator leakage impedance drop:

$$V_1 = E_1 + I_1(r_1 + jx_1)$$

........................eq1

The stator current $_1$consists of following two components, $'_1$ and . The component $_1'$ the load component and counteracts the rotor m.m.f. The other component creates the resultant air gap flux ∅ and provides the core loss. This current can be resolved into two components: $_c I$ in phase with $_1 E$ and I_Φ lagging $_1 E$ by 90o. In the equivalent circuit of the stator shown in **Figure 6**, and ∅ are taken into account by a parallel branch, consisting of core-loss resistance in parallel to magnetizing reactance ∅.

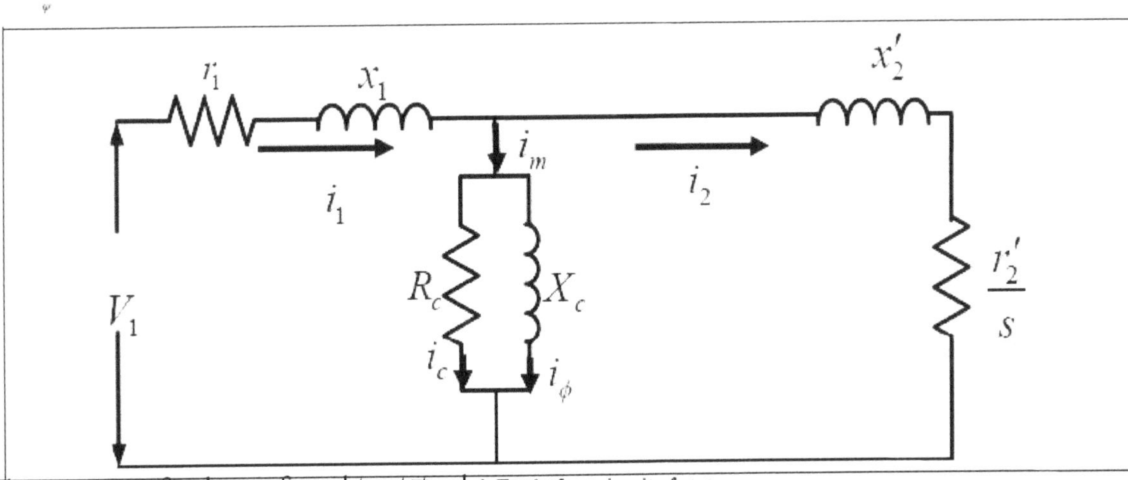

Figure 6: Equivalent circuit of stator

The rotor e.m.f. when referred to stator becomes

$$E_1 = \frac{E_2}{N_2'} N_1'$$

................................eq2

Where N'_1 and N'_2 are the no of turns in stator and Rotor respectively The rotor leakage impedance when referred to the stator is

$$Z'_2 = \left(\frac{r_2}{s} + jx_2\right)\left(\frac{N'_1}{N'_2}\right)^2 = \frac{r'_2}{s} + jx'_2$$

where

$$r'_2 = \left(\frac{N'_1}{N'_2}\right)^2 r_2;\ x'_2 = \left(\frac{N'_1}{N'_2}\right)^2 x_2 \qquad \text{..............................eq3}$$

After referred the rotor quantities towards stator, the combined equivalent circuit of the machine is shown in **Figure 7**. For simplicity the prime notations will not be used in the further discussions and all the rotor quantities henceforth will be referred to the stator side. Moreover, all the quantities are at stator frequency.

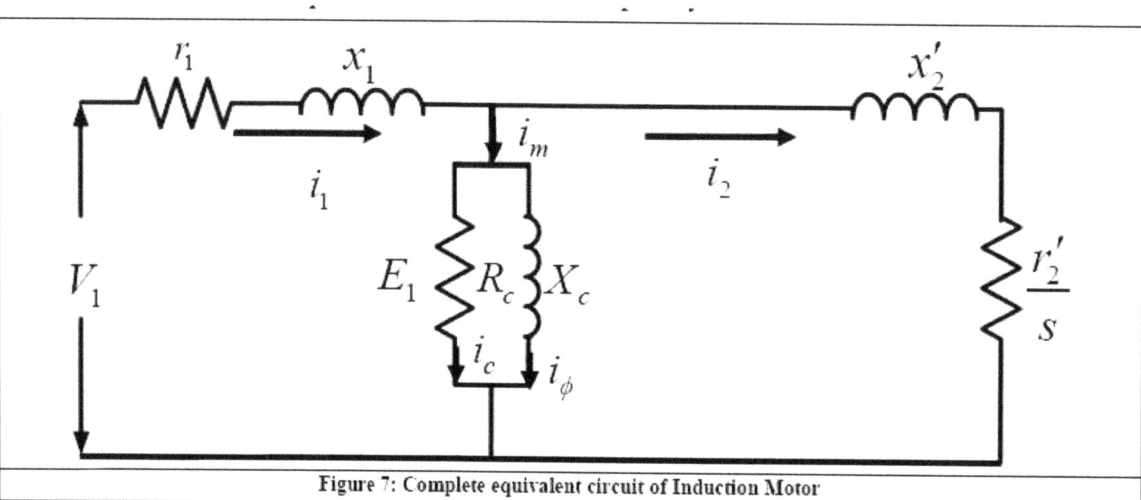

Figure 7: Complete equivalent circuit of Induction Motor

SIMPLIFICATION EQUIVALENT CIRCUIT:

The use of exact equivalent circuit is laborious; hence some simplifications are done in the equivalent circuit. Under normal operating conditions of constant voltage and frequency, core loss in induction motors is usually constant. Hence, the core loss component can be omitted from the equivalent circuit, **Figure 8**. However, to determine the shaft power, the constant core loss must be taken into account along with friction, windage and stray load losses. It should be noted that all the quantities used in the equivalent circuit are per phase quantities. Steady state performance parameters of the induction motor, such as current, speed, torque, losses etc. can be computed from the equivalent circuit shown in **Figure 8**.

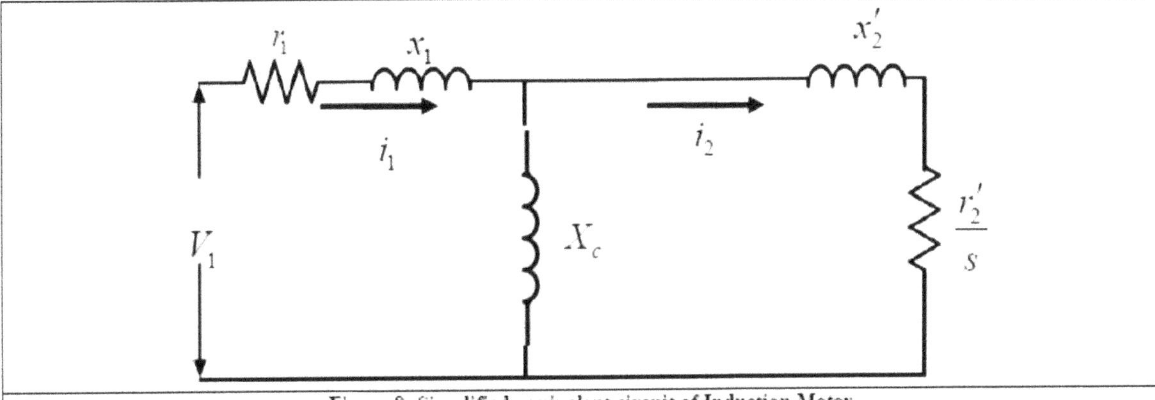

Figure 8: Simplified equivalent circuit of Induction Motor

ANALYSIS OF EQUIVALENT CIRCUIT:

The total power transferred across the air gap ( ) from the stator is

$$P_{gap} = n_{ph} i_2^2 \left(\frac{r_2}{s} \right)$$
$$= n_{ph} \left(i_2^2 r_2 + i_2^2 r_2 \left(\frac{1-s}{s} \right) \right) \qquad \text{................................eq4}$$

Where is the no of phases

Hence, the rotor Ohmic loses and the internal mechanical power are given as

$$P_{rotor} = n_{ph} i_2^2 r_2 = n_{ph} s P_{gap} \qquad \text{..................................eq5}$$

$$P_{mech} = n_{ph} i_2^2 r_2 \left(\frac{1-s}{s} \right) \qquad \text{..........................eq6}$$

The internal (gross or air gap or the electromagnetic torque) torque developed per phase is given by

$$T_e = \frac{P_{mech}}{\omega_r} = \frac{(1-s) P_{gap}}{(1-s)\omega_s} = \frac{P_{gap}}{\omega_s} \qquad \text{.............................eq7}$$

where is the rotor speedand is the synchronous speed

The output or the shaft power is

$$P_{shaft} = P_{mech} - Mechanical\ losses$$

$$or$$

$$P_{shaft} = P_{gap} - Rotor\ Ohmic\ losses - Mechanical\ losses \qquad \text{...........eq8}$$

3.2.8.THEVENIN'S EQUIVALENT CIRCUIT OF INDUCTION MOTOR:

When the torque-slip or power-slip characteristics are required, application of Thevenin's theorem to the induction motor equivalent circuit reduces the computation complexity. For applying Thevenin's theorem to the equivalent circuit shown in **Figure 8**, two points ***a***, ***b*** are considered as shown in **Figure 9**. From these points the voltage source is viewed and the equivalent voltage at point ***a*** and ***b*** is 1 V

$$V_{eq} = \frac{V_1(jX_c)}{R_1 + j(X_1 + X_c)}$$

..............................eq9

The equivalent impedance of the circuit as seen from points ***a*** and ***b*** is

$$Z_{eq} = \frac{(R_1 + jX_1)(jX_c)}{R_1 + j(X_1 + X_c)}$$

.................................eq10

For most induction motors ($_1$+) is much greater than $_1$. Hence, $_1$can be neglected from the denominator of **equation 22** and **equation 23**. The simplified expression for and are

$$V_{eq} = \frac{V_1(jX_c)}{j(X_1 + X_c)} = \frac{V_1 X_c}{X_1 + X_c}$$

.........................eq11

$$Z_{eq} = R_{eq} + jX_{eq} = \frac{R_1 X_c}{X_1 + X_c} + \frac{jX_1 X_c}{X_1 + X_c}$$

...............................eq12

From the Thevenin's equivalent circuit, the rotor current can be determined as

$$I_2 = \frac{V_{eq}}{\left(R_{eq} + \frac{r_2}{s}\right) + j(X_{eq} + X_2)}$$

.................................eq13

The airgap torque produced by the motor is

$$T_e = \frac{n_{ph}}{\omega_s} \frac{V_{eq}^2}{\left(R_{eq} + \frac{r_2}{s}\right)^2 + \left(X_{eq} + X_2\right)^2} \frac{r_2}{s}$$

$$= \frac{K_t}{\left(R_{eq} + \frac{r_2}{s}\right)^2 + X^2} \frac{r_2}{s}$$

....................................eq14

where

$$K_t = \frac{n_{ph} V_{eq}^2}{\omega_s} \text{ and } X = X_2 + X_{eq}$$

...........................eq15

A typical torque versus slip curve for IM obtained from **equation 27** is shown in **Figure 10**.

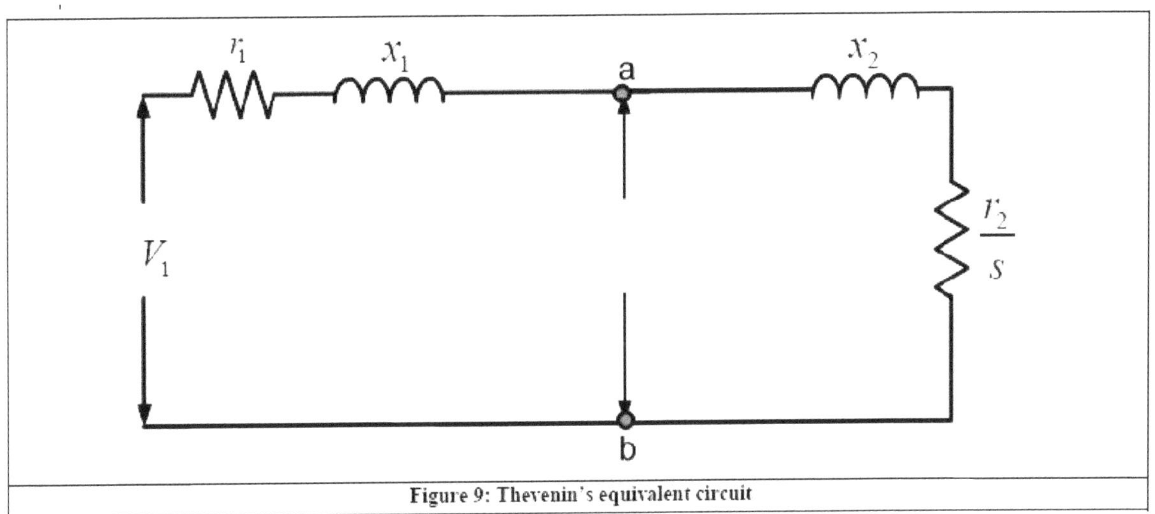

Figure 9: Thevenin's equivalent circuit

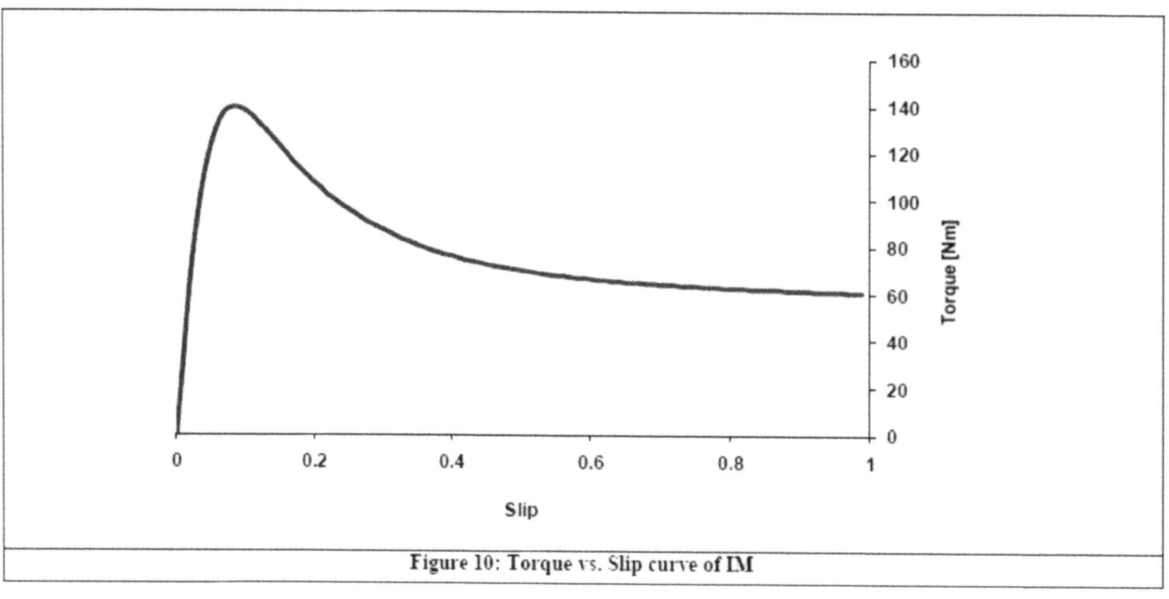

Figure 10: Torque vs. Slip curve of IM

PERMANENT MAGNET MOTORS:

By using high energy magnets such as rare earth-based magnets, a PM machine drive can be designed with high power density, high speed and high operation efficiency. These advantages are attractive for their application in EVs and HEVs. The major advantages of PM machines are:

- ***High efficiency***: The PM machines have a very high efficiency due to the use of PMs for excitation which consume no power. Moreover, the absence of mechanical commutators and brushes results in low mechanical friction losses.
- ***High Power density***: The use of high energy density magnets has allowed achieving very high flux densities in the PM machines. As a result of high flux densities, high torque can be produced from a given volume of motor compared to other motors of same volume.
- ***Ease of Control***: THE PM motors can be controlled as easily as DC motors because the control variables are easily accessible and constant throughout the operation of the motor.
- ***Cost***: Rare-earth magnets commonly used in PM machines are very expensive.
- ***Magnet Demagnetization***: The magnets can be demagnetized by large opposing magnetomotive force and high temperatures.
- ***Inverter Failure***: Due to magnets on the rotor, PM motors present major risks in the case of short circuit failures of the inverters. The rotor is always energized and constantly induces EMF in the short-circuited windings. A very large current circulates in those windings and an accordingly large torque tends to block the rotor. The dangers of blocking one or several wheels of a vehicle are non-negligible.

Based on the shape of the back e.m.f induced in the stator windings, the PM motors can be classified into two types:

- Permanent Magnet Synchronous Machine with sinusoidal back e.m.f (**Figure 1a**)

- Brushless Permanent Magnet DC Machines (BLDC) with trapezoidal back e.m.f (**Figure 1b**)

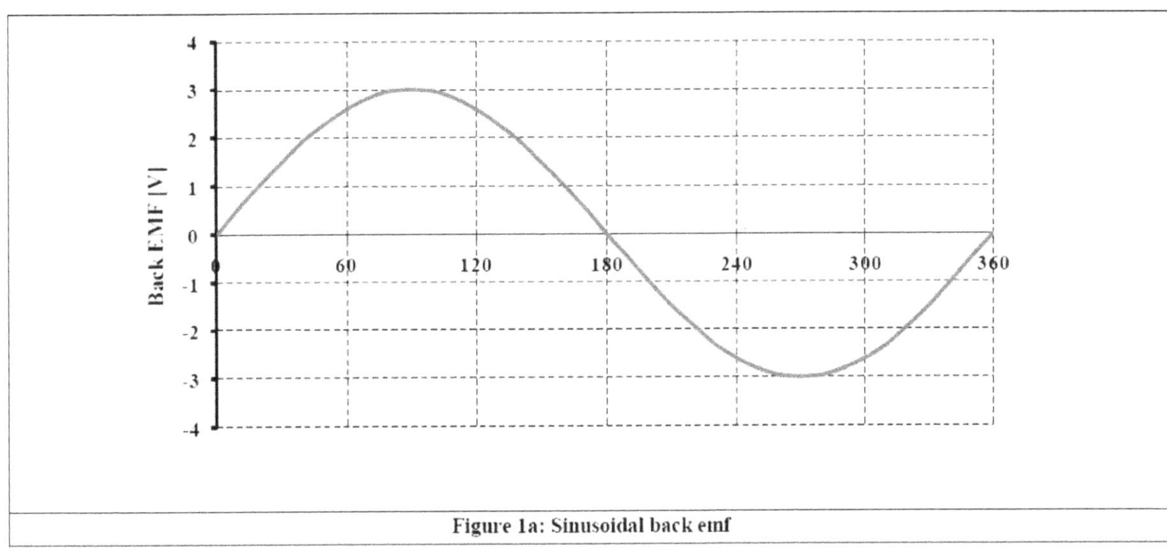

Figure 1a: Sinusoidal back emf

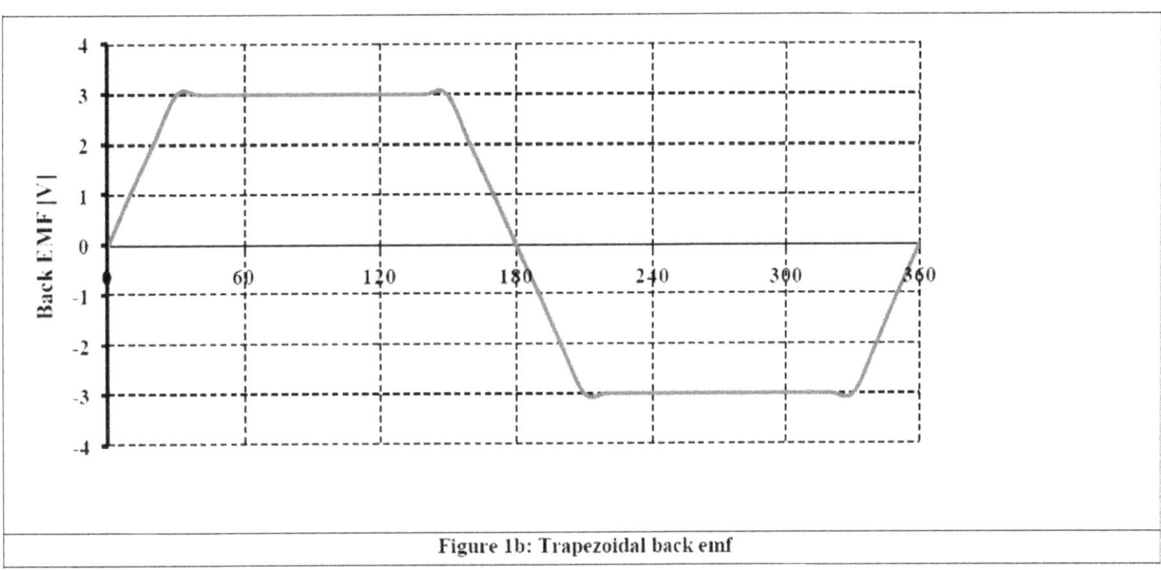

Figure 1b: Trapezoidal back emf

PRINCIPLE OF OPERATION OF PM MACHINE:

To produce torque, in general, a rotor flux and a stator mmf has to be present that are stationary with respect to each other but having a nonzero phase shift between them. In PM machines, the necessary rotor flux is present due to rotor PMs. Currents in the stator windings generate the stator mmf. The zero-relative speed between the stator mmf and the rotor flux is achieved if the stator mmf is revolving at the same speed as the rotor flux, that is, rotor speed and also in the same direction. The revolving stator mmf is the result of injecting a set of polyphase currents phase shifted from each other by the same amount of phase shift between the polyphase windings. For example, a three phase machine with three windings shifted in space by electrical 120o between them produces a rotating magnetic field constant in magnitude and travelling at an angular frequency of the currents (just as in case of Induction machines). The rotor has permanent magnets on it, hence the flux produced by the rotor magnets start to chase the stator mmf and as a result torque is produced. Since the relative speed between the stator mmf and rotor flux has to be zero, the rotor moves at the same speed as the speed of the stator mmf. Hence, the PM machines are inherently synchronous machines. As the coils in the stator experience a change of flux linkages caused by the moving magnets, there is an induced e.m.f in the windings. The shape of the induced e.m.f is very dependent on the shape of the flux linkage. If the rotational electrical speed of the machine and the air gap flux is sinusoidal then it can be expressed as (**Figure 3**)

$$\phi = \phi_m \sin(\omega_r t)$$

$$\omega_r = \frac{N_p}{2} \omega_{mech} \qquad \text{......................eq1}$$

where∅ is the peak flux produced

ω is the electrical speed of the rotation

is the mechanical speed of the rotor

is the no of poles of motor

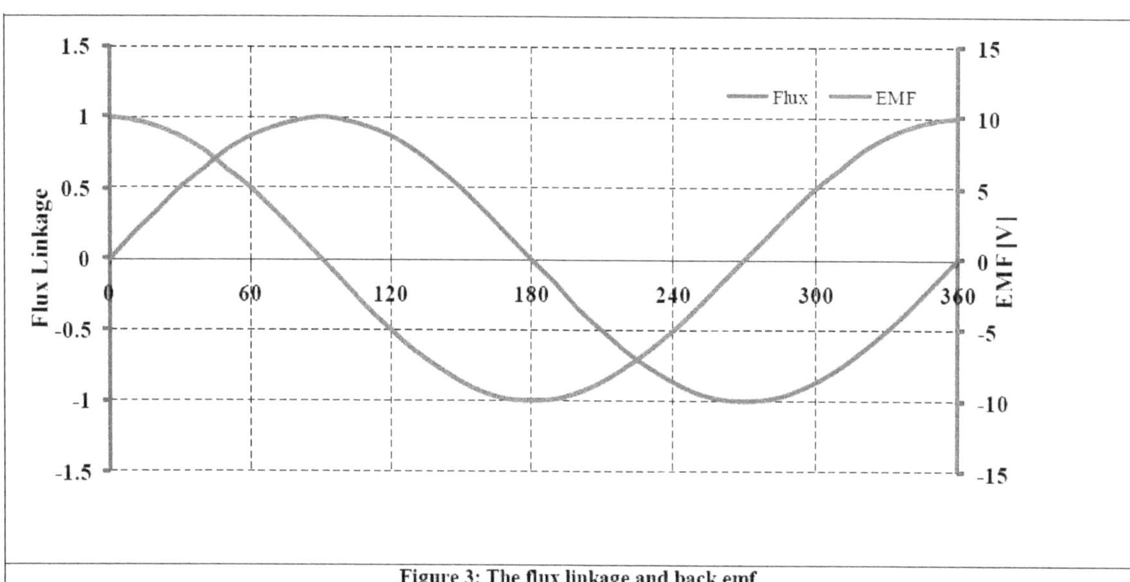

Figure 3: The flux linkage and back emf.

Given the number of turns ( ), then the flux linkages (λ) are equal to the product ∅ . The induced emf is equal to the rate of flux linkages and is given by (**Figure 3**):

$$e = -\frac{d\lambda}{dt} = -N_{turns}\phi_m\omega_r \cos(\omega_r t) = -\lambda_m\omega_r \cos(\omega_r t) = -\lambda_m\omega_r \cos(\theta_r)$$

where

$$\lambda_m = N_{turns}\phi_m$$

$$\theta_r = \omega_r t \qquad \text{..........eq2}$$

The –ve sign in **equation 2** indicates that the induced e.m.f opposes the applied voltage. Some observations based on **equation 2** are:

- The emf is proportional to the product of the rotational frequency and air gap for a constant number of turns.
- Assuming that air gap flux is constant, it can be seen that the e.m.f is influenced only by the rotational speed of rotor which is same as the stator current frequency

(

- By changing the frequency of stator current, the speed of the motor can be changed and a speed control of the motor can be achieved. However, beyond a certain speed known as base speed, an increase in stator frequency will result in voltage demand exceeding the supply capability. During that operation, keeping the voltage constant and increasing the excitation frequency reduces the airgap flux and thus allowing the excitation frequency reduces the air gap flux, thus allowing going to higher speed over and above the base speed. This operation is known as ***flux weakening***.

The PM machines are fed by DC-AC converter. By changing the frequency at which the gates are turned on, the frequency of the output wave can be varied. In the next sections the operation of a three phase PM machines with 120o and 180o conduction modes are explained. The following assumptions are made in the following analysis:

- The phases of the machines are **Y** connected.
- The current entering the neutral point (n) is considered to be positive and leaving it is considered to be negative. n
- The back e.m.f induced in the phases is sinusoidal.
- All the phases of the machine are balanced, that is, the inductances and resistances of the phases are equal.

STEADY STATE CHARACTERISTICS OF PERMANENT MAGNET MOTORS:

STEADY STATE MODELLING OF PERMANENT MAGNET MACHINES:

The PM machines are driven by the inverter and the triggering of the DC-AC converter switches is symmetric, the waveforms of the applied stator voltage exhibit the following relationships

$$V_{an}\left(\omega_r t+\frac{\pi}{3}\right)=-V_{bn}\left(\omega_r t\right);\ V_{bn}\left(\omega_r t+\frac{\pi}{3}\right)=-V_{cn}\left(\omega_r t\right);\ V_{cn}\left(\omega_r t+\frac{\pi}{3}\right)=-V_{an}\left(\omega_r t\right) \qquad (1)$$

The voltage and current relations given in

$$p\begin{bmatrix} i_a \\ i_b \\ i_c \end{bmatrix}=\begin{bmatrix} -\frac{R_s}{L_s} & 0 & 0 \\ 0 & -\frac{R_s}{L_s} & 0 \\ 0 & 0 & -\frac{R_s}{L_s} \end{bmatrix}\begin{bmatrix} i_a \\ i_b \\ i_c \end{bmatrix}+\begin{bmatrix} \frac{1}{L_s} & 0 & 0 \\ 0 & \frac{1}{L_s} & 0 \\ 0 & 0 & \frac{1}{L_s} \end{bmatrix}+\begin{bmatrix} V_{an}-e_a \\ V_{bn}-e_b \\ V_{cn}-e_c \end{bmatrix}$$

……………………………..................................eq2(a)

$$e_a=\lambda_m\omega_r\cos\left(\omega_r t\right);e_b=\lambda_m\omega_r\cos\left(\omega_r t-\frac{2\pi}{3}\right);e_c=\lambda_m\omega_r\cos\left(\omega_r t+\frac{2\pi}{3}\right)$$

…………………………………………………eq2(b)

The differential equations given in **equation 2** are time-invariant. Hence, the stator currents which form the response of the system, obey the same symmetry relations as the input voltage and can be

$$i_a\left(\omega_r t+\frac{\pi}{3}\right)=-i_b\left(\omega_r t\right);\ i_b\left(\omega_r t+\frac{\pi}{3}\right)=-i_c\left(\omega_r t\right);\ i_c\left(\omega_r t+\frac{\pi}{3}\right)=-i_a\left(\omega_r t\right)$$

....eq3

STEADY STATE SOLUTION FOR ◦ CONDUCTION OF THE DC-AC CONVERTER

Due to the symmetries for the voltages and currents given by **equations 1** and **3**, if thesolution is known for one basic switching interval, it can be used to generate the solutionfor the remaining intervals. ◦In conduction mode of DC-AC inverter, each switchconducts for ◦. The analysis starts when switch $_2$is turned ***on*** and $_6$is turned ***off*** Due to the inductance of the stator windings, the current in phase **B** does not become zero instantaneously and continues to flow through the freewheeling diodes $_3$or $_6$depending on the direction of the current. Once the current through the phase **B** becomes zero, the diode stops conducting and only phase **A** and **C** conduct and the equivalent circuit. The duration for which the freewheeling diodes conduct is known as ***commutation period*** and the duration when only two phases conduct is known as ***conduction period***. At the start of the commutation period (when switch $_6$is turned off), the rotor angle is defined to be

$$\theta_r=-\phi+\frac{\pi}{6}$$

........................eq4

Where θ is the advance firing angle,

The duration of the ***commutation period*** is given by the commutation angle and is a function of∅ , the winding inductances and resistances and rotor speed ω making it difficult to estimate. The determination of current is achieved in two steps:

- **Step 1:** In this step the general solution of the currents is obtained
- **Step 2:** In this step the angle is determined using the symmetries given

in **equations 1** and **3**.

Step 1: General Solution:

At time t=0 the switch $_2$ is turned ***on*** and $_2$is turned ***off***. As discussed in the previous section, the current does not become zero immediately and remains nonzero till the time t= . Hence, the commutation period lasts for 0≤t≤ .In this period all the three phases are connected to the DC-AC converter and the stator voltages for < 0 are

$$\begin{bmatrix} V_{an} \\ V_{bn} \\ V_{cn} \end{bmatrix}=\begin{bmatrix} \frac{V_{in}}{3} \\ \frac{V_{in}}{3} \\ -\frac{2V_{in}}{3} \end{bmatrix}$$

.................eq5

In case > 0 , the stator phase voltages are

$$\begin{bmatrix} V_{an} \\ V_{bn} \\ V_{cn} \end{bmatrix} = \begin{bmatrix} \frac{2V_{in}}{3} \\ -\frac{V_{in}}{3} \\ -\frac{V_{in}}{3} \end{bmatrix}$$ ……………………… eq6

Substituting from **equation 2b** and replacing with -∂ - in **equation 2a** gives,

$$p\begin{bmatrix} i_a \\ i_b \\ i_c \end{bmatrix} = \begin{bmatrix} -\frac{R_s}{L_s} & 0 & 0 \\ 0 & -\frac{R_s}{L_s} & 0 \\ 0 & 0 & -\frac{R_s}{L_s} \end{bmatrix}\begin{bmatrix} i_a \\ i_b \\ i_c \end{bmatrix} + \begin{bmatrix} \frac{1}{L_s} & 0 & 0 \\ 0 & \frac{1}{L_s} & 0 \\ 0 & 0 & \frac{1}{L_s} \end{bmatrix}\begin{bmatrix} V_{an} - \omega_r \lambda_m \cos\left(\theta_r - \phi + \frac{\pi}{6}\right) \\ V_{bn} - \omega_r \lambda_m \sin\left(\theta_r - \phi\right) \\ V_{cn} - \omega_r \lambda_m \cos\left(\theta_r - \phi + \frac{5\pi}{6}\right) \end{bmatrix}$$

………………………………… eq7

The system of first order differential **equation 7** can be expressed in standard state variable form as

$$pi_{abc}(t) = Ai_{abc}(t) + Bu(t)$$

where

$$i_{abc} = \begin{bmatrix} i_a \\ i_b \\ i_c \end{bmatrix}, A = \begin{bmatrix} -\frac{R_s}{L_s} & 0 & 0 \\ 0 & -\frac{R_s}{L_s} & 0 \\ 0 & 0 & -\frac{R_s}{L_s} \end{bmatrix}$$ ……………………eq8

$$B=\begin{bmatrix}\frac{1}{L_s} & 0 & 0\\ 0 & \frac{1}{L_s} & 0\\ 0 & 0 & \frac{1}{L_s}\end{bmatrix}, u(t)=\begin{bmatrix}V_{an}-\omega_r\lambda_m\cos\left(\theta_r-\phi+\frac{\pi}{6}\right)\\ V_{bn}-\omega_r\lambda_m\sin(\theta_r-\phi)\\ V_{cn}-\omega_r\lambda_m\cos\left(\theta_r-\phi+\frac{5\pi}{6}\right)\end{bmatrix}$$

The solution of **equation 8** is

$$i_{abc}(t)=e^{At}i_o+\int_0^{t_c}e^{A(-\tau)}Bu(\tau)d\tau$$

..................eq9

where the initial conditions vector is

$$i_o=\begin{bmatrix}i_a(0)\\ i_b(0)\\ i_c(0)\end{bmatrix}=\begin{bmatrix}i_a(0)\\ i_b(0)\\ -(i_a(0)+i_b(0))\end{bmatrix}$$

.... eq10

The solution of **equation 9** for the time interval $0\leq t\leq$, using the initial conditions given in **equation 10**, is

$$i_a(t)=i_a(0)e^{-\frac{R_s}{L_s}t}+\frac{V_{an}}{R_s}\left(1-e^{-\frac{R_s}{L_s}t}\right)+\frac{\omega_r\lambda_m}{2(R_s^2+\omega_r^2L_s^2)}\left[(\omega_rL_s+\sqrt{3}R_s)\cos\phi+(R_s-\sqrt{3}\omega_rL_s)\sin\phi\right]e^{-\frac{R_s}{L_s}t}$$

$$-\frac{\omega_r\lambda_m}{2(R_s^2+\omega_r^2L_s^2)}\left[(\omega_rL_s+\sqrt{3}R_s)\cos(\theta_r-\phi)-(R_s-\sqrt{3}\omega_rL_s)\sin(\theta_r-\phi)\right]$$

..................eq11

$$i_b(t)=i_b(0)e^{-\frac{R_s}{L_s}t}+\frac{V_{bn}}{R_s}\left(1-e^{-\frac{R_s}{L_s}t}\right)-\frac{\omega_r\lambda_m}{(R_s^2+\omega_r^2L_s^2)}\left[\omega_rL_s\cos\phi+R_s\sin\phi\right]e^{-\frac{R_s}{L_s}t}$$

$$+\frac{\omega_r\lambda_m}{(R_s^2+\omega_r^2L_s^2)}\left[\omega_rL_s\cos(\theta_r-\phi)-R_s\sin(\theta_r-\phi)\right]$$

.....................eq12

Since the three phases are connected in Y, the phase **C** current is given by

$$i_c(t)=-(i_a(t)+i_b(t))$$

.....................eq13

When the becomes zero at t = , the commutation period ends and the conduction period starts with just phases **A** and **C** conducting. The duration of conduction period is ≤ ≤ . The

differential equation given in **equation 11** holds for the conduction period and the only change is in u(t) and initial values of current given by

$$u(t)=\begin{bmatrix} \frac{V_{in}}{2}-\frac{\omega_r\lambda_m}{2}\cos\left(\theta_r-\phi+\frac{\pi}{6}\right) \\ \omega_r\lambda_m\sin(\theta_r-\phi) \\ -\frac{V_{in}}{2}-\frac{\omega_r\lambda_m}{2}\cos\left(\theta_r-\phi+\frac{5\pi}{6}\right) \end{bmatrix};\ i_o=\begin{bmatrix} i_a(t_c) \\ i_b(t_c) \\ i_c(t_c) \end{bmatrix}=\begin{bmatrix} i_a(t_c) \\ 0 \\ -i_a(t_c) \end{bmatrix}$$

……………………………….eq14

The solution of **equation 9** for conduction period is

$$i_{abc}(t)=e^{A(t-t_c)}i_o+\int_0^{\frac{\pi}{3\omega_r}}e^{A(t-\tau)}Bu(\tau)d\tau$$

……………eq15

The evaluation of the integration given in **equation 15**gives

$$i_a(t)=i_a(t_c)e^{-\frac{R_s}{L_s}(t-t_c)}+\frac{V_{in}}{2R_s}\left(1-e^{-\frac{R_s}{L_s}(t-t_c)}\right)+\frac{\sqrt{3}\omega_r\lambda_m}{2\left(R_s^2+\omega_r^2L_s^2\right)}\left[R_s\cos(\phi-\theta_c)-\omega_rL_s\sin(\phi-\theta_c)\right]e^{-\frac{R_s}{L_s}(t-t_c)}$$

$$-\frac{\sqrt{3}\omega_r\lambda_m}{2\left(R_s^2+\omega_r^2L_s^2\right)}\left[R_s\cos(\theta_r-\phi)+\omega_rL_s\sin(\theta_r-\phi)\right]$$

…………………………………………………………………...eq16

The phase **C** current is same as phase **A** current ((t) = - ( )) and phase B current is zero (= 0)

Step 2: Determination of Commutation Angle:

At time t = 0, the switch 6is turned off and 2is turned on. Hence, at t = 0 the current in phase **C** is zero and the phase **A** and **B** currents are equal in magnitude. Therefore, the initial conditions are given by

$$i_o=\begin{bmatrix} i_a(0) \\ i_b(0) \\ i_c(0) \end{bmatrix}=\begin{bmatrix} I_o \\ -I_o \\ 0 \end{bmatrix}$$

…………………...eq17

At the end of the conduction period, the currents are

$$\begin{bmatrix} i_a\left(\dfrac{\pi}{3\omega_r}\right) \\ i_b\left(\dfrac{\pi}{3\omega_r}\right) \\ i_c\left(\dfrac{\pi}{3\omega_r}\right) \end{bmatrix} = \begin{bmatrix} I_o \\ 0 \\ -I_o \end{bmatrix}$$

.... eq18

The commutation period ends when phase **B** current becomes zero, that is ( )=0. Using this condition and initial conditions given by **equation 17**in **equation 18** gives

$$0 = -I_o e^{-\frac{R_s}{L_s}t_c} + \frac{V_{in}}{R_s}\left(1-e^{-\frac{R_s}{L_s}t_c}\right) - \frac{\omega_r\lambda_m}{\left(R_s^2+\omega_r^2 L_s^2\right)}\left[\omega_r L_s\cos\phi + R_s\sin\phi\right]e^{-\frac{R_s}{L_s}t_c}$$

$$+\frac{\omega_r\lambda_m}{\left(R_s^2+\omega_r^2 L_s^2\right)}\left[\omega_r L_s\cos\left(\theta_c-\phi\right) - R_s\sin\left(\theta_c-\phi\right)\right]$$

....eq19

Using the boundary condition given by

$$I_o = i_a(t_c)e^{-\frac{R_s}{L_s}\left(\frac{\pi}{3\omega_r}-t_c\right)} + \frac{V_{in}}{2R_s}\left(1-e^{-\frac{R_s}{L_s}\left(\frac{\pi}{3\omega_r}-t_c\right)}\right) + \frac{\sqrt{3}\omega_r\lambda_m}{2\left(R_s^2+\omega_r^2 L_s^2\right)}\left[R_s\cos\left(\phi-\theta_c\right)-\omega_r L_s\sin\left(\phi-\theta_c\right)\right]e^{-\frac{R_s}{L_s}\left(\frac{\pi}{3\omega_r}-t_c\right)}$$

$$-\frac{\sqrt{3}\omega_r\lambda_m}{2\left(R_s^2+\omega_r^2 L_s^2\right)}\left[R_s\cos\left(\frac{\pi}{3}-\phi\right)+\omega_r L_s\sin\left(\frac{\pi}{3}-\phi\right)\right]$$

....eq20

Using the boundary condition given by

CONTROL STRATEGIES OF PM MACHINES:

There are various control strategies and depending on the application a suitable strategy can bechosen. For example, a mutual flux air gap linkages control gives a smooth transition to flux weakening above the base speed. Similarly, a maximum efficiency control is suitable forapplications where energy saving is important such as hybrid and electric vehicles. The most commonly used control strategies are:

- Constant torque angle control
- Unity power factor control
- Constant mutual air gap flux linkages control
- Angle control of air gap flux and current phasors
- Optimum torque per ampere control
- Constant loss based maximum torque speed boundary control
- Minim loss or maximum efficiency control.

The control strategies marked in bold are discussed in the following sections.

Constant Torque Angle Control:

Consider that the PM motor is supplied three phase currents given as follows:

$$i_{as} = I_m \sin\left(\omega_r t + \delta\right)$$

$$i_{bs} = I_m \sin\left(\omega_r t + \delta - \frac{2\pi}{3}\right)$$

$$i_{cs} = I_m \sin\left(\omega_r t + \delta - \frac{4\pi}{3}\right) \quad \text{.......................eq1}$$

The q and d axes stator currents in the rotor reference frames are obtained through the transformation matrix as

$$\begin{bmatrix} i_{qs}^r \\ i_{ds}^r \end{bmatrix} = \frac{2}{3}\begin{bmatrix} \cos\omega_r t & \cos\left(\omega_r t - \frac{2\pi}{3}\right) & \cos\left(\omega_r t - \frac{4\pi}{3}\right) \\ \sin\omega_r t & \sin\left(\omega_r t - \frac{2\pi}{3}\right) & \sin\left(\omega_r t - \frac{4\pi}{3}\right) \end{bmatrix}\begin{bmatrix} i_{as} \\ i_{bs} \\ i_{cs} \end{bmatrix}$$

$$= \frac{2}{3}\begin{bmatrix} \cos\omega_r t & \cos\left(\omega_r t - \frac{2\pi}{3}\right) & \cos\left(\omega_r t - \frac{4\pi}{3}\right) \\ \sin\omega_r t & \sin\left(\omega_r t - \frac{2\pi}{3}\right) & \sin\left(\omega_r t - \frac{4\pi}{3}\right) \end{bmatrix}\begin{bmatrix} I_m \sin(\omega_r t + \delta) \\ I_m \sin\left(\omega_r t + \delta - \frac{2\pi}{3}\right) \\ I_m \sin\left(\omega_r t + \delta - \frac{4\pi}{3}\right) \end{bmatrix}$$

$$= I_m \begin{bmatrix} \sin\delta \\ \cos\delta \end{bmatrix}$$

……………………………………………………………………….eq2

$$T_e = \frac{3}{2}\frac{N_p}{2}\left[\lambda_{af} i_{qs}^r + \left(L_d - L_q\right) i_{qs}^r i_{ds}^r\right]$$

………………. eq3

Substituting the values of and from **equation 2** into **equation 3a** gives

$$T_e = \frac{3}{2}\frac{N_p}{2}\left[\lambda_{af} I_m \sin\delta + \frac{1}{2}\left(L_d - L_q\right) I_m^2 \sin(2\delta)\right]$$

……………………………………………………………….eq4

Having developed the basic equations, we now focus on the ***Constant Torque Angle Control***. In this strategy the torque angle is maintained at90°. Hence, the above torque equation becomes:

$$T_e = \frac{3}{2}\frac{N_p}{2}\lambda_{af} I_m$$

……………………. eq5

The *q* and *d* axis voltage for the PM machine is given by

$$\begin{bmatrix} v_{qs}^r \\ v_{ds}^r \end{bmatrix} = \begin{bmatrix} R_s + L_q p & \omega_r L_d \\ -\omega_r L_q & R_s + L_d p \end{bmatrix}\begin{bmatrix} i_{qs}^r \\ i_{ds}^r \end{bmatrix} + \begin{bmatrix} \omega_r \lambda_{af} \\ 0 \end{bmatrix}$$

…………………………….eq6

Since the load angle = 90°, from **equation 2**,. and **equation 5** can be written as:

$$\begin{bmatrix} v_{qs}^r \\ v_{ds}^r \end{bmatrix} = \begin{bmatrix} R_s + L_q p & \omega_r L_d \\ -\omega_r L_q & R_s + L_d p \end{bmatrix} \begin{bmatrix} I_m \\ 0 \end{bmatrix} + \begin{bmatrix} \omega_r \lambda_{af} \\ 0 \end{bmatrix}$$

$$v_{qs}^r = \left(R_s + L_q p\right) I_m + \omega_r \lambda_{af}$$

.... eq7

$$v_{ds}^r = -\omega_r L_q I_m$$

For the analysis of the control strategy, it is convenient to convert **equation 4** and **equation 6** into per unit (p.u) values. The base values chosen are:

base value of stator current

base value of magnet flux

ω base speed

base voltage =

base Resistance

base Inductance

base value of torque =

2 2

base value of reactance = ω

Using the base values given in **equation 7** the normalized can be written as

$$T_{en} = \frac{T_e}{T_b} = \frac{\frac{3}{2}\frac{N_p}{2}\lambda_{af} I_m}{\frac{3}{2}\frac{N_p}{2}\lambda_{af} I_b} = I_{mn}$$

..........................eq8

From **equation 8** it can be seen that the normalized torque ( ) is equal to the normalized stator current . The voltage equation for steady state analysis can be obtained by making P=0 (because in steady state the time variation is zero) in **equation 6** and is written as

$$v_{qs}^r = R_s I_m + \omega_r \lambda_{af}; \quad v_{ds}^r = -\omega_r L_q I_m$$

$$v_{qs}^r = R_s I_m + \omega_r \lambda_{af}; \quad v_{ds}^r = -\omega_r L_q I_m$$

.........................eq9

The magnitude of the stator voltage is given by

$$V_s = \sqrt{\left(v_{qs}^r\right)^2 + \left(v_{ds}^r\right)^2}$$

............................eq10

The normalized stator voltage is obtained as

$$V_{sn} = \frac{V_s}{V_b} = \frac{V_s}{\omega_b \lambda_{af}} = \sqrt{\left(R_{sn} I_{mn} + \omega_m\right)^2 + \left(\omega_m L_{qn} I_{mn}\right)^2}$$

.....................eq11

The phasor diagram for this control strategy is shown in **Figure 1**. From this figure the power factor is obtained as

$$\cos\phi = \frac{v_{qs}^{r}}{V_{s}} = \frac{v_{qs}^{r}}{\sqrt{\left(v_{qs}^{r}\right)^{2} + \left(v_{ds}^{r}\right)^{2}}} = \frac{1}{\sqrt{1 + \left(\frac{v_{ds}^{r}}{v_{qs}^{r}}\right)^{2}}} = \frac{1}{\sqrt{1 + \left(\frac{L_{qn} I_{sn}}{1 + \frac{R_{sn} I_{sn}}{\omega_{m}}}\right)^{2}}}$$ ……………..eq12

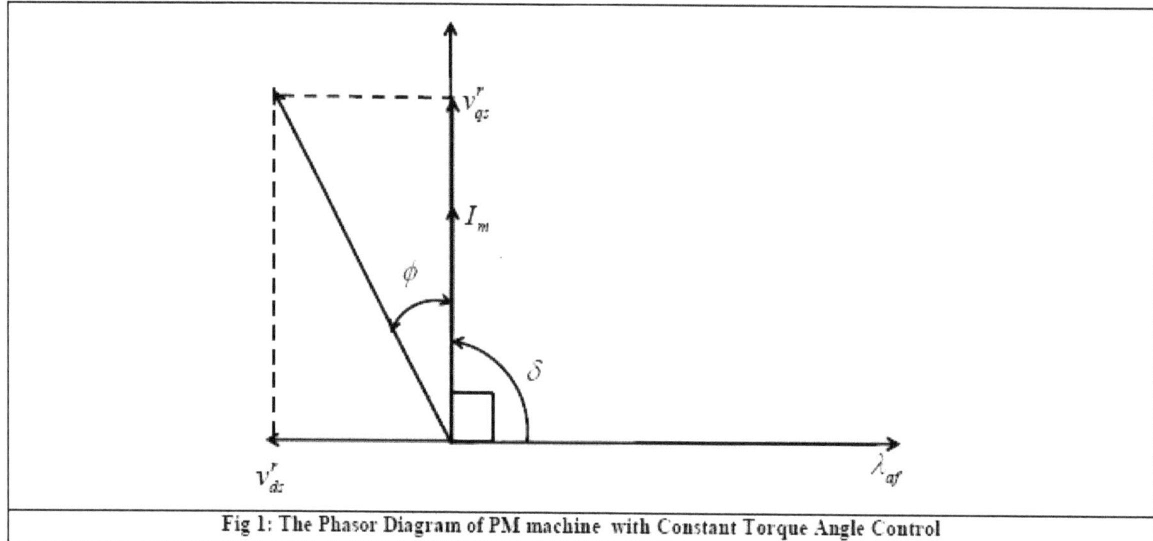

Fig 1: The Phasor Diagram of PM machine with Constant Torque Angle Control

The **equation 12** shows that the power factor deteriorates as the rotor speed goes up. The maximum rotor speed with this control strategy can be obtained by solving **equation 11** for , neglecting the stator resistive drop (∽ 0), and is given as

$$\omega_{rn(\max)} = \frac{{}_{sn(\max)}}{\sqrt{1 + \left(L_{qn} I_{sn}\right)^{2}}}$$ ………………..eq13

Assuming that the motor is driven by a three phase DC-AC converter, the maximum voltage is given by:

$$V_{sn(\max)} = \frac{\sqrt{2} \times 0.45 V_{dc}}{V_{b}}$$ ……………………..eq14

The performance characteristics of the PM machine are shown in **Figure 2**. The parameters of the machine for a speed of 1p.u. (=1) used to plot the curves are given in **Table 1**. From the **Figure 2** the following can be observed:

- The power factor falls as the current rises.
- The torque is proportional to the current as is evident from **equation 8**.
- The normalized increases with the increase in current. The impedance of the machine remains constant because its speed is constant at 1p.u. hence, when the current through the machine has to increase the applied voltage also has to increase (**equation 11**).

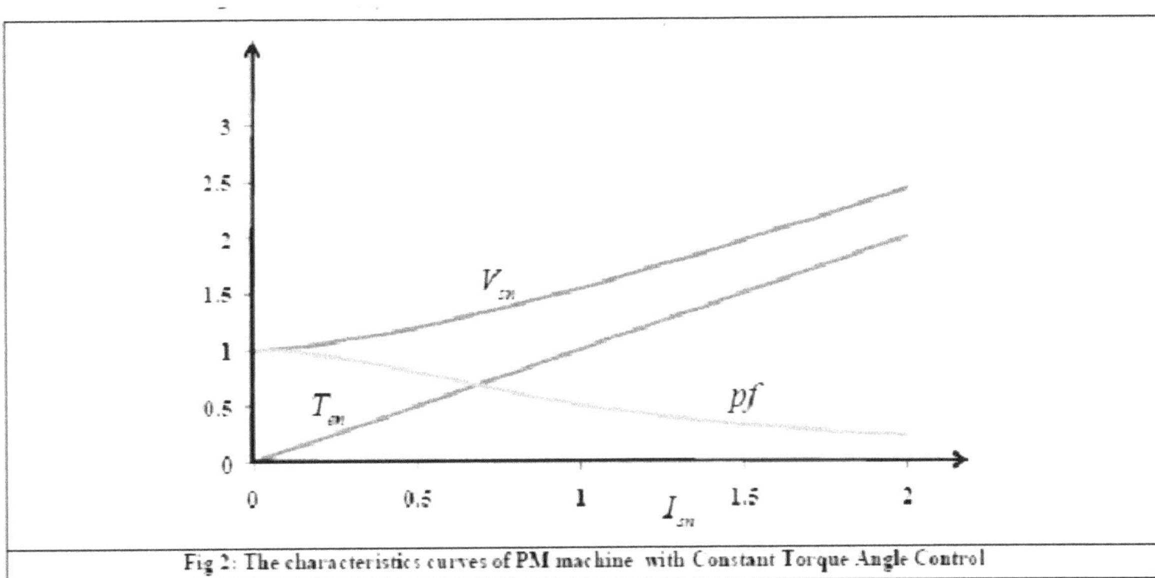

Fig 2: The characteristics curves of PM machine with Constant Torque Angle Control

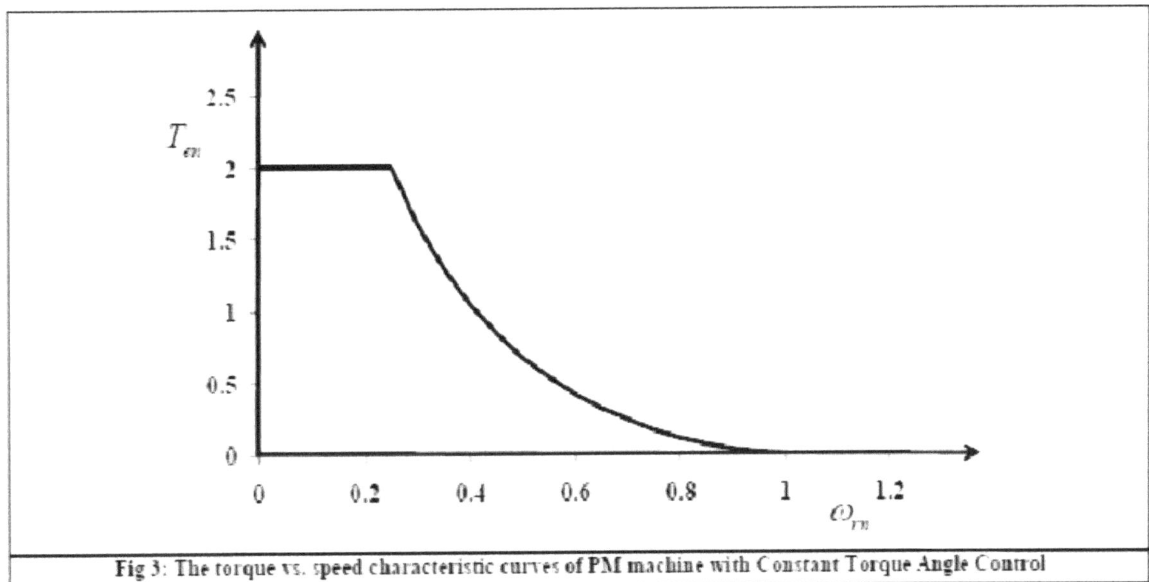

Fig 3: The torque vs. speed characteristic curves of PM machine with Constant Torque Angle Control

Table 1: The parameters of a salient pole PM machine

Base Voltage (V_b)	Base Current (I_b)	Base Inductance (L_b)	Base Speed (ω_b)	Base Flux Linkage (λ_b)	Resistance (R)	d-axis inductance (L_d)	q-axis inductance (L_q)
100 V	10 A	0.02 H	600 rad/s	0.167 Vs/rad	1.8 Ω	0.011 H	0.022 H

The torque vs. speed curve for the machine, whose parameters are given in **Table 1**, is shown in **Figure 3**. In determining the curve it has been assumed that the magnitude of the normalized stator voltage (   ) is 1 p.u. and the maximum value of normalized stator current (   ) is fixed to 2 p.u. From the **Figure 3** the following can be observed:

- Through this control strategy, the PM machine is able to produce 2 p.u. torques up to a speed of 0.25 p.u.
- The machine is able to produce 1 p.u. torque up to a speed of 0.4 p.u.

Constant Mutual Flux Linkage Control:

In this control strategy, the resultant flux linkage of the stator *q* and *d* axis and rotor is Maintained constant. The main advantage of this control strategy is that it keeps the stator Voltage requirement is kept low. To start with the analyses consider the flux linkage Expressionfor the *q* and *d* axis:

$$\lambda_{qs}^r = L_q i_{qs}^r \quad \text{............eq15}$$

$$\lambda_{ds}^r = L_d i_{ds}^r + \lambda_{af} \quad \text{................eq16}$$

The magnitude of the flux linkage is given by

$$\lambda_m = \sqrt{\left(\lambda_{qs}^r\right)^2 + \left(\lambda_{ds}^r\right)^2} = \sqrt{\left(L_q i_{qs}^r\right)^2 + \left(L_d i_{ds}^r + \lambda_{af}\right)^2} \quad \text{............eq17}$$

In this strategy, the mutual flux linkage given by **equation 17** is held constant and its magnitude is made equal to . Substituting the values of , and from **equation 2** into **equation 17** gives

$$\lambda_m = \lambda_{af} = \sqrt{\left(L_q I_m \sin\delta\right)^2 + \left(L_d I_m \cos\delta + \lambda_{af}\right)^2} \quad \text{..........................eq18}$$

Solving **equation 18** for gives

$$I_m = -\frac{2\lambda_{af}}{L_d}\left(\frac{\cos\delta}{\cos^2\delta + \rho^2\sin^2\delta}\right) \quad \text{..............................eq19}$$

Where

$$\rho = \frac{L_q}{L_d}$$

The normalized current is given bu

$$I_{mn} = \frac{I_m}{I_b} = -\frac{2}{L_{dn}}\left(\frac{\cos\delta}{\cos^2\delta + \rho^2\sin^2\delta}\right) \quad \text{......................eq20}$$

The stator voltage is given

$$V_s = \sqrt{\left(v_{qs}^r\right)^2 + \left(v_{ds}^r\right)^2} = \sqrt{\left(R_s i_{qs}^r + \omega_r L_d i_{ds}^r + \omega_r \lambda_{af}\right)^2 + \left(-\omega_r L_q i_{qs}^r + R_s i_{ds}^r\right)^2} \quad \text{..........eq21}$$

The normalized values of the stator voltage is

$$V_{sn} = \frac{V_s}{V_b} = \frac{\sqrt{\left(R_s i_{qs}^r + \omega_r L_d i_{ds}^r + \omega_r \lambda_{af}\right)^2 + \left(-\omega_r L_q i_{qs}^r + R_s i_{ds}^r\right)^2}}{\omega_b \lambda_{af}}$$

$$= \sqrt{\left(R_{sn} i_{qsn}^r + \omega_{rn} L_{dn} i_{dsn}^r + \omega_{rn}\right)^2 + \left(-\omega_{rn} L_{qn} i_{qsn}^r + R_{sn} i_{dsn}^r\right)^2} \quad \text{.............eq22}$$

The normalized voltage given by **can** be written as

......eq23

In order to determine the value of angle δ, two distinct cases have to be considered:

When $\rho = 1$ and $\rho \neq 1$. Once the angle δ is known, the torque can be obtained from equation **3**. Each of these cases are explained in the following subsections.

Case when $\rho = 1$

Substituting $\rho = 1$ into **equation 20** and solving for δ gives

$$\delta = \cos^{-1}\left(\frac{-L_{dn}I_{mn}}{2}\right) \qquad \text{............eq24}$$

The torque produced by the machine is given by

$$T_e = \frac{3}{2}\frac{N_p}{2}\left[\lambda_{af}I_m \sin\delta\right] \qquad \text{....................eq25}$$

The normalized torque is given by

$$T_{en} = \frac{T_e}{T_b} = I_{mn}\sin\delta \qquad \text{.................eq26}$$

The performance characteristics of a PM machine at a speed of 1 p.u. are shown in **Figure 4a** and the parameters of this machine are given in **Table 2**. The torque versus the speed characteristics of the PM Machine are shown in **Figure 4b**.

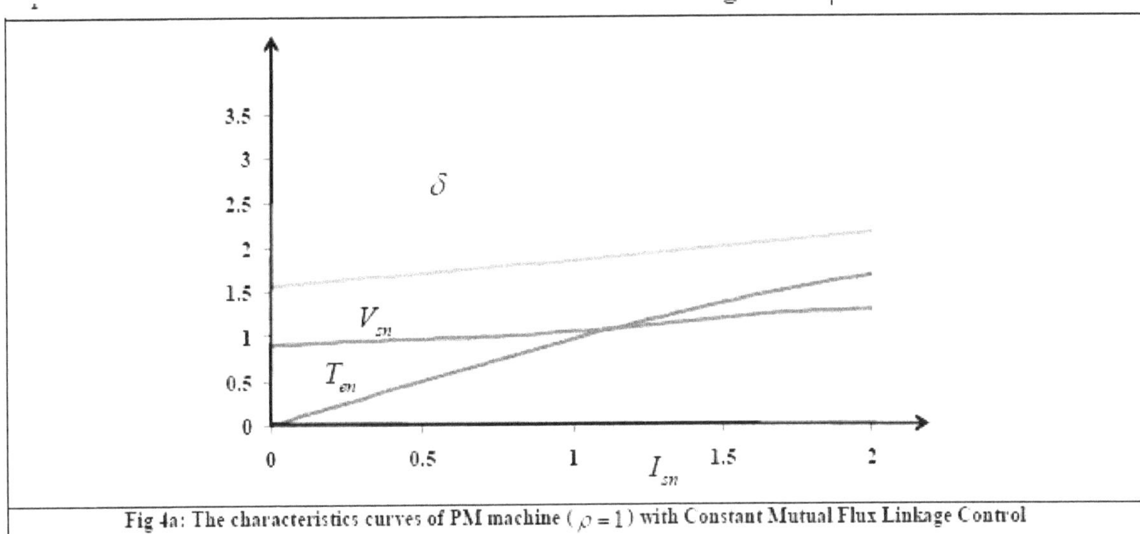

Fig 4a: The characteristics curves of PM machine ($\rho = 1$) with Constant Mutual Flux Linkage Control

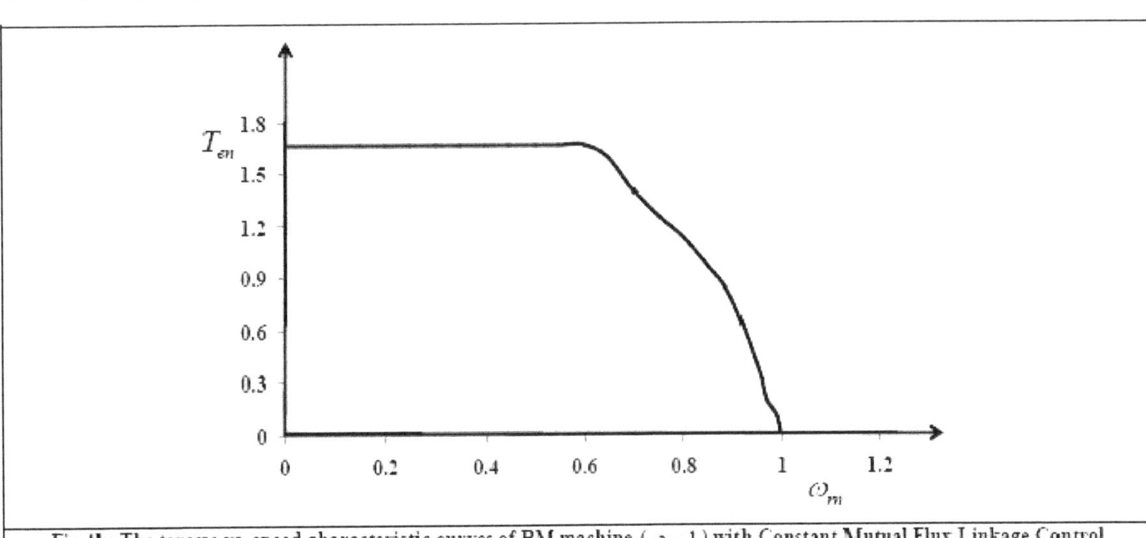

Fig 4b: The torque vs. speed characteristic curves of PM machine ($\rho = 1$) with Constant Mutual Flux Linkage Control

Table 2: The parameters of a non salient pole PM machine

Base Voltage (V_b)	Base Current (I_b)	Base Inductance (L_b)	Base Speed (ω_b)	Base Flux Linkage (λ_b)	Resistance (R)	d-axis inductance (L_d)	q-axis inductance (L_q)
100 V	10 A	0.02 H	600 rad/s	0.167 Vs/rad	1.8 Ω	0.011 H	0.011 H

***Case when* ρ ≠1**

When ρ ≠1, using **equation 20** the expression for is obtained as

$$\delta = \cos^{-1}\left[\frac{-1}{L_{dn}I_{mn}(1-\rho)^2} \pm \sqrt{\left\{\frac{1}{L_{dn}(1-\rho^2)I_{sn}}\right\}^2 - \frac{\rho^2}{(1-\rho^2)}}\right]$$

…………eq27

The performance characteristics of the machine, whose parameters are given in **Table 1**, are shown in **Figure 5a** and the torque versus speed characteristics is shown in **Figure 5b**.

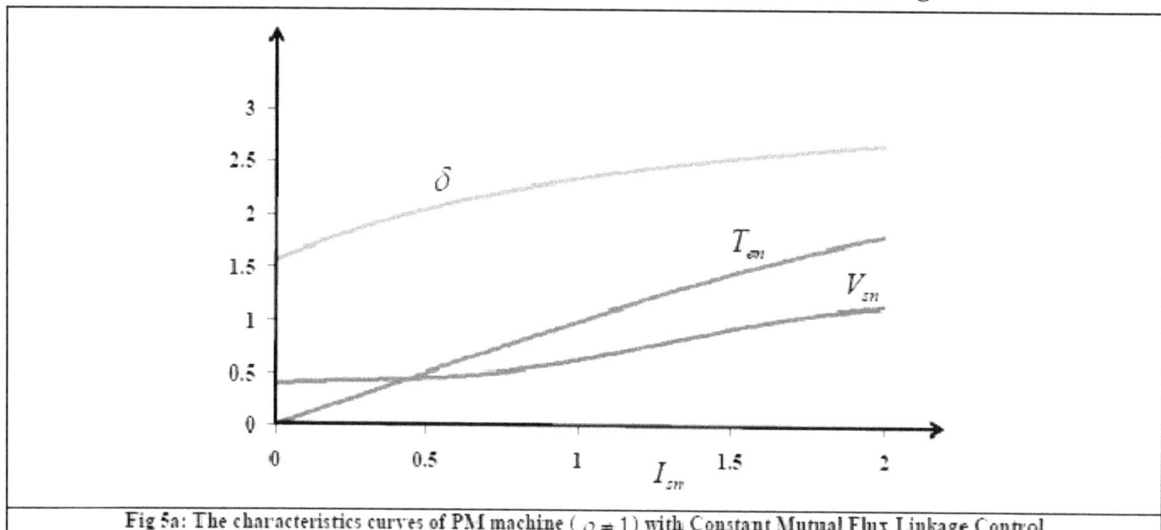

Fig 5a: The characteristics curves of PM machine ($\rho \neq 1$) with Constant Mutual Flux Linkage Control

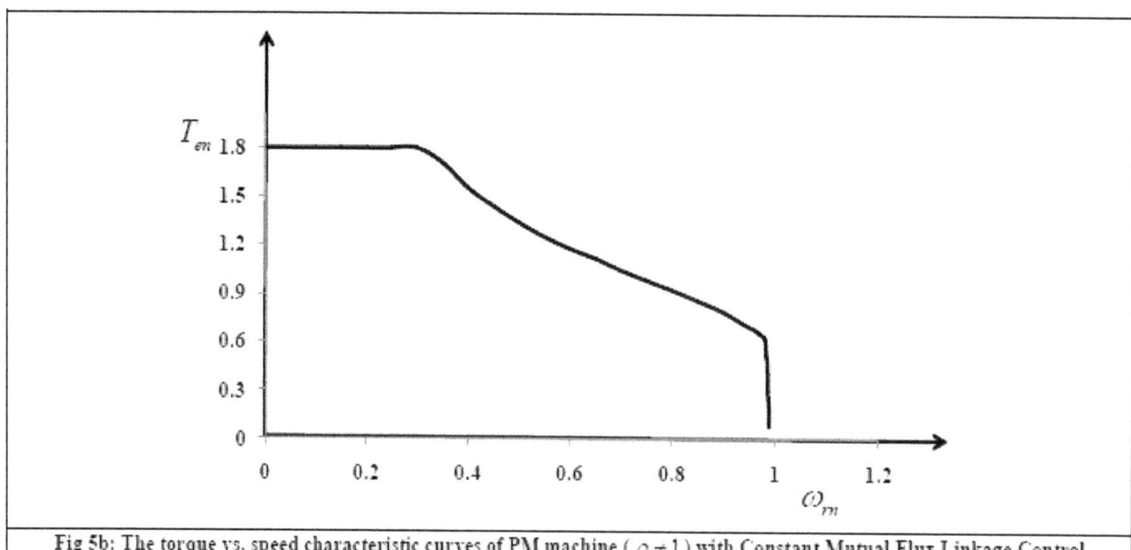

Fig 5b: The torque vs. speed characteristic curves of PM machine ($\rho \neq 1$) with Constant Mutual Flux Linkage Control

Optimum Torque per Unit Current Control:

The aim of this control strategy is to maximize electromagnetic torque for a unit stator current. By using this strategy the PM machine will produce maximum torque for a given magnitude of current. To develop the mathematical models of this strategy, consider the torque equation of the PM machine given in **equation 3** and normalize it into p.u. system. The normalized torque expression is

$$T_{en} = \frac{T_e}{T_b} = I_{mn}\left[\sin(\delta) + \frac{1}{2}\left(L_{dn} - L_{qn}\right)I_{mn}\sin(2\delta)\right] \qquad \text{.............eq28}$$

The torque per unit stator current is defined as

$$\frac{T_{en}}{I_{mn}} = \left[\sin(\delta) + \frac{1}{2}\left(L_{dn} - L_{qn}\right)I_{mn}\sin(2\delta)\right] \qquad \text{............eq29}$$

The condition under which the machine produces maximum torque per unit stator current is obtained by differentiating **equation 29** with respect to and equating it to zero, that is

$$\frac{d\left[\sin(\delta) + \frac{1}{2}\left(L_{dn} - L_{qn}\right)I_{mn}\sin(2\delta)\right]}{d\delta} = 0$$

$$\Rightarrow \cos(\delta) + \left(L_{dn} - L_{qn}\right)I_{mn}\cos(2\delta) = 0 \qquad \text{..................eq30}$$

Using the trigonometric identity 2cos(2) =2 2( )-1 in **equation 30** gives

$$\cos(\delta) + \left(L_{dn} - L_{qn}\right)I_{mn}\left[2\cos^2(\delta) - 1\right] = 0 \qquad \text{.....................eq31}$$

The solution of **equation 31** gives

$$\delta = \cos^{-1}\left[-\frac{1}{4K} \pm \sqrt{\left(\frac{1}{4K}\right)^2 + \frac{1}{2}}\right] \qquad \text{..............................eq32}$$

$$\text{where } K = \frac{1}{\left(L_{dn} - L_{qn}\right)I_{mn}}$$

In **equation 32**, only the value of greater than 90o is considered so as to reducethe field in the air gap. The performance characteristics of the PM machine (parameters of the machine are given in **Table 1**) for this control strategy are shown in **Figure 6a** and the torque versus speed characteristics are shown in **Figure 6b**.

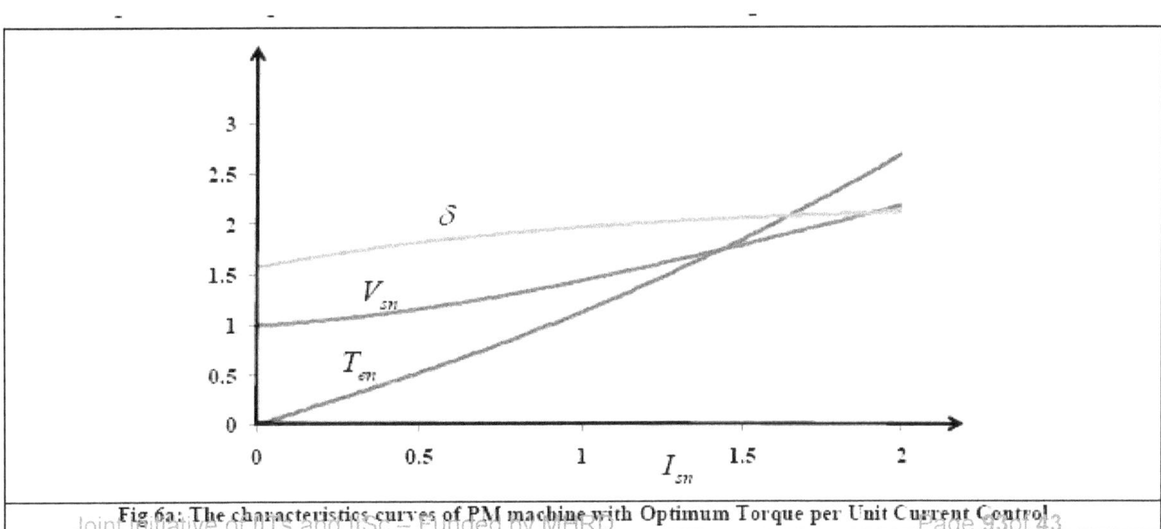

Fig 6a: The characteristics curves of PM machine with Optimum Torque per Unit Current Control

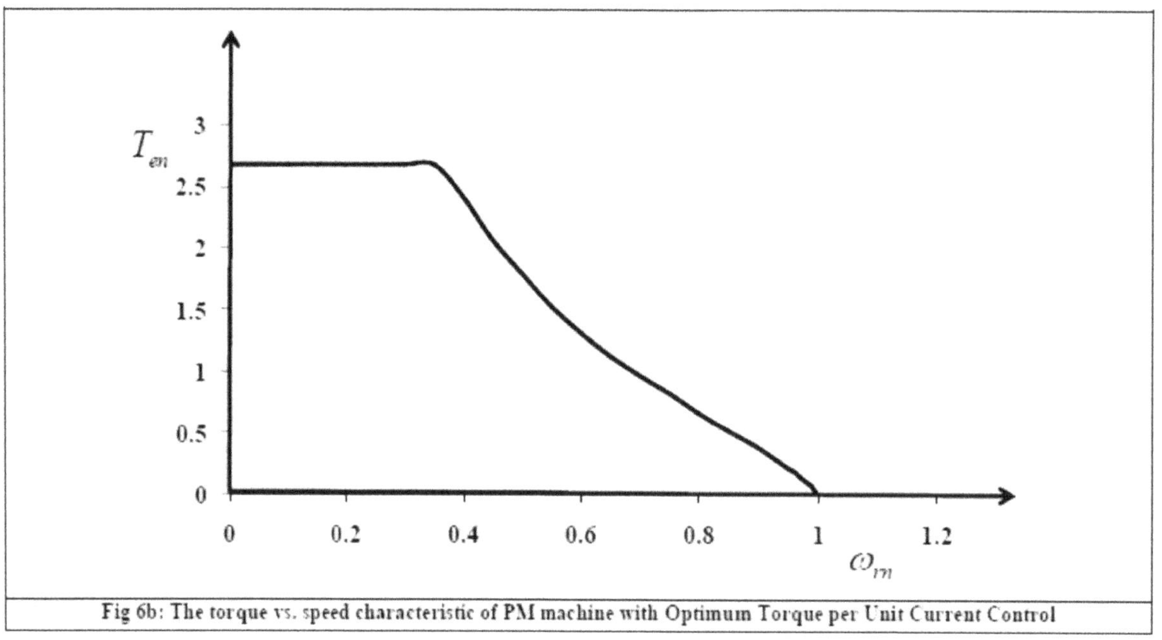

Fig 6b: The torque vs. speed characteristic of PM machine with Optimum Torque per Unit Current Control

SWITCHED RELUCTANCE MOTOR DRIVES:

The switched reluctance motor (SRM) drive is considered to be an attractive candidate for variable speed motor drives due to its low cost, rugged structure, reliable converter topology, high efficiency over a wide speed range, and simplicity in control.43,44 These drives are suitable for EVs, electric traction applications, automotive applications, aircraft starter/generator systems, mining drives, washing machines, door actuators, etc.48,50,51The SRM has a simple, rugged, and low-cost structure. It has no PM or winding on the rotor. This structure not only reduces the cost of the SRM butalso offers high-speed operation capability for this motor. Unlike the induction and PM machines, the SRM is capable of high-speed operation without the concern of mechanical failures that result from the high-level centrifugal force. In addition, the inverter of the SRM drive has a reliable topology. The stator windings are connected in series with the upper and lower switches of the inverter. This topology can prevent the shoot-through fault that exists in the induction and permanent motor drive inverter. Moreover, high efficiency over a wide speed range and control simplicity are known merits of the SRM drive.43,47A conventional SRM drive system consists of the switched reluctance motor, power inverter, sensors such as voltage, currentandpositionsensors, and controlcircuitry such as the DSP controller and its peripherals, as shownin Figure 6.54. Through proper control, high performance can be achieved in the SRM drive system.43,44The SRM drive inverter is connected to a DC power supply, which can be derived from the utility lines through a front-end diode rectifier or from batteries. The phase windings of the SRM are connected to the power inverter, as shown in Figure 6.55. The control circuit provides a gating signal to the switches of the inverter according to particular control strategies and the signals from various sensors.

FIELD ORIENTED CONTROL (FOC):

In an Electric Vehicle, it is required that the traction motor is able to deliver the required torque almost instantaneously. In an induction motor (IM) drive, such performance can be achieved using a class of algorithms known as Field Oriented Control (FOC). There are varieties of FOC such as:

- Stator flux oriented
- Rotor flux oriented
- Air gap flux oriented

The basic premise of FOC may be understood by considering the current loop in a uniform magnetic field as shown in Figure 1a. From Lorenz force equation, it can be seen that the torque acting on the current loop is given by

$$T_e = -2BiNLr\sin\theta \quad \text{.............eq1}$$

Where
B is the flux density
I is the current
N is the no of turns
L is the length of the coil
r is the radius of the coil

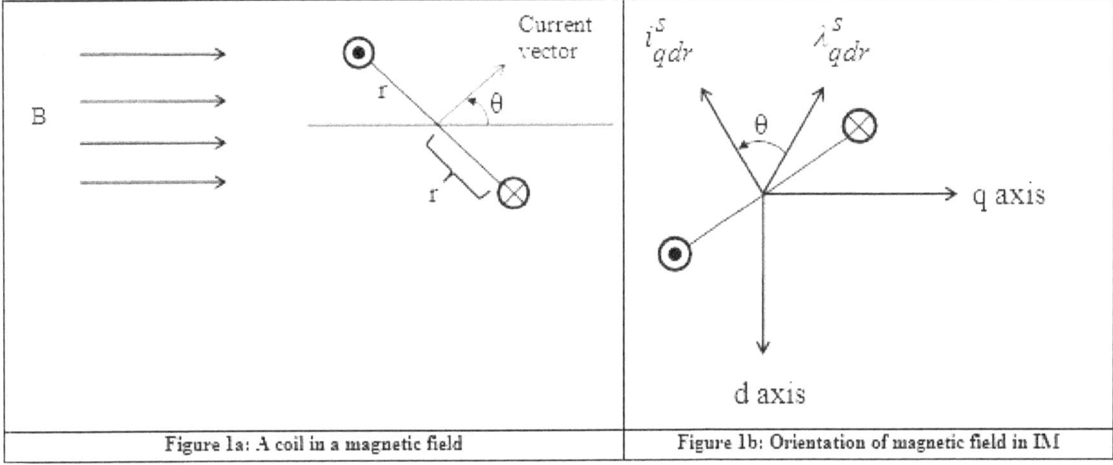

Figure 1a: A coil in a magnetic field

Figure 1b: Orientation of magnetic field in IM

From equation 1 it is evident that the torque is maximized when the current vector is perpendicular to the magnetic field. The same conclusion can be applied to an IM. In Figure 1b orientations of magnetic fields and currents in an IM are shown. The rotor current and flux linkage vectors are shown in Figure 1 at some instant of time. Hence, the torque produced by the motor is given by

$$T_e = \frac{3}{2}\frac{P}{2}\left(\lambda'_{qr} i'_{dr} - \lambda'_{dr} i'_{qr}\right) \qquad \text{................eq2}$$

The equation 2 can be re-written as

$$T_e = -\frac{3}{2}\frac{P}{2}\left|\lambda'_{qdr}\right|\left|i'_{qdr}\right|\sin\theta \qquad \text{................eq3}$$

The equation 3 is analogous to equation 1. Hence, for a given magnitude of flux linkage, torque is maximized when the flux linkage and current vectors are perpendicular. Therefore, it is desirable to keep the rotor flux linkage perpendicular to rotor current vector.

In the analysis of FOC the following convention will be used: The parameters with a superscript —s‖ are in stator frame of reference.

- The parameters with a superscript —e‖ are in synchronous frame of reference.
- The parameters with subscript —r‖ indicate rotor parameters.
- The parameters with subscript —s‖ indicate stator parameters.
- All rotor quantities are referred to stator using the turns ratio of the windings

In case of singly excited IMs (in singly excited IM, the rotor winding is not fed by any external voltage source. In case of wound rotor machines, they are short circuited using slip rings. For cage IMs, the rotor bars are short circuited at the terminals), the rotor flux linkage vector and rotor current vector are always perpendicular. The voltage equations for the IM (refer to Lecture 19) in synchronous frame of reference are

$$v_{qs}^e = r_s i_{qs}^e + \omega_e \lambda_{ds}^e + p\lambda_{qs}^e$$
$$v_{ds}^e = r_s i_{ds}^e - \omega_e \lambda_{qs}^e + p\lambda_{ds}^e$$
$$v_{os}^e = r_s i_{os}^e + p\lambda_{os}^e$$
$$v_{qr}^e = r_r i_{qr}^e + (\omega_e - \omega_r)\lambda_{dr}^e + p\lambda_{qr}^e$$
$$v_{dr}^e = r_r i_{dr}^e - (\omega_e - \omega_r)\lambda_{qr}^e + p\lambda_{dr}^e$$
$$v_{or}^e = r_r i_{or}^e + p\lambda_{or}^e$$

..............................eq4

Where   is the rotational speed of Synchronous frame of reference

In case of singly excited IM, the rotor voltages are zero, that is =0, =0, =0. Hence, the rotor currents can be obtained as

$$0 = r_r i_{qr}^e + (\omega_e - \omega_r)\lambda_{dr}^e + p\lambda_{qr}^e \Rightarrow i_{qr}^e = -\frac{1}{r_r}(\omega_e - \omega_r)\lambda_{dr}^e - p\lambda_{qr}^e$$

$$0 = r_r i_{dr}^e - (\omega_e - \omega_r)\lambda_{qr}^e + p\lambda_{dr}^e \Rightarrow i_{dr}^{\prime e} = \frac{1}{r_r}(\omega_e - \omega_r)\lambda_{qr}^e - p\lambda_{dr}^e$$

$$0 = r_r i_{or}^e + p\lambda_{or}^e \Rightarrow i_{or}^e = -\frac{p\lambda_{or}^e}{r_r}$$

.......eq5

Since steady state operation of IM is considered, the time derivative term of flux linkage in equation 2 will vanish. Hence, the rotor currents are:

$$i_{qr}^e = -\frac{1}{r_r}(\omega_e - \omega_r)\lambda_{dr}^e$$

$$i_{dr}^e = \frac{1}{r_r}(\omega_e - \omega_r)\lambda_{qr}^e$$

$$i_{or}^e = 0$$

.....................eq6

The dot product of the rotor flux linkage and rotor current vectors may be expressed as

$$\lambda_{qdr}^e . i_{qdr}^e = \lambda_{qr}^e . i_{qr}^e + \lambda_{dr}^e . i_{dr}^e$$

........................eq7

Substituting the values of   and   from equation 6 into equation 7gives

$$\lambda_{qdr}^e . i_{qdr}^e = -\frac{\lambda_{qr}^e}{r_r}(\omega_e - \omega_r)\lambda_{dr}^e + \frac{\lambda_{dr}^e}{r_r}(\omega_e - \omega_r)\lambda_{qr}^e = 0$$

.........eq8

Form equation 5 it can be seen that the dot product between the rotor flux and rotor current vectors is zero in case of singly excited IM. Hence, it can be concluded that the rotor flux and rotor current vectors are perpendicular to each other in steady state operation. The defining feature of FOC is that this characteristic (that the rotor flux and rotor current vectors are perpendicular to each other) is maintained during transient conditions as well. In both direct and indirect FOC, the 90o shift between the rotor flux and rotor current vector can be achieved in two steps:

- The first step is to ensure that

$$\lambda_{qr}^e = 0$$

....eq8

- The second step is to ensure that

$$i^e_{dr} = 0$$ ………………………………eq9

By suitable choice of on an instantaneous basis, equation 6 can be achieved. Satisfying equation 7 can be accomplished by forcing d -axis stator current to remain constant. To see this, consider the d -axis rotor voltage equation

$$0 = r_r i^e_{dr} + (\omega_e - \omega_r)\lambda^e_{qr} + p\lambda^e_{dr}$$ ………………eq10

Since = 0, eq10 can be written as

$$0 = r_r i^e_{dr} + p\lambda^e_{dr}$$ ……………………eq11

The d -axis rotor flux linkage is given by :

$$\lambda^e_{dr} = L_{lr} i^e_{dr} + L_m\left(i^e_{ds} + i^e_{dR}\right)$$ ………………….eq12

Substituting the value of from equation 10 into equation 11 gives

$$pi^e_{dr} = -\frac{r_r}{L_{lr}} i^e_{dr} - \frac{L_m}{L_{lr}} pi^e_{ds}$$ ……………………eq13

Is is held constant, then p =0 and the solutions of equations 13 becomes

$$i^e_{dr} = Ce^{-\left(\frac{r_r'}{L_{lr}}\right)t}$$ ……………………eq14

Where C is Constant of integration

It is evident from equation 12 that the rotor current will decay to zero and stay at zero regardless of other transients that may be taking place. Hence, the torque is given by

$$T_e = \frac{3}{2}\frac{P}{2}\lambda^e_{dr} i^e_{qr}$$ ………………..eq15

The q-axis rotor flux is given by

$$\lambda^e_{qr} = L_{lr} i^e_{qr} + L_m\left(i^e_{qs} + i^e_{qr}\right)$$ ……………..eq16

The above equation can be rewritten as

$$\lambda^e_{dr} = L_m i^e_{ds}$$ ……………...eq17

The generic rotor flux-oriented control shown in Figure 2.

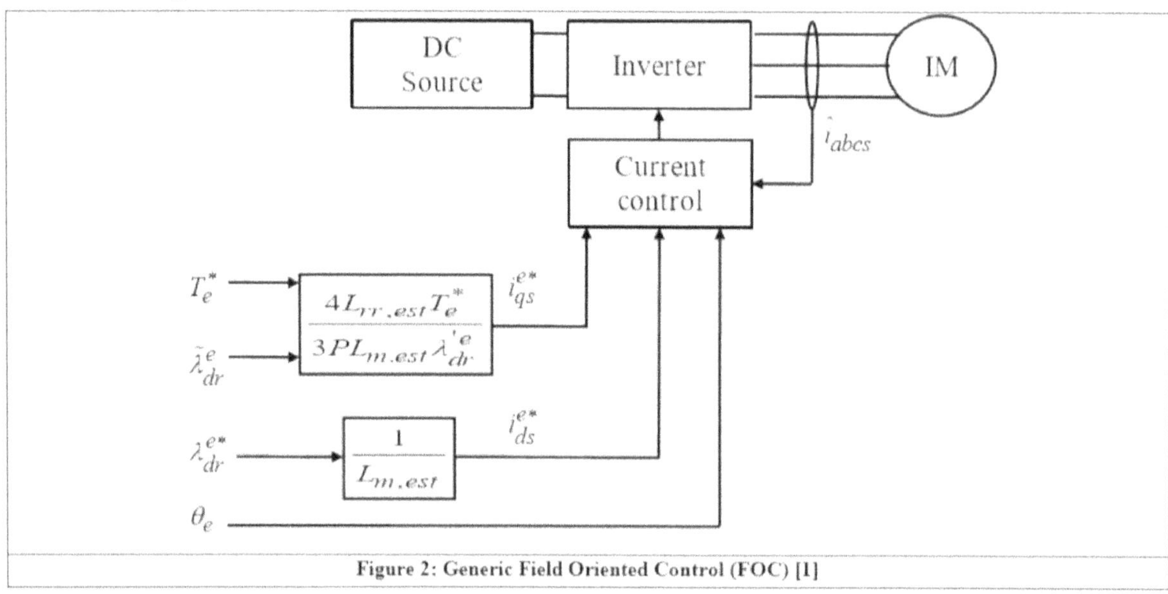

Figure 2: Generic Field Oriented Control (FOC) [1]

In Figure 2 the variables of the form, and ·, , denote command, measured and estimated values respectively. In case of parameters that are estimated, a subscript‖ est‖ is used. The working of the controller is as follows:

i. Based on the torque command (·), the assumed values of the parameters and the estimated value of d -axis rotor flux ˜ is used to formulate a q-axis stator current command ˚

ii. The d -axis stator current command is · calculated such as to achieve a rotor flux command ˆ .

iii. The q-axis and d -axis stator current command is then achieved using a current source control.

The above description of rotor flux oriented FOC is incomplete with determination of ˜ and .

The difference between direct and indirect FOC is in how these two variables are determined.

DIRECT ROTOR ORIENTED FOC:

In direct FOC, the position of the synchronous reference frame ( ) is determined based on the values of q-axis and d-axis rotor flux linkages in the stationary reference frame. The relation of flux linkages in synchronous reference frame and stationary reference frame is

$$\begin{bmatrix} \lambda_{qr}^e \\ \lambda_{dr}^e \end{bmatrix} = \begin{bmatrix} \cos\theta_e & -\sin\theta_e \\ \sin\theta_e & \cos\theta_e \end{bmatrix} \begin{bmatrix} \lambda_{qr}^s \\ \lambda_{dr}^s \end{bmatrix}$$

......................eq18

where

=is the rotor d -axis flux linkage in stationary frame of reference

= is the rotor q -axis flux linkage in stationary frame of reference

In order to achieve , it is sufficient to define the position of the synchronous reference frame as

$$\theta_e = \tan^{-1}\left(\frac{\lambda_{qr}^s}{\lambda_{dr}^s}\right) + \frac{\pi}{2}$$

.... eq19

The difficulty with this approach is that and are not directly measurable quantities.flux, hall-effect sensors are placed in the air gap and used to measure the air-gap flux in q-axis and d-axis. Since the hall-effect sensors are stationary, the flux measured by them is in stationary reference frame. The flux measured by the sensors is the net flux in the air gap (combination of stator and rotor flux). The net flux in the air gap is given by:

$$\lambda_{qm}^{s} = L_{m}\left(i_{qs}^{s} + i_{qr}^{s}\right) \quad \text{.................................eq20}$$

where

is the magnetization inductance

From **equation 20**, the rotor q -axis current is obtained as

$$i_{qr}^{s} = \frac{\lambda_{qm}^{s} - L_{m} i_{qs}^{s}}{L_{m}} \quad \text{.. eq21}$$

The q -axis rotor flux linkage is given by

$$\lambda_{qr}^{s} = L_{lr} i_{qr}^{s} + L_{m}\left(i_{qs}^{s} + i_{qr}^{s}\right) \quad \text{.......................................eq22}$$

Substituting the rotor q -axis current from **equation 21**into **equation 22**gives

$$\lambda_{qr}^{s} = \frac{L_{lr}}{L_{m}} \lambda_{qm}^{s} - L_{lr} i_{qs}^{s} \quad \text{.. eq23}$$

An identical derivation for d-axis gives

$$\lambda_{dr}^{s} = \frac{L_{lr}}{L_{m}} \lambda_{dm}^{s} - L_{lr} i_{ds}^{s} \quad \text{.......................................eq24}$$

The implementation of this control strategy is shown in **Figure 3a** and **b**

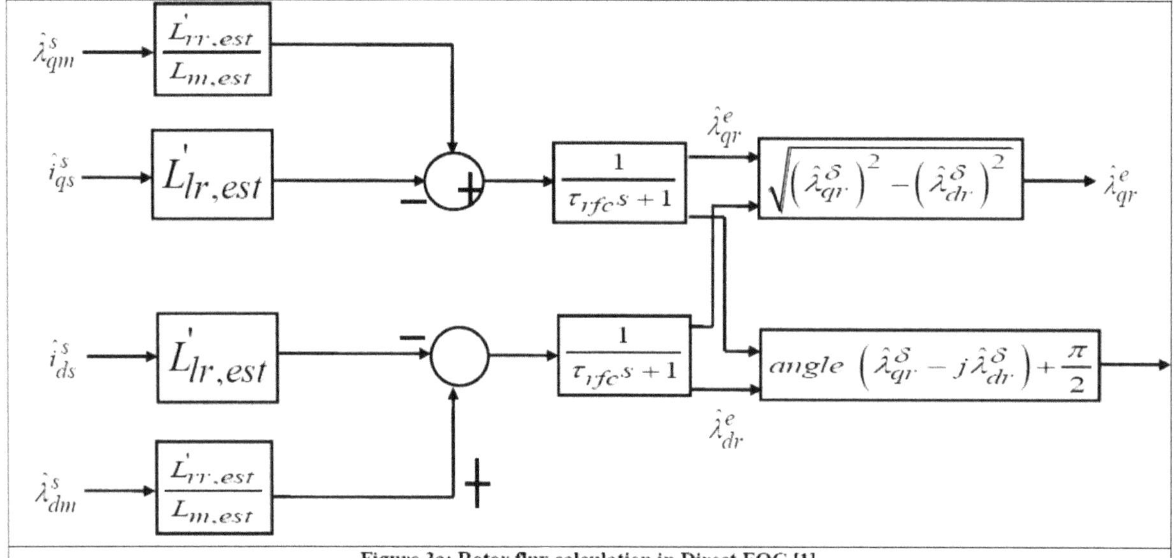

Figure 3a: Rotor flux calculation in Direct FOC [1]

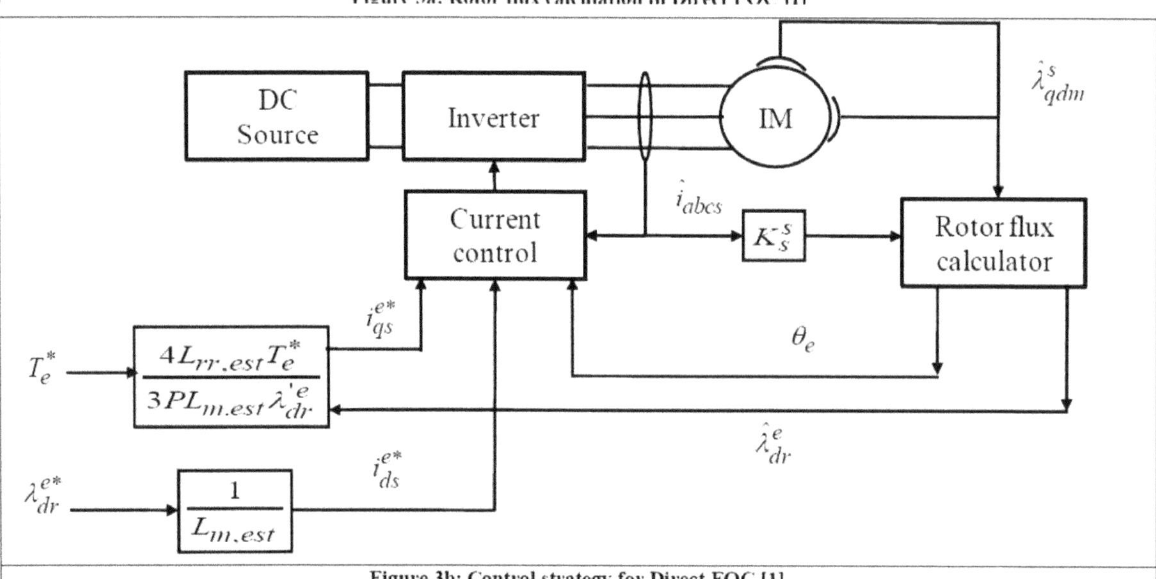

Figure 3b: Control strategy for Direct FOC [1]

INDIRECT ROTOR ORIENTED FOC:

The direct FOC is problematic and expensive due to use of hall-effect sensors. Hence, indirect FOC methods are gaining considerable interest. The indirect FOC methods are more sensitive to knowledge of the machine parameters but do not require direct sensing of the rotor flux linkages. The q-axis rotor voltage equation in synchronous frame is.

$$0 = r_r i_{qr}^e + (\omega_e - \omega_r)\lambda_{dr}^e + p\lambda_{qr}^e$$

.... eq25

Since for direct field-oriented control, **equation 25**becomes

$$0=r_r i_{qr}^e+(\omega_e-\omega_r)\lambda_{dr}^e$$

$$\Rightarrow \omega_e=\omega_r-r_r\frac{i_{qr}^e}{\lambda_{dr}^e}$$ eq26

Substituting the values of and substitute in above equations

$$\omega_e=\omega_r+\frac{r_r}{L_{lr}}\frac{i_{qs}^e}{\lambda_{ds}^e}$$ eq27

From **equation 27**it can be observed that instead of establishing θ using the rotor fluxas shown in **Figure 3**, it can be determined by integrating ω given by **equation 27**whereω is given as

$$\omega_e=\omega_r+\frac{r_r}{L_{lr}}\frac{i_{qs}^{e*}}{\lambda_{ds}^{e*}}$$ eq28

The **equation 28**does satisfy the conditions of FOC. In order to check it, consider the rotor voltage equations for the q -axis and d -axis:

$$0=r_r i_{qr}^e+(\omega_e-\omega_r)\lambda_{dr}^e+p\lambda_{qr}^e$$ eq29

$$0=r_r i_{dr}^e+(\omega_e-\omega_r)\lambda_{qr}^e+p\lambda_{dr}^e$$ eq30

Substituting from **equation 28** into **equations 29** and **30**gives

$$0=r_r i_{qr}^e+\frac{r_r}{L_{lr}}\frac{i_{qs}^{e*}}{i_{ds}^{e*}}\lambda_{dr}^e+p\lambda_{qr}^e$$ eq31

$$0=r_r i_{dr}^e+\frac{r_r}{L_{lr}}\frac{i_{qs}^{e*}}{i_{ds}^{e*}}\lambda_{qr}^e+p\lambda_{dr}^e$$ eq32

Substituting the value of from*d*-axis rotor flux **intoequation 32**gives

$$0=r_r\left(\frac{\lambda_{qr}^e-L_m i_{qs}^{e*}}{L_{lr}}\right)i_{qr}^e+\frac{r_r}{L_{lr}}\frac{i_{qs}^{e*}}{i_{ds}^{e*}}\left(L_{lr}i_{dr}^{e*}+L_m i_{ds}^{e*}\right)+p\lambda_{qr}^e$$

......eq33

$$0 = r_r i_{dr}^e - \frac{r_r}{L_{lr}} \frac{i_{qs}^{e*}}{i_{ds}^{e*}} \lambda_{qr}^e + p\left(L_{lr} i_{qr}^e + L_m i_{ds}^{e*}\right)$$

.........................eq34

If the d -axis rotor current is held constant, then •and rearranging **equations 33**and **34**gives

$$p\lambda_{qr}^e = -\frac{r_r}{L_{lr}} \lambda_{qr}^e - r_r \frac{i_{qs}^{e*}}{i_{ds}^{e*}} i_{dr}^e$$

....eq35

In **Figure 4** the implementation of ***indirect FOC*** is shown and it is much simpler than the ***direct FOC***.

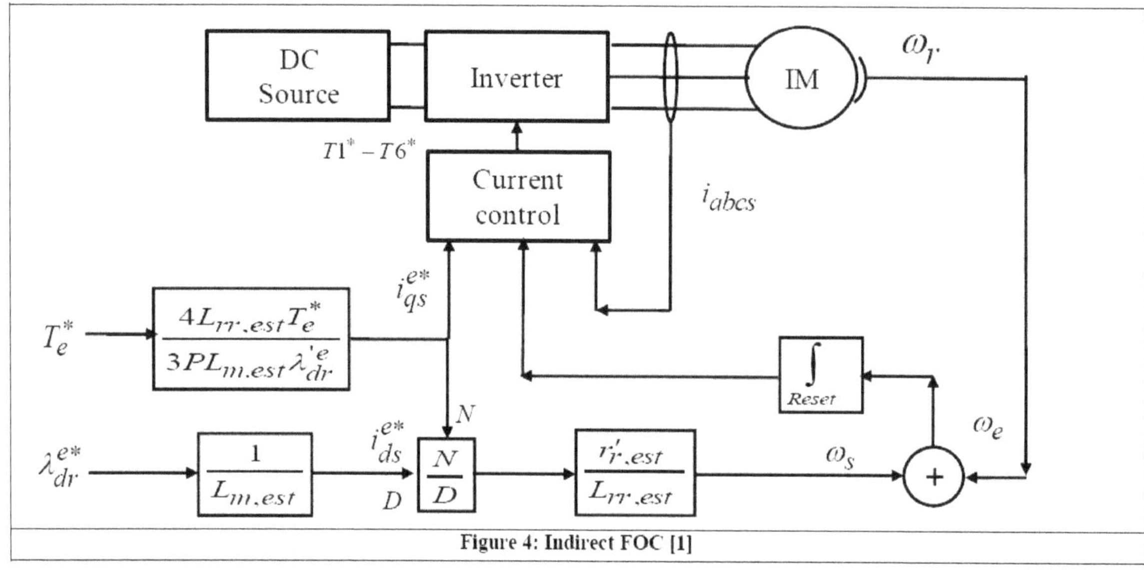

Figure 4: Indirect FOC [1]

UNIT –IV

ENERGY STORAGE

—Energy storages‖ are defined in this book as the devices that store energy, deliver energy outside (discharge), and accept energy from outside (charge). There are several types of energy storages that have been proposed for electric vehicle (EV) and hybrid electric vehicle (HEV) applications. These energy storages, so far, mainly include chemical batteries, ultra capacitors or super capacitors, and ultrahigh-speed flywheels. The fuel cell, which essentially is a kind of energy converter, will be discussed in Chapter12.There are a number of requirements for energy storage applied in an automotive application, such as specific energy, specific power, efficiency, maintenance management, cost, environmental adaptation and friendliness, and safety. For allocation on an EV, specific energy is the first consideration since it limits the vehicle range. On the other hand, for HEV applications specific energy becomes less important and specific power is the first consideration, because all the energy is from the energy source (engine or fuel cell) and sufficient power is needed to ensure vehicle performance, particularly during acceleration, hill climbing, and regenerative braking. Of course, other requirements should be fully considered in vehicle drive train development.

4.1 ELECTROCHEMICAL BATTERIES:

Electrochemical batteries, more commonly referred to as —batteries,‖ are electrochemical devices that convert electrical energy into potential chemical energy during charging, and convert chemical energy into electric energy during discharging. A —battery‖ is composed of several cells stacked together. A cell is an independent and complete unit that possesses all the electrochemical properties. Basically, a battery cell consists of three primary elements: two electrodes (positive and negative) immersed into an electrolyte shown in Figure 4.1.

Battery manufacturers usually specify the battery with coulometric capacity(amp-hours), which is defined as the number of amp-hours gained when discharging the battery from a fully charged state until the terminal voltage drops to its cut-off voltage, as shown in Figure 4.2. It should be noted that the same battery usually has a different number of amp-hours at different discharging current rates. Generally, the capacity will become smaller with a large discharge current rate, as shown in Figure 4.3.

Battery manufacturers usually specify a battery with a number of amp-hours along with a current rate. For example, a battery labelled 100 Ah at C5 rate has a 100 amp-hour capacity at 5 hours discharge rate (discharging current_100/5_20 A).Another important parameter of a battery is the state-of-charge (SOC).SOC is defined as the ratio of the remaining capacity to the fully charged capacity. With this definition, a fully charged battery has an SOC of100% and a fully discharged battery has an SOC of 0%. However, the term —fully discharged‖ sometimes causes confusion because of the different capacity at different discharge rates and different cut-off voltage (refer to Figure4.3).

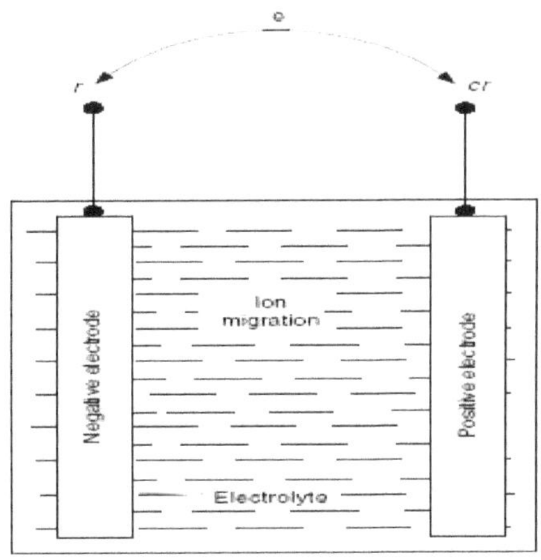

FIGURE 4.1.A typical electrochemical battery cell

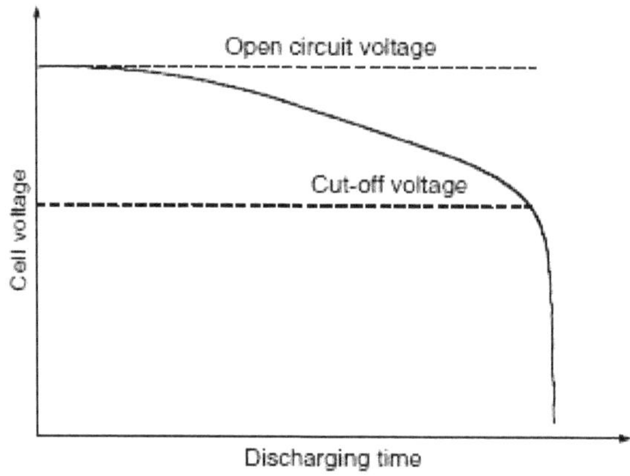

FIGURE 4.2 Cut-off voltage of a typical battery

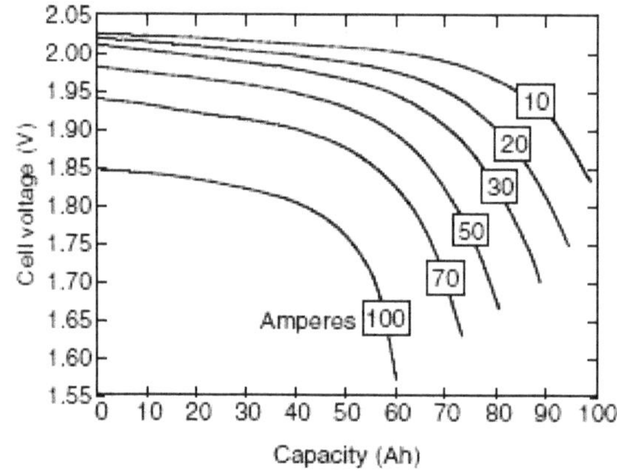

FIGURE 4.3. Discharge characteristics of a lead-acid battery

The change in SOC in a time interval, *dt*, with discharging or charging current *i* may be expressed as

$$\Delta SOC = \frac{i\,dt}{Q(i)}, \qquad \text{.........................eq1}$$

Where$Q(i)$ is amp-hour capacity of the battery at current rate *i*. For discharging,*i*is positive, and for charging, *i* is negative. Thus, the SOC of the battery can be expressed as

$$SOC = SOC_0 - \int \frac{i\,dt}{Q(i)}, \qquad \text{...................eq2}$$

where $SOC0$ is the initial value of the SOC.

For EVs and HEVs, the energy capacity is considered to be more importantthan the coulometric capacity (Ahs), because it is directly associated with the vehicle operation. The energy delivered from the battery can be expressed as

$$EC = \int_0^t V(i, SOC)\, i(t)\, dt, \qquad \text{....................... eq3}$$

Where V (i, SOC*)* is the voltage at the battery terminals, which is a function of the battery current and SOC.

ELECTROCHEMICAL REACTIONS:

For simplicity, and because it is the most widespread battery technology intoday's automotive applications, the lead-acid battery case is used as anexample to explain the operating principle theory of electrochemical batteries. Lead-acid battery uses an aqueous solution of sulfuric acid (2H SO2_4)as the electrolyte.

The electrodes are made of porous lead (Pb, anode, electrically negative) and porous lead oxide

Figure 4.4(a), where lead is consumed and lead sulfate is formed. The chemical reaction on the anode can be written as

$$Pb + SO_4^{2-} \rightarrow PbSO_4 + 2e^- \quad \text{.....................eq1}$$

This reaction releases two electrons and, thereby, gives rise to an excess negative charge on the electrode that is relieved by a flow of electrons through the external circuit to the positive (cathode) electrode. At the positive electrode, the lead of PbO2 is also converted to PbSO4 and, at the same time, water is formed. The reaction can be expressed as

$$PbO_2 + 4H^+ + SO_4^{2-} + 2e^- \rightarrow PbSO_4 + 2H_2O \quad \text{...................eq2}$$

During charging, the reactions on the anode and cathode are reversed as shown in Figure 4.4(b) that can be expressed by

Anode:

$$PbSO_4 + 2e^- \rightarrow Pb + SO_4^{2-} \quad \text{.......................eq3 and}$$

Cathode:

$$PbSO_4 + 2H_2O \rightarrow PbO_2 + 4H^+ + SO_4^{2-} + 2e^- \quad \text{........................eq4}$$

The overall reaction in a lead-acid battery cell can be expressed as

Overall:

$$Pb + PbO_2 + 2H_2SO_4 \underset{\text{charge}}{\overset{\text{discharge}}{\rightleftarrows}} 2PbSO_4 + 2H_2O. \quad \text{......................eq5}$$

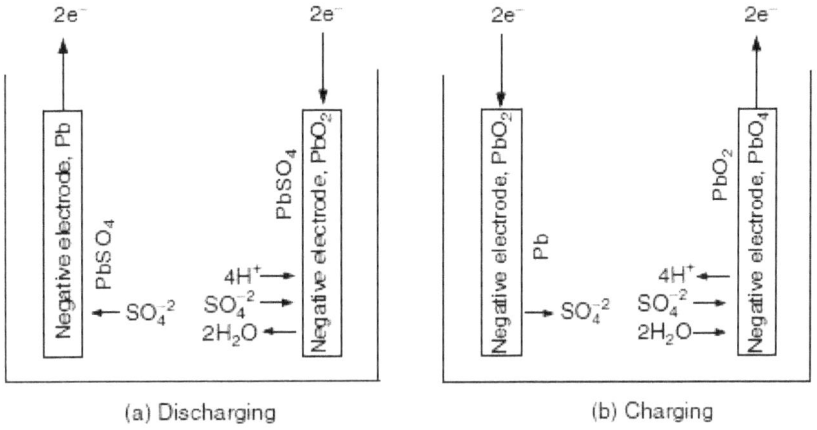

FIGURE 4.4. Electrochemical processes during the discharge and charge of a lead-acid battery cell The lead-acid battery has a cell voltage of about 2.03 V at standard condition, which is affected by the concentration of the electrolyte.

THERMODYNAMIC VOLTAGE:

The thermodynamic voltage of a battery cell is closely associated with the energy released and the number of electrons transferred in the reaction. The energy released by the battery cell reaction is given by the change in Gibbs free energy, ΔG, usually expressed in per mole quantities. The change in Gibbs free energy in a chemical reaction can be expressed as

$$\Delta G = \sum_{\text{Products}} G_i - \sum_{\text{Reactants}} G_j, \quad \text{.....................eq6}$$

Where *Gi* and *Gj*are the free energy in species *i* of products and species *j* of reactants. In a reversible process, ΔG is completely converted into electric energy, that is,

$$\Delta G = -nFV_r, \quad \text{................eq7}$$

Where*n* is the number of electrons transferred in the reaction, *F*_96,495 is the Faraday constant in

coulombs per mole, and *Vr*is the reversible voltage of the cell. At standard condition (25°C temperature and 1 atm pressure), the open circuit (reversible) voltage of a battery cell can be expressed as

$$V_r^0 = -\frac{\Delta G^0}{nF},$$
..................eq8

Where$\Delta G0$ is the change in Gibbs free energy at standard conditions.

The change of free energy, and thus the cell voltage, in a chemical reaction is a function of the activities of the solution species. From equation (7)and the dependence of ΔG on the reactant activities, the *Nernst relationship* is derived as

$$V_r = V_r^0 - \frac{RT}{nF}\ln\left[\frac{\Pi(activities\ of\ products)}{\Pi(activities\ of\ reactants)}\right],$$
..................eq9

Where$R$ is the universal gas constant, 8.31J/mol K, and T is absolute temperature in K.

SPECIFIC ENERGY:

Specific energy is defined as the energy capacity per unit battery weight (Wh/kg). The theoretical specific energy is the maximum energy that can be generated per unit total mass of the cell reactant. As discussed above, the energy in a battery cell can be expressed by the Gibbs free energy ΔG. With respect to theoretical specific energy, only the effective weights (molecular weight of reactants and products) are involved; then

$$E_{spe,theo} = -\frac{\Delta G}{3.6\sum M_i} = \frac{nFV_r}{3.6\sum M_i}(\mathrm{Wh/kg}),$$
..................eq10

Where$\Sigma Mi$is the sum of the molecular weight of the individual species involved in the battery reaction. Taking the lead-acid battery as an example, *Vr*_2.03 V, *n*_2, and ΣMi_642 g; then *Espe,the*_170 Wh/kg. From (10), it is clear that the —idealǁ couple would be derived from a highly electronegative element and a highly electropositive element, both of low atomic weight. Hydrogen, lithium, or sodium would be the best choice for the negative reactants, and the lighter halogens, oxygen, or sulfur would be the best choice for the positive. To put such couples together in a battery requires electrode designs for effective utilization of the contained active materials, as well as electrolytes of high conductivity compatible with the materials in both electrodes. These constraints result in oxygen and sulfur being used in some systems as oxides and sulfides rather than as the elements themselves. For operation at ambient temperature, aqueous electrolytes are advantageous because of their high conductivities. Here, alkali-group metals cannot be used as electrodes since these elements react with water. It is necessary to choose other metals, which have a reasonable degree of electro positivity, such as zinc, iron, or aluminum. When considering electrode couples, it is preferable to exclude those elements that have a low abundance in the earth's crust, are expensive to produce, or are unacceptable from a health or environmental point of view.

Examination of possible electrode couples has resulted in the study of morethan 30 different battery systems with a view of developing a reliable, highperformance, inexpensive high-power energy source for electric traction. The theoretical specific energies of the systems championed for EVs and HEVs are presented in Table 4.6. Practical specific energies, however, are well below the theoretical maxima. Apart from electrode kinetic and other restrictions that serve to reduce the cell voltage and prevent full utilization of the reactants, there is a need for construction materials which add to the battery weight but which are not involved in the energy-producing reaction.

In order to appreciate the extent to which the practical value of the specific energy is likely to differ from the theoretical values, it is instructive to consider the situation of the well-established lead-acid battery. A breakdown ofthe various components of a lead-acid battery designed to give a practical specific energy of 45 Wh/kg is shown in Figure 4.5.It shows that only about 26% of the total weight of the battery is directly involved in producing electrical energy. The remainder is made up of (1) potential call reactants that are not discharged at the rates required for EV operation, (2) water used as the solvent for the electrolyte (sulfuric acid alone is not suitable), (3) lead grids for current collection, (4) —top leadǁ, that is, terminals, straps and intercellconnectors, and (5) cover, connector, and separators. A similar ratio of practical-to-theoretical specific energy is expected for each of the candidate systems listed in Table 4.6.

Theoretical Specific Energies of Candidate Batteries for EVs and HEVs[1]

Battery ⊕	⊖	Cell Reaction: Charge ⇐	Cell Reaction: Discharge ⇒	Specific Energy (Wh/kg)
Acidic aqueous solution				
PbO_2	Pb	$PbO_2 + 2H_2SO_4 + Pb$	⇔ $2PbSO_4 + 2H_2O$	170
Alkaline aqueous solution				
NiOOH	Cd	$2NiOOH + 2H_2O + Cd$	⇔ $2Ni(OH)_2 + Cd(OH)_2$	217
NiOOH	Fe	$2NiOOH + 2H_2O + Fe$	⇔ $2Ni(OH)_2 + Fe(OH)_2$	267
NiOOH	Zn	$2NiOOH + 2H_2O + Zn$	⇔ $2Ni(OH)_2 + Zn(OH)_2$	341
NiOOH	H_2	$2NiOOH + H_2$	⇔ $2Ni(OH)_2$	387
MnO_2	Zn	$2MnO2 + H_2O + Zn$	⇔ $2MnOOH + ZnO$	317
O_2	Al	$4Al + 6H_2O + 3O_2$	⇔ $4Al(OH)_3$	2815
O_2	Fe	$2Fe + 2H_2O + O_2$	⇔ $2Fe(OH)_2$	764
O_2	Zn	$2Zn + 2H_2O + O_2$	⇔ $2Zn(OH)_2$	888
Flow				
Br_2	Zn	$Zn + Br_2$	⇔ $ZnBr_2$	436
Cl_2	Zn	$Zn + Cl_2$	⇔ $ZnCl_2$	833
$(VO_2)_2SO_4$	VSO_4	$(VO_2)_2SO_4 + 2HVSO_4 + 2H_2SO_4$	⇔ $2VOSO_4 + V_2(SO_4)_3 + 2H_2O$	114
Molten salt				
S	Na	$2Na + 3S$	⇔ Na_2S_3	760
$NiCl_2$	Na	$2Na + NiCl_2$	⇔ $2NaCl$	790
FeS_2	LiAl	$4LiAl + FeS_2$	⇔ $2Li_2S + 4Al + Fe$	650
Organic lithium				
$LiCoO_2$	Li-C	$Li_{(y-x)}C_6 + Li_{(1-(y-x))}CoO_2$	⇔ $Li_yC6 + Li_{(1-y)}CoO_2$	320[a]

[a] For a maximum value of $x = 0.5$ and $y = 0$.

TABLE 4.6. Theoretical Specific Energies of Candidate Batteries for EVs and HEVs1 **SPECIFIC POWER:**

Specific power is defined as the maximum power of per unit battery weight that the battery can produce in a short period. Specific power is important in the reduction of battery weight, especially in high power demand applications, such as HEVs. The specific power of a chemical battery depends mostly on the battery's internal resistance. With the battery model as shown in Figure 10.6, the maximum power that the battery can supply to the load is

$$P_{peak} = \frac{V_0^2}{4(R_c + R_{int})}, \qquad \text{..........................eq11}$$

Where*Rohm* is the conductor resistance (ohmic resistance) and *Rint*is the internalresistance caused by chemical reaction.

Internal resistance, *Rint*, represents the voltage drop, ΔV, which is associatedwith the battery current. The voltage dropΔV, termed over potential in

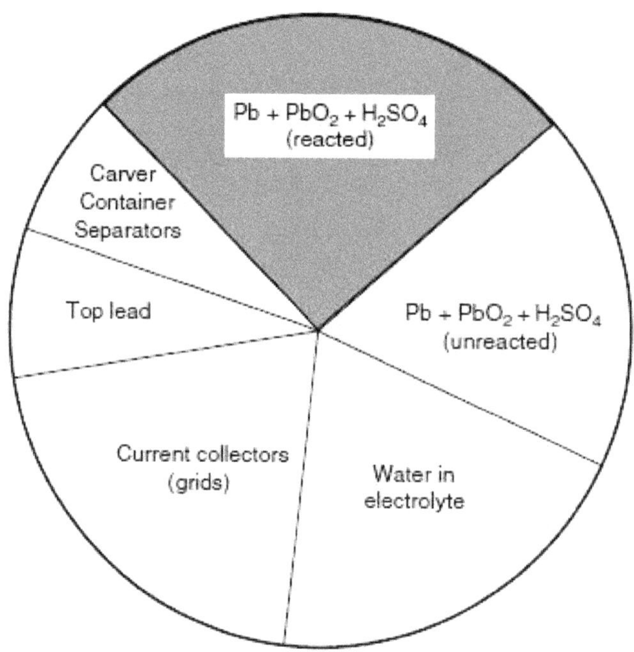

FIGURE 4.7: Weight distribution of the components of a lead-acid EV battery with a specific energy of 45Wh/kg at the C5/5 rate1

Battery terminology includes two components: one is caused by reaction activity ΔVA, and the other by electrolyte concentration ΔVC. General expressions of ΔVA and ΔVC are

$$\Delta V_A = a + b \log I$$

.....................eq12

And

$$\Delta V_C = -\frac{RT}{nF}\ln\left(1 - \frac{I}{I_L}\right),$$

. ...eq13

where a and b are constants, R is the gas constant, 8.314 J/K mol, T is the absolute temperature, n is the number of electrons transferred in the reaction,F is the Faraday constant — 96,495 ampere-seconds per mole — and $IL$is the limit current. Accurate determination of battery resistance or voltagedrop by analysis is difficult and is usually obtained by measurement.1 Thevoltage drop increases with increasing discharging current, decreasing thestored energy in it (refer to Figure 4.3).Table 4.8 also shows the status of battery systems potentially availablefor EV. It can be seen that although specific energies are high in advancedbatteries, the specific powers have to improve. About 300 W/kg might be

System	Specific Energy (Wh/kg)	Peak Power (W/kg)	Energy Efficiency (%)	Cycle Life	Self-Discharge (% per 48 h)	Cost (US$/kWh)
Acidic aqueous solution						
Lead/acid	35–50	150–400	>80	500–1000	0.6	120–150
Alkaline aqueous solution						
Nickel/cadmium	50–60	80–150	75	800	1	250–350
Nickel/iron	50–60	80–150	75	1500–2000	3	200–400
Nickel/zinc	55–75	170–260	65	300	1.6	100–300
Nickel/metal hydride	70–95	200–300	70	750–1200+	6	200–350
Aluminum/air	200–300	160	<50	?	?	?
Iron/air	80–120	90	60	500+	?	50
Zinc/air	100–220	30–80	60	600+	?	90–120
Flow						
Zinc/bromine	70–85	90–110	65–70	500–2000	?	200–250
Vanadium redox	20–30	110	75–85	—	—	400–450
Molten salt						
Sodium/sulfur	150–240	230	80	800+	0[a]	250–450
Sodium/nickel chloride	90–120	130–160	80	1200+	0[a]	230–345
Lithium/iron sulfide (FeS)	100–130	150–250	80	1000+	?	110
Organic/lithium						
Lithium-ion	80–130	200–300	>95	1000+	0.7	200

[a]No self-discharge, but some energy loss by cooling.

TABLE 4.8: Status of Battery Systems for Automotive Applications

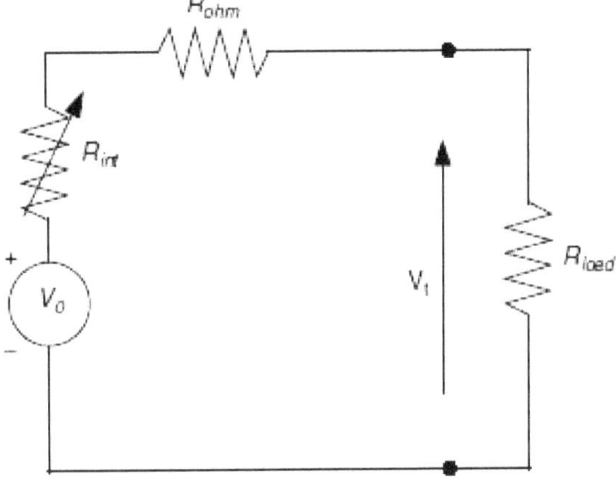

FIGURE 4.9. Battery circuit model

The optimistic estimate. However, SAFT has reported their Li-ion highpower for HEV application with a specific energy of 85 Wh/kg and aspecific power of 1350 W/kg and their high-energy batteries for EV applicationwith about 150 Wh/kg and 420 W/kg (at 80% SOC, 150A current and30 sec), respectively.

ENERGY EFFICIENCY:

The energy or power losses during battery discharging and charging appear in the form of voltage loss. Thus, the efficiency of the battery during discharging and charging can be defined at any operating point as the ratio of the cell operating voltage to the thermodynamic voltage, that is: During Discharging:

$$\eta = \frac{V}{V_0} \qquad \text{......................eq14}$$

And

During charging:

$$\eta = \frac{V_0}{V}. \qquad \text{eq15}$$

The terminal voltage, as a function of battery current and energy stored in itor SOC, is lower in discharging and higher in charging than the electrical potential produced by a chemical reaction. Figure 4.10 shows the efficiency of the lead-acid battery during discharging and charging. The battery has ahigh discharging efficiency with high SOC and a high charging efficiency with low SOC. The net cycle efficiency has a maximum in the middle range of the SOC. Therefore, the battery operation control unit of an HEV should control the battery SOC in its middle range so as to enhance the operating efficiency and depress the temperature rise caused by energy loss. High temperature would damage the battery.

BATTERY TECHNOLOGIES:

The viable EV and HEV batteries consist of the lead-acid battery, nickel based batteries such as nickel/iron, nickel/cadmium, and nickel–metal hydride batteries, and lithium-based batteries such as lithium polymer and lithium-ion batteries.3 In the near term, it seems that lead-acid batteries will still be the major type due to its many advantages. However, in the middle and long term, it seems that cadmium- and lithium-based batteries will be major candidates for EVs and HEVs.

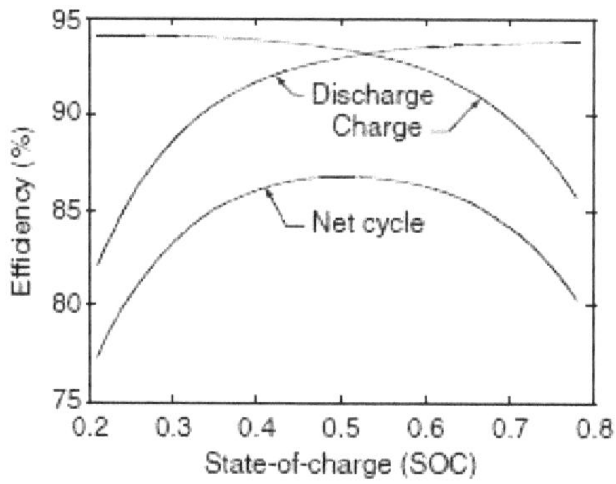

FIGURE 4.10 Typical battery charge and discharge efficiency

LEAD-ACID BATTERIES:

The lead-acid battery has been a successful commercial product for over a century and is still widely used as electrical energy storage in the automotive field and other applications. Its advantages are its low cost, mature

technology, relative high-power capability, and good cycle. These advantagesare attractive for its application in HEVs where high power is the firstconsideration. The materials involved (lead, lead oxide, sulfuric acid) are rather low in cost when compared to their more advanced counterparts. Lead-acid batteries also have several disadvantages. The energy density of lead-acid batteries is low, mostly because of the high molecular weight of lead. The temperature characteristics are poor.2 Below 10°C, its specific power and specific energy are greatly reduced. This aspect severely limits the application of lead-acid batteries for the traction of vehicles operating in cold climates.

The presence of highly corrosive sulfuric acid is a potential safety hazard for vehicle occupants. Hydrogen released by the self-discharge reactions is another potential danger, since this gas is extremely flammable even intiny concentrations. Hydrogen emission is also a problem for hermetically sealed batteries. Indeed, in order to provide a good level of protection against acid spills, it is necessary to seal the battery, thus trapping the parasitic gases in the casing. As a result, pressure may build up in the battery, causing swelling and mechanical constraints on the casing and sealing. The lead in the electrodes is an environmental problem because of its toxicity. The emission of lead consecutive to the use of lead-acid batteriesmay occur during the fabrication of the batteries, in case of vehicle wreck (spill of electrolyte through cracks), or during their disposal at the end of battery life.

Different lead-acid batteries with improved performance are beingdeveloped for EVs and HEVs. Improvements of the sealed lead-acid batteries in specific energy over 40 Wh/kg, with the possibility of rapid charge, have been attained. One of these advanced sealed lead-acid batteries isElectro source's Horizon battery. It adopts the lead wire woven horizontalplate and hence offers long cycle life (over 600 cycles for on-road EV application), rapid recharge capability (50% capacity in 8 minand 100% in less than 30 min), low cost (US$2000–3000 an EV), mechanicalruggedness (robust structure of horizontal plate), maintenance-free conditions(sealedbatterytechnology), and environmental friendliness. Otheradvanced lead-acid batterytechnologies include bipolar designs and microtubular griddesigns. Advanced lead-acid batteries have been developed to remedy these disadvantages. The specific energy has been increased through the reductionof inactive materials such as the casing, current collector, separators, etc. The lifetime has been increased by over 50% — at the expense of cost, however. The safety issue has been addressed and improved, with electrochemical processes designed to absorb the parasitic releases ofhydrogen and oxygen.

NICKEL-BASED BATTERIES:

Nickel is a lighter metal than lead and has very good electrochemical properties desirable for battery applications. There are four different nickel-based battery technologies: nickel–iron, nickel–zinc, nickel–cadmium, and nickel–metal hydride.

NICKEL/IRON SYSTEM:

The nickel/iron system was commercialized during the early years of the20th century. Applications included fork-lift trucks, mine locomotives, shuttle vehicles, railway locomotives, and motorized hand-trucks.1 The system comprises a nickel (III) hydroxy-oxide (NiO OH) positive electrode and a metallic iron negative electrode. The electrolyte is a concentrated solution of potassium hydroxide (typically 240 g/l) containing lithium hydroxide (50 g/l). The cell reaction is given in Table 4.6 and its nominal open-circuit voltage is1.37v

NICKEL-BASED BATTERIES:

Nickel is a lighter metal than lead and has very good electrochemical properties desirable for battery applications. There are four different nickel-based battery technologies: nickel–iron, nickel–zinc, nickel–cadmium, andnickel–metal hydride.

NICKEL/IRON SYSTEM:

The nickel/iron system was commercialized during the early years of the20th century. Applications included fork-lift trucks, mine locomotives, shuttle vehicles, railway locomotives, and motorized hand-trucks.1 The system comprises a nickel (III) hydroxy-oxide (NiOOH) positive electrode and a metallic iron negative electrode. The electrolyte is a concentrated solution of potassium hydroxide (typically 240 g/l) containing lithium hydroxide (50 g/l). The cell reaction is given in Table 10.1 and its nominal open-circuit

voltage is 1.37 V.Nickel/iron batteries suffer from gassing, corrosion, and self-discharge problems. These problems have been partially or totally solved in prototypes that have yet to reach the market. These batteries are complex due to the need to maintain the water level and the safe disposal of the hydrogen and

oxygen released during the discharge process. Nickel–iron batteries also suffer from low temperatures, although less than lead-acid batteries. Finally, the cost of nickel is significantly higher than that of lead. Their greatest advantages are high power density compared with lead-acid batteries, and a capability of withstanding 2000 deep discharges.

NICKEL/CADMIUM SYSTEM:

The nickel/cadmium system uses the same positive electrodes and electrolyteas the nickel/iron system, in combination with metallic cadmiumnegative electrodes. The cell reaction is given in Table 10.1 and its nominal open-circuit voltage is 1.3 V. Historically, the development of the battery hascoincided with that ofnickel/iron and they have a similar performance. Nickel/cadmium technology has seen enormous technical improvementbecause of the advantages of high specific power (over 220 W/kg), longcycle life (up to 2000 cycles), a high tolerance of electric and mechanical abuse, a small voltage drop over a wide range of discharge currents, rapid charge capability (about 40 to 80% in 18 min), wide operating temperature(_40 to 85°C), low self-discharge rate (_0.5% per day), excellent long-termstorage due to negligible corrosion, and availability in a variety of sizedesigns. However, the nickel/cadmium battery has some disadvantages, including high initial cost, relatively low cell voltage, and the carcinogenicityand environmental hazard of cadmium. Nickel/iron batteries suffer from gassing, corrosion, and self-discharge problems. These problems complex due to the need to maintain the water level and the safe disposal of the hydrogen and oxygen released during the discharge process. Nickel–iron batteries also suffer from low temperatures, although less than lead-acid batteries. Finally, the cost of nickel is significantly higher than that of lead. Their greatest advantages are high power density compared with lead-acid batteries, and a capability of withstanding 2000 deep discharges.

NICKEL/CADMIUM SYSTEM:

The nickel/cadmium system uses the same positive electrodes and electrolyte as the nickel/iron system, in combination with metallic cadmium negative electrodes. The cell reaction is given in Table 10.1 and its nominal open-circuit voltage is 1.3 V. Historically, the development of the battery has coincided with that of nickel/iron and they have a similar performance. Nickel/cadmium technology has seen enormous technical improvement because of the advantages of high specific power (over 220 W/kg), long cycle life (up to 2000 cycles), a high tolerance of electric and mechanicalabuse, a small voltage drop over a wide range of discharge currents, rapidcharge capability (about 40 to 80% in 18 min), wide operating temperature(_40 to 85°C), low self-discharge rate (_0.5% per day), excellent long-termstorage due to negligible corrosion, and availability in a variety of size designs. However, the nickel/cadmium battery has some disadvantages, including high initial cost, relatively low cell voltage, and the carcinogenicity and environmental hazard of cadmium.

The nickel/cadmium battery can be generally divided into two major categories, namely the vented and sealed types. The vented type consists of many alternatives. The vented sintered-plate is a more recent development, which has a high specific energy but is more expensive. It is characterized by a flat discharge voltage profile, and superior high current rate and low-temperature performance. A sealed nickel/cadmium battery incorporates a specific cell design feature to prevent a build-up of pressure in the cell caused by gassing during overcharge. As a result, the battery requires no maintenance.

The major manufacturers of the nickel/cadmium battery for EV and HEVallocation are SAFT and VARTA. Recent EVs powered by the nickel/cadmium battery have included the Chrysler TE Van, Citroën AX, Mazda Roadster, Mitsubishi EV, Peugeot 106, and Renault Clio.3,6

NICKEL–METAL HYDRIDE (NI–MH) BATTERY

The Nickel-metal hydride battery has been on the market since 1992. Its characteristics are similar to those of the nickel/cadmium battery. The principal difference between them is the use of hydrogen, absorbed in a metal hydride, for the active negative electrode material in place of cadmium. Because of its superior specific energy when compared to the Ni–Cd and its freedom from toxicity or carcinogenicity, the Ni–MH battery is superseding the Ni–Cd battery. The overall reaction in a Ni– MH battery is

$$MH + NiOOH \leftrightarrow M + Ni(OH)_2.$$

…………………...eq1

When the battery is discharged, the metal hydride in the negative electrode is oxidized to form metal alloy, and nickel oxyhydroxide in the positive electrode is reduced to nickel hydroxide. During charging, the reverse reaction occurs.

At present, Ni–MH battery technology has a nominal voltage of 1.2 V and attains a specific energy of 65 Wh/kg and a specific power of 200 W/kg. Akey component of the Ni–MH battery is the hydrogen storage metal alloy, which is formulated to obtain a material that is stable over a large number of cycles. There are two major types of these metal alloys being used. These are the rare-earth alloys based around lanthanum nickel, known as AB5, and alloys consisting of titanium and zirconium, known as AB2. The AB2 alloys have a higher capacity than the AB5 alloys. However, the trend is to use AB5alloys because of better charge retention and stability characteristics. Since the Ni–MH battery is still under development, its advantages based on present technology are summarized as follows: it has the highest specific energy (70 to 95 Wh/kg) and highest specific power (200 to 300 W/kg) of nickel-based batteries, environmental friendliness (cadmium free), a flat discharge profile (smaller voltage drop), and rapid recharge capability. However, this battery still suffers from its high initial cost. Also, it may havea memory effect and may be exothermic on charge.

The Ni–MH battery has been considered as an important near-term choice for EV and HEV applications. A number of battery manufacturers, such asGM Ovonic, GP, GS, Panasonic, SAFT, VARTA, and YUASA, have activelyengaged in the development of this battery technology, especially for poweringEVs and HEVs. Since1993, Ovonic battery has installed its Ni–MH batteryin the Solectron GT Force EV for testing and demonstration. A 19-kWhbattery has delivered over 65 Wh kg, 134 km/h, acceleration from zero to 80km/h in 14 sec, and a city driving range of 206 km. Toyota and Honda haveused the Ni–MH battery in their HEVs — Prius and Insight, respectively.

LITHIUM-BASED BATTERIES

Lithium is the lightest of all metals and presents very interesting characteristics from an electrochemical point of view. Indeed, it allows a very highthermodynamic voltage, which results in a very high specific energy and specific power. There are two major technologies of lithium-based batteries: lithium–polymer and lithium-ion.

LITHIUM–POLYMER (LI–P) BATTERY:

Lithium–polymer batteries use lithium metal and a transition metal intercalation oxide (M*y*O*z*) for the negative and positive electrodes, respectively. This M*y*O*z* possesses a layered structure into which lithium ions can be inserted, or from where they can be removed on discharge and charge, respectively. A thin solid polymer electrolyte (SPE) is used, which offers themerits of improved safety and flexibility in design. The general electrochemical reactions are

$$x\mathrm{Li} + \mathrm{M}_y\mathrm{O}_z \leftrightarrow \mathrm{Li}_x\mathrm{M}_y\mathrm{O}_z.$$ eq2

On discharge, lithium ions formed at the negative electrode migrate through the SPE, and are inserted into the crystal structure at the positive electrode. On charge, the process is reversed. By using a lithium foil negative electrode and vanadium oxide (V6O13) positive electrode, the Li/SPE/V6O13 cell is the most attractive one within the family of Li–polymer. It operates at a nominal voltage of 3 V and has a specific energy of 155 Wh/kg and a specific power of 315 W/kg. The corresponding advantages are a very low self-discharge rate (about 0.5% per month), capability of fabrication in a variety of shapes and sizes, and safe design (reduced activity of lithium with solid electrolyte). However, it has the drawback of a relatively weak low-temperature performance due to the temperature dependence of ionic conductivity.

LITHIUM-ION (LI-ION) BATTERY:

Since the first announcement of the Li-ion battery in 1991, Li-ion battery technology has seenanunprecedented rise to what is now considered to bethe most promising rechargeable battery of thefuture. Although still atthedevelopment stage, the Li-ion battery has already gained acceptance for EVand HEV applications.

The Li-ion battery uses a lithiated carbon intercalation material (Li*x*C) forthe negative electrode instead of metallic lithium, a lithiated transitionmetal intercalation oxide (Li1_*x* M*y*O*z*) for the positive electrode, and a liquidorganic solution or a solid polymer for the electrolyte. Lithium ions swing through the electrolyte between the positive and negative electrodesduring discharge and charge. The general electrochemical reaction is described as

$$\mathrm{Li}_x\mathrm{C} + \mathrm{Li}_{1-x}\mathrm{M}_y\mathrm{O}_z \leftrightarrow \mathrm{C} + \mathrm{LiM}_y\mathrm{O}_z.$$ eq3

On discharge, lithium ions are released from the negative electrode, migrate via the electrolyte, and are taken up by the positive electrode. On charge, themprocess is reversed. Possible positive electrode materials include Li1_*x*CoO2, Li1_*x*NiO2, and Li1_*x*Mn2O4, which have the advantages of stability in air, high voltage, andreversibility for the lithium intercalation reaction. The Li*x*C/Li1_*x*NiO2 type, loosely written as C/LiNiO2 or simply calledthe nickel-based Li-ion battery, has a nominal voltage of 4 V, a specificenergy of 120 Wh/kg, an energy density of 200 Wh/l, and a specific powerof 260 W/kg. The cobalt-based type has a higher specific energy and energydensity, but at a higher cost and significant increase in the self-discharge

rate. The manganese-based type has the lowest cost and its specific energyand energy density lie betweenthose of the cobalt- and nickel-based types. It is anticipated that the development of the Li-ion battery will ultimately move to the manganese-based type because of the low cost, abundance, and environmental friendliness of the manganese-based materials. Many battery manufacturers, such as SAFT, GS Hitachi, Panasonic, SONY, and VARTA, have actively engaged in the development of the Li-ion battery. Starting in 1993, SAFT focused on the nickel-based Li-ion battery. Recently, SAFT reported the development of Li-ion high-power batteries forHEV applications with a specific energy of 85 Wh/kg and a specific powerof 1350 W/kg. They also announced high-energy batteries for EV applicationswith about 150 Wh/kg and 420 W/kg (at 80% SOC, 150 A current, and30 sec), respectively.

ULTRACAPACITORS OR SUPER CAPACITORS:

Because of the frequent stop/go operation of EVs and HEVs, the discharging and charging profile of the energy storage is highly varied. The average power required from the energy storage is much lower than the peak power of relatively short duration required for acceleration and hill climbing. In fact, the energy involved in the acceleration and deceleration transients is roughly two thirds of the total amount of energy over the entire vehicle mission in urban driving (Chapters 8 and 9). In HEV design, the peak power capacity of the energy storage is more important than its energy capacity, and usually constrains its size reduction. Based on present battery technology, battery design has to carry out the trade-off among the specific energy and specific power and cycle life. The difficulty in simultaneously obtaining high values of specific energy, specific power, and cycle life has led to some suggestions that the energy storage system of EV and HEV should be a hybridization of an energy source and a power source. The energy source, mainly batteries and fuelcells, has high specific energy whereas the power source has high specific power. The power sources can be recharged from the energy source during less demanding driving or regenerative braking. The power source that has received wide attention is the ultracapacitor

4.7.1. FEATURES OF ULTRACAPACITORS:

The ultracapacitor is characterized by much higher specific power, but much lower specific energy compared to the chemical batteries. Its specific energy is in the range of a few watt-hours per kilogram. However, its specific power can reach up to 3 kW/kg, much higher than any type of battery. Due to their low specific energy density and the dependence of voltage onthe SOC, it is difficult to use ultracapacitors alone as an energy storage forEVs and HEVs. Nevertheless, there are a number of advantages that can result from using the ultracapacitor as an auxiliary power source. One promising application is the so-called battery and ultracapacitor hybrid energy storage system for EVs and HEVs. Specific energy and specificpower requirements can be decoupled, thus affording an opportunity todesign a battery that is optimized for the specific energy and cycle life withlittle attention being paid to the specific power. Due to the load levelling effect of the ultracapacitor, the high-current discharging from the batteryand the high-current charging to the battery by regenerative braking is minimized so that the available energy, endurance, and life of the battery can besignificantly increased.

BASIC PRINCIPLES OF ULTRACAPACITORS

Double-layer capacitor technology is the major approach to achieving theultracapacitor concept. The basic principle of a double-layer capacitor isillustrated in Figure 10.8. When two carbon rods are immersed in a thin sulfuric acid solution, separated from each other and charged with voltage increasing from zero to 1.5 V, almost nothing happens up to 1 V; then at alittle over 1.2 V, a small bubble will appear on the surface of both the electrodes. Those bubbles at a voltage above 1 V indicate electrical decompositionof water. Below the decomposition voltage, while the current does not

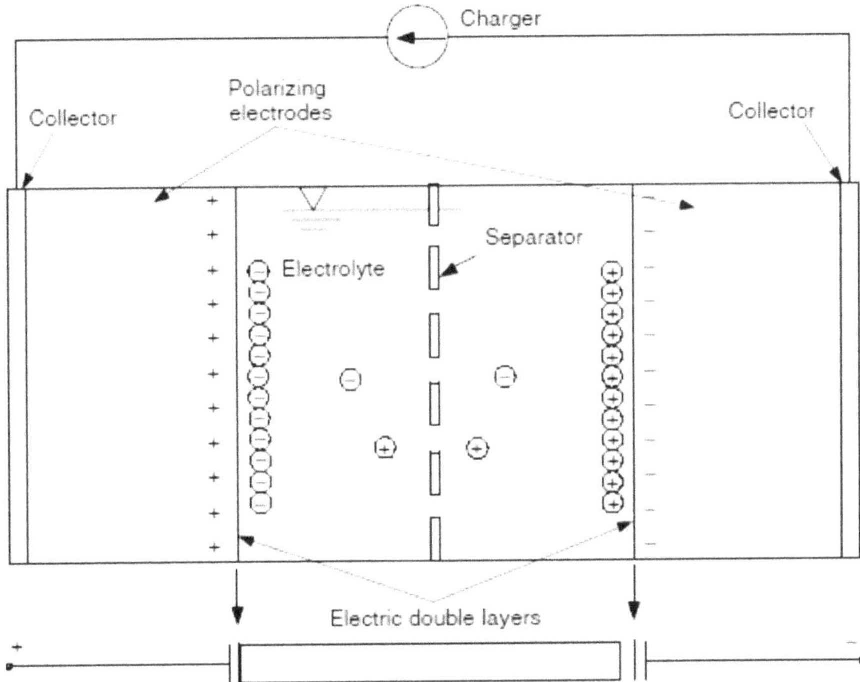

FIGURE 4.11: Basic principles of a typical electric double-layer capacitor

flow, an —electric double layer‖ then occurs at the boundary of electrode and electrolyte. The electrons are charged across the double layer and for a capacitor.

An electrical double layer works as an insulator only below the decomposing voltage. The stored energy, *Ecap*, is expressed as

$$E_{cap} = \frac{1}{2}CV^2,$$

.... eq4

where C is the capacitance in Faraday and V is the usable voltage in volt.This equation indicates that the higher rated voltage V is desirable for larger energy density capacitors. Up to now, capacitors' rated voltage with an aqueous electrolyte has been about 0.9 V per cell, and 2.3 to 3.3 V for each cell with a nonaqueous electrolyte.

There is great merit in using an electric double layer in place of plastic oraluminium oxide films in a capacitor, since the double layer is very thin — as thin as one molecule with no pin holes — and the capacity per area is quite large, at 2.5 to 5 µF/cm2.Even if a few µF/cm2 are obtainable, the energy density of capacitors is not large when using aluminium foil. For increasing capacitance, electrodes aremade from specific materials that have a very large area, such as activated carbons, which are famous for their surface areas of 1,000 to 3,000 m2/g. To those surfaces, ions are adsorbed and result in 50 F/g (1,000 m2/g_5F/cm2_10,000 cm2/m2_50 F/g). Assuming that the same weight of electrolyteis added, 25 F/g is quite a large capacity density. Nevertheless, theenergy density of these capacitors is far smaller than secondary batteries; the typical specific energy of ultracapacitors at present is about 2 Wh/kg, only1/20 of 40 Wh/kg, which is the available value of typical lead-acid batteries.

PERFORMANCE OF ULTRACAPACITORS:

The performance of an ultracapacitor may be represented by terminal voltages during discharge and charge with different current rates. There arethree parameters in a capacitor: the capacitance itself (its electric potential*VC*), the series resistance *RS*, and the dielectric leakage resistance, *RL*, asshown in Figure 4.12. The terminal voltage of the ultracapacitor during dischargecan be expressed as

$$V_t = V_C - iR_S.$$

................eq5

$$\frac{dV_C}{dt} = -\left(\frac{i+i_L}{C}\right),$$
…………eq6

where C is the capacitance of the ultracapacitor. On the other hand, the leakagecurrent iLcan be expressed as

$$i_L = \frac{V_c}{R_L}.$$
…………....eq7

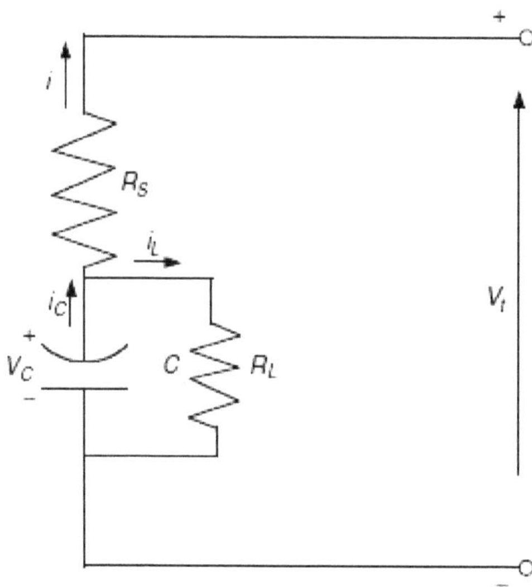

FIGURE 4.12: Ultracapacitor equivalent circuit

$$\frac{dV_C}{dt} = \frac{V_c}{CR_L} - \frac{i}{C}.$$
…………..........eq8

The terminal voltage of the ultracapacitor cell can be represented by the diagramas shown in Figure 10.10. The analytical solution of (eq8) is

$$V_C = \left[V_{C0}\int_0^t \frac{i}{C} e^{t/CR_L}\, dt\right] e^{t/CR_L},$$
............eq9

where i is the discharge current, which is a function of time in real operation. The discharge characteristics of the Maxwell 2600 F ultracapacitor are shown in Figure 4.14. At different discharge current rates, the voltage decreases linearlywith discharge time. At a large discharge current rate, the voltage decreases much faster than at a small current rate.

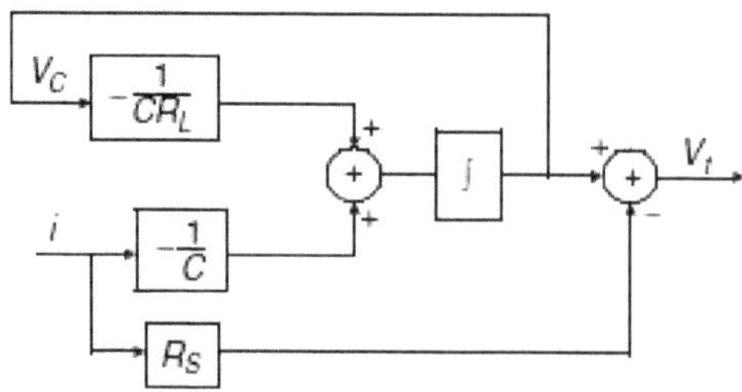

FIGURE 4.13: Block diagram of the ultracapacitor model

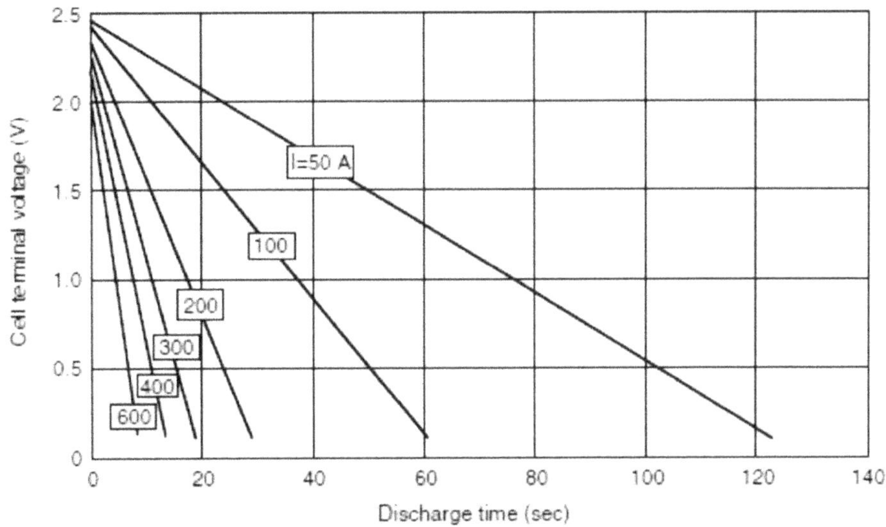

FIGURE 4.14: Discharge characteristics of the 2600 F Maxwell Technologies ultracapacitor

A similar model can be used to describe the charging characteristics of anultracapacitor, and readers who are interested may do their own analysisand simulation.
The operation efficiency in discharging and charging can be expressed as:
discharging:

$$\eta_d = \frac{V_t I_t}{V_C I_C} = \frac{(V_C - I_t R_S) I_t}{V_C (I_t + I_L)}$$

..........eq10

and

charging:

$$\eta_c = \frac{V_C I_C}{V_t I_t} = \frac{V_C (I_t - I_L)}{(V_C + I_t R_s) I_t},$$

...............eq11

where *Vt* is the terminal voltage and *It* is the current input to or output fromthe terminal. In actual operation, the leakage current *IL* is usually very small(few mA) and can be ignored. Thus, equations (10) and (11) can berewritten
as: *discharging*:

$$\eta_d = \frac{V_C - R_S I_t}{V_C} = \frac{V_t}{V_C}$$

.................eq12

And
charging:

$$\eta_c = \frac{V_C}{V_C + R_s I_t} = \frac{V_C}{V_t}.$$

.....................eq13

The above equations indicate that the energy loss in an ultracapacitor iscaused by the presence of seriesresistance. The efficiency decreases at a highcurrent rate and low cell voltage, as shown in Figure 4.15. Thus, in actual

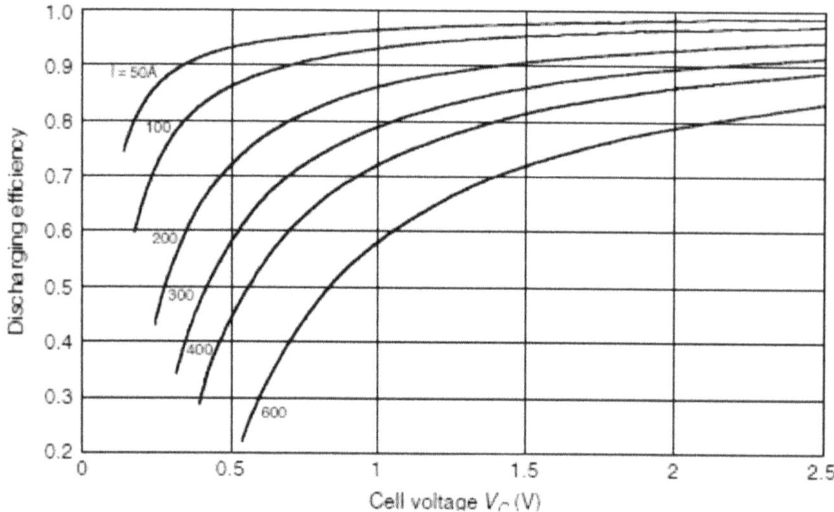

FIGURE 4.15: Discharge efficiency of the 2600 F Maxwell Technologies ultracapacitor operation, the ultracapacitor should be maintained at its high voltage region, for more than 60% of its rated voltage.

The energy stored in an ultracapacitor can be obtained through the energyneeded to charge it to a certain voltage level, that is,

$$E_C = \int_0^t V_C I_C \, dt = \int_0^V C V_C \, dV_C = \frac{1}{2} C V_C^2,$$

......................eq14

where VC is the cell voltage in volts. At its rated voltage, the energy stored in the ultracapacitor reaches its maxima. Equation (10.31) indicates that increasing the rated voltage can significantly increase the stored energy since the energy increases with the voltage squared. In real operation, itis impossible to utilize the stored energy completely because of the low power in the low SOC (low voltage). Thus, an ultracapacitor is usually given a bottom voltage, VCb, below which the ultracapacitor will stop delivering energy. Consequently, the available or useful energy for use is less than its fully charged energy, which can be expressed as

$$E_u = \frac{1}{2} C \left(V_{CR}^2 - V_{Cb}^2 \right),$$

....................eq15

where VCR is the rated voltage of the ultracapacitor. At its bottom voltage, theSOC can be written as

$$SOC = \frac{0.5 C V_{Cb}^2}{0.5 C V_{CR}^2} = \frac{V_{Cb}^2}{V_{CR}^2}.$$

..........................eq16

For example, when the cell voltage drops from rated voltage to 60% of therated voltage, 64% of the total energy is available for use, as shown inFigure 415.

4.7.4. ULTRACAPACITOR TECHNOLOGIES:

According to the goals set by the U.S. Department of Energy for the inclusionof ultracapacitors in EVs and HEVs, the near-term specific energyand specific power should be better than 5 Wh/kg and 500 W/kg, respectively, while the advanced performance values should be over 15 Wh/kgand 1600 W/kg. So far, none of the available ultracapacitors can fully satisfy these goals. Nevertheless, some companies are actively engaged in the
research and development of ultracapacitors for EV and EHV applications. Maxwell Technologies hasclaimed that its power BOOSTCAP ultracapacitor cells (2600 F at 2.5 V) and integrated modules (145 F at 42 Vand435 F at 14 V) are in production. The technical specifications are listedin Table 4.9.

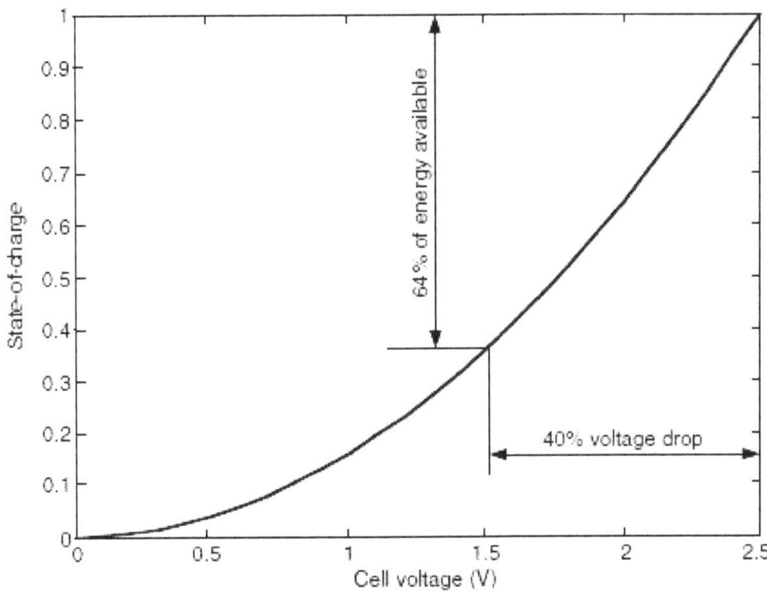

FIGURE 4.16: SOC vs. cell voltage

TABLE 4.9: Technical Specifications of the Maxwell Technologies Ultracapacitor Cell andIntegrated Modules5

	BCAP0010 (Cell)	BMOD0115 (Module)	BMOD0117 (Module)
Capacitance (farads, −20%/+20%)	2600	145	435
maximum series resistance ESR at 25°C (mΩ)	0.7	10	4
Voltage (V), continuous (peak)	2.5 (2.8)	42 (50)	14 (17)
Specific power at rated voltage (W/kg)	4300	2900	1900
Specific energy at rated voltage (Wh/kg)	4.3	2.22	1.82
Maximum current (A)	600	600	600
Dimensions (mm) (reference only)	60 × 172 (Cylinder)	195 × 165 × 415 (Box)	195 × 265 × 145 (Box)
Weight (kg)	0.525	16	6.5
Volume (l)	0.42	22	7.5
Operating temperature[a] (°C)	−35 to +65	−35 to +65	−35 to +65
Storage temperature (°C)	−35 to +65	−35 to +65	−35 to +65
Leakage current (mA) 12 h, 25°C	5	10	10

[a]Steady-state case temperature.

ULTRAHIGH-SPEED FLYWHEELS:

The use of flywheels for storing energy in mechanical form is not a new concept. More than 25 years ago, the Oerlikon Engineering Company inSwitzerland made the first passenger bus solely powered by a massive flywheel. This flywheel, which weighed 1500 kg and operated at 3000 rpm, wasrecharged by electricity at each bus stop. The traditional flywheel is a massive steel rotor with hundreds of kilograms that spins on the order of ten hundreds of rpm. On the contrary, the advanced flywheel is a lightweight composite rotor with tens of kilograms and rotates on the order of 10,000rpm; it is the so-called ultrahigh-speed flywheel. The concept of ultrahigh-speed flywheels appears to be a feasible means for fulfilling the stringent energy storage requirements for EV and HEVapplications, namely high specific energy, high specific power, long cycle life, high-energy efficiency, quick recharge, maintenance free characteristics, costeffectiveness, and environmental friendliness.

OPERATION PRINCIPLES OF FLYWHEELS:

A rotating flywheel stores energy in the kinetic form as

$$E_f = \frac{1}{2} J_f \omega_f^2$$ eq1

where *Jf* is the moment of inertia of the flywheel in kgm2/sec and ω*f* is the angular velocity of the flywheel in rad/sec. Equation (10.32) indicates that enhancing the angular velocity of the flywheel is the key method of increasing its energy capacity and reducing its weight and volume. At present, a speed of over 60,000 rpm has been achieved in some prototypes. With current technology, it is difficult to directly use the mechanical energy stored in a flywheel to propel a vehicle, due to the need for continuous variation transmission (CVT) with a wide gear ratio variation range. The commonly used approach is to couple an electric machine to the flywheel directly or through a transmission to constitute a so-called mechanical battery. The electric machine, functioning as the energy input and output port, converts the mechanical energy into electric energy or vice versa, as shown in Figure 4.17. Equation (1) indicates that the energy stored in a flywheel is proportional to the moment of inertia of the flywheel and flywheel rotating speed squared. A lightweight flywheel should be designed to achieve moment of inertia per unit mass and per unit volume by properly designing its geometric shape.

The moment of inertia of a flywheel can be calculated by

$$J_f = 2\pi\rho \int_{R_1}^{R_2} W(r) r^3 \, dr,$$ eq2

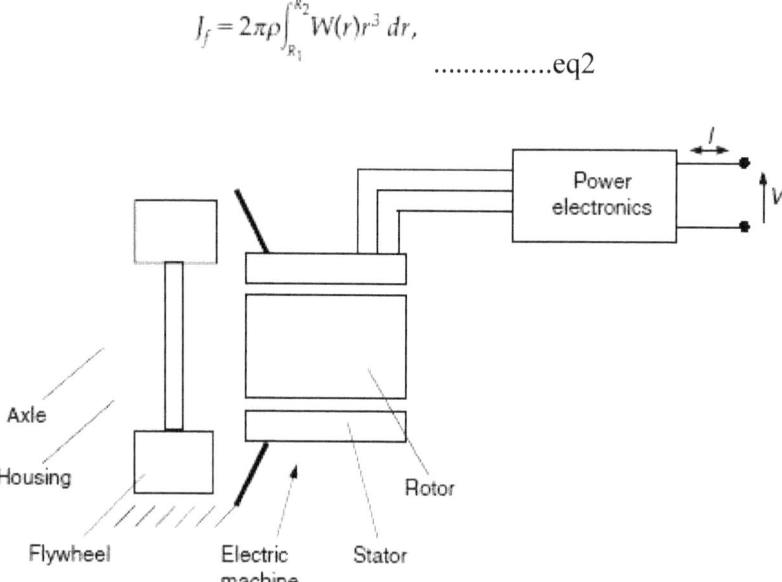

FIGURE 4.17: Basic structure of a typical flywheel system (mechanical battery)

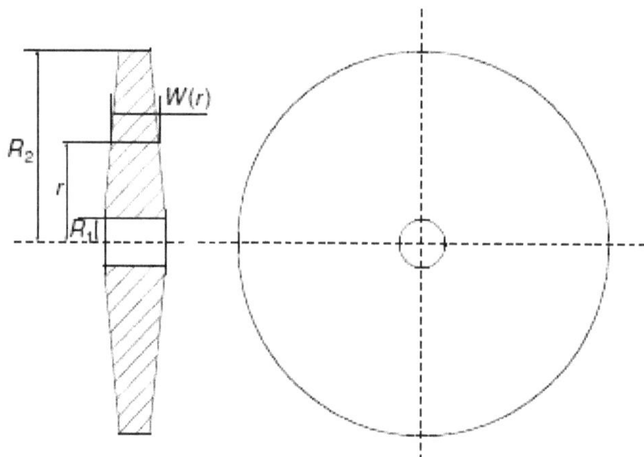

where ρ is the material mass density and $W(r)$ is the width of the flywheelcorresponding to the radius r, as shown in Figure 4.18. The mass of the flywheelcan be calculated by

$$M_f = 2\pi\rho\int_{R_1}^{R_2} W(r)r\,dr.$$

.............eq3

Thus, the specific moment of inertia of a flywheel, defined as the moment ofinertia per unit mass, can be expressed as

$$J_{fs} = \frac{\int_{R_1}^{R_2} W(r)r^3\,dr}{\int_{R_1}^{R_2} W(r)r\,dr}.$$

...........................eq4

Equation (1) indicates that the specific moment of inertia of a flywheel isindependent of its material mass density and dependent solely on its geometricshape $W(r)$.

For a flywheel with equal width, the moment of inertia is

$$J_f = 2\pi\rho\left(R_2^4 - R_1^4\right) = 2\pi\rho\left(R_2^2 + R_1^2\right)\left(R_2^2 - R_1^2\right).$$

...........................eq5

The specific moment of inertia is

$$J_{fs} = R_2^2 + R_1^2.$$

.........................eq6

The volume density of the moment of inertia, defined as the moment of inertiaper unit volume, is, indeed, associated with the mass density of the material.

The volume of the flywheel can be obtained by

$$V_f = 2\pi\int_{R_2}^{R_2} W(r)r\,dr.$$

.......................eq7

The volume density of the moment of inertia can be expressed as

$$J_{fV} = \frac{\rho\int_{R_1}^{R_2} W(r)r^3\,dr}{\int_{R_1}^{R_2} W(r)r\,dr}.$$

..............................eq8

For a flywheel with equal width, the volume density of the moment of inertialS

$$J_{fV} = \rho\left(R_2^2 + R_1^2\right).$$ eq9

Equations (8) and (9) indicate that heavy material can, indeed, reduce the volume of the flywheel with a given moment of inertia.

POWER CAPACITY OF FLYWHEEL SYSTEMS:

The power that a flywheel delivers or obtains can be obtained by differentiatingequation (1) with respect to time, that is,

$$P_f = \frac{dE_f}{dt} = J_f\omega_f\frac{d\omega_f}{dt} = \omega_f T_f,$$

...................eq10

where Tf is the torque acting on the flywheel by the electric machine. When the flywheel discharges its energy, the electric machine acts as a generator and converts the mechanical energy of the flywheel into electric energy. On the other hand, when the flywheel is charged, the electric machine acts as a motor and converts electric energy into mechanical energy stored in the flywheel. Equation (10.44) indicates that the power capacity of a flywheel system depends completely on the power capacity of the electric machine. An electric machine usually has the characteristics as shown in — constant torque and cregion.

In the constant torque region, the voltage of the electric machine is proportional to its angular velocity, and the magnetic flux in the air gap isconstant. However, in the constant power region, the voltage is constant and the magnetic field is weakened with increasing machine angular velocity. In charge of the flywheel, that is, accelerating the flywheel from a low speed, ω0, to a high speed, maximum speed, ω*max*, for example, the torque delivered from the electric machine is

$$T_m = J_f \frac{d\omega_f}{dt},$$

.....................eq11

where it is supposed that the electric machine is directly connected to the flywheel.
The time, *t*, needed can be expressed as

$$t = \int_{\omega_0}^{\omega_{max}} \frac{J_f}{T_m} d\omega = \int_{\omega_0}^{\omega_b} \frac{J_f}{P_m/\omega_b} \omega + \int_{\omega_b}^{\omega_{max}} \frac{J_f}{P_m/\omega} d\omega.$$

.........................eq12

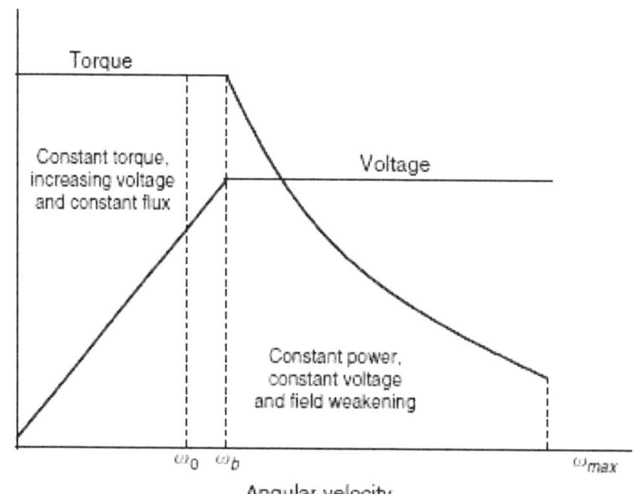

FIGURE 4.19. Typical torque and voltage profile vs. rotational speed

With the given accelerating time, *t*, the maximum power of the electricmachine can be obtained from (12) as

$$P_m = \frac{J_f}{2_t}\left(\omega_b^2 - 2\omega_0\omega_b + \omega_{max}^2\right).$$

.....................eq13

Equation (13) indicates that the power of the electric machine can be minimized by the design of its corner speed or base speed, ω*b*, equal to the bottom speed of the flywheel, ω0. This conclusion implies that the effective operating speed range of the flywheel should coincide with the constant speed region of the electric machine. The power of the electric machine can be minimized as

$$P_m = \frac{J_f}{2_t}\left(\omega_0^2 + \omega_{max}^2\right).$$

.....................eq14

Another advantage achieved by coinciding the operating speed range of the flywheel with the constant power speed range is that the voltage of the electric machine is always constant (refer to Figure 4.19), therefore significantly simplifying the power management system, such as DC/DC converters and their controls.

FLYWHEEL TECHNOLOGIES:

Although higher rotational speed can significantly increase the stored energy (equation [10.35]), there is a limit to which the tensile strength σ ofthe material constituting the flywheel cannot withstand the stress resulting from the centrifugal force. The maximum stress acting on the flywheeldepends on its geometry, specific density ρ, and rotational speed. The maximum benefit can be obtained by adopting flywheel materials that have a maximum ratio of σ/ρ. Notice that if the speed energy is proportional to the ratio of σ/ρ. Table 10.4 summarizes thecharacteristics of some composite materials for ultrahigh-speed flywheels. A constant-stress principle maybe employed for the design of ultrahigh speedflywheels. To achieve the maximum energy storage, every element inthe rotor should be stressed equally to its maximum limit.

Due to the extremely high rotating speed and in order to reduce the aerodynamic loss and frictional loss, the housing inside the flywheel in spinning is always highly vacuumed, and noncontact, magnetic bearings are employed. The electric machine is one of the most important components in the flywheel system, since it has critical impact on the performance of the system. At present, permanent magnet (PM) brushless DC motors are usually accepted in the flywheel system. Apart from possessing high power density and high efficiency, the PM brushless DC motor has a unique advantage that no heat is generated inside the PM rotor, which is particularly essential for the rotor to work in a vacuum environment to minimize the windage loss A switched reluctance machine (SRM) is also a very promising candidate for the application in a flywheel system. SRM has a very simple structure and can operate efficiently at very high speed. In addition, SRM presents a large extended constant power speed region, which allows more energy in the flywheel that can be delivered. In this extended speed region, only the machine excitation flux is varied, and is easily realized. On the contrary, the PM brushless motor shows some difficulty in weakening the field flux induced by the PM. In contrast to applying the ultrahigh-speed flywheel for energy storage in stationary plants, its application to EVs and HEVs suffers from two specific problems. First, gyroscopic forces occur whenever a vehicle departs from its straight-line course, such as in turning and in pitching upward or downward

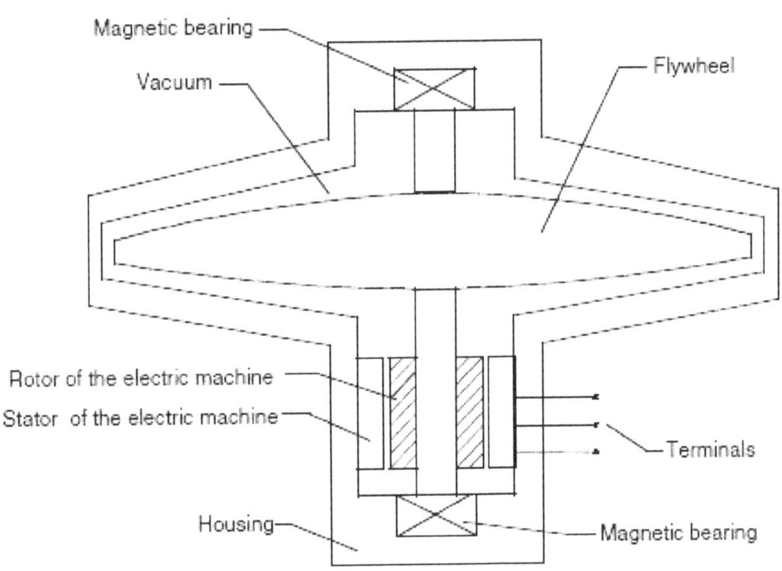

FIGURE4.20. Basic structure of a typical flywheel system

from road grades. These forces essentially reduce the manoeuvrability of the vehicle. Secondly, if the flywheel is damaged, its stored energy in mechanical form will be released in a very short period of time. The corresponding power released will be very high, which can cause severe damage to the vehicle. For example, if a 1-kWh flywheel breaks apart in 1 to 5 sec, it will generate a huge power output of 720 to 3600 kW. Thus, containment in case of failure is presently the most significant obstacle to implementing the ultra-high speed flywheel in EVs and HEVs.

The simplest way to reduce the gyroscopic forces is to use multiple smaller flywheels. By operating them in apair (one half spinning in one direction and another in the opposite direction), the net gyroscopic effect becomes theoretically zero. Practically, it still has some problems related to the distribution and coordination of these flywheels. Also, the overall specific energy and specific power of all flywheels may be smaller than a single one. Similarly, the simplest way to minimize the damage due to the breakage ofthe ultrahigh-speed flywheel is to adopt multiple small modules, but specific power. Recently, a new failure containment has beenproposed. Instead of diminishing the thickness of the rotor's rim to zerobased on the maximum stress principle, the rim thickness is purposely enlarged. Hence, the neck area just before the rim (virtually a mechanical fuse) will break first at the instant that the rotor suffers from a failure. Dueto the use of this mechanical fuse, only the mechanical energy stored in therim needs to be released or dissipated in the casing upon failure.6Many companies and research agencies have engaged in the development ofultrahigh-speedflywheels as the energy storages of EVs and HEVs, such as Lawrence Livermore National Laboratory (LLNL) in the U.S., Ashman Technology, AVCON, Northrop Grumman, Power R&D, Rocketdyne/Rockwell Trinity Flywheel US Flywheel Systems, Power Centre at UT Austin, etc. However, technologies of ultrahigh-speed flywheel are still in their infancy. Typically, the whole ultrahigh-speed flywheel system can achieve a specific energy of 10 to 150 Wh/kg and a specific power of 2 to 10 kW. LLIL has built prototype (20 cm diameter and 30 cm height) that can achieve 60,000 rpm,1 kWh, and 100 kW.

HYBRIDIZATION OF ENERGY STORAGES:

The hybridization of energy storage is to combine two or more energy storages together so that the advantages of each one can be brought out and the disadvantages can be compensated by others. For instance, the hybridization of a chemical battery with an ultracapacitor can overcome such problems as low specific power of electrochemical batteries and low specific energy of ultracapacitors, thereforeachieving high specific energy and high specific power Basically, the hybridized energy storage consists of two basic energy storages: one with high specific energy and the other with high specific power. The basic operation of this system is illustrated in Figure 10.18. In high power demand operations, such as acceleration and hill climbing, both basic energy storages deliver their power to the load as shown in Figure 21 (a). On the other hand, in low power demand operation, such as constant speed cruising operations, the high specific energy storage will deliver its power to the load and charge the high specific power storage to recover its charge lost during high power demand operation, as shown in Figure 21 (b). In regenerative brakingoperations, the peak power will be absorbed by the high specific

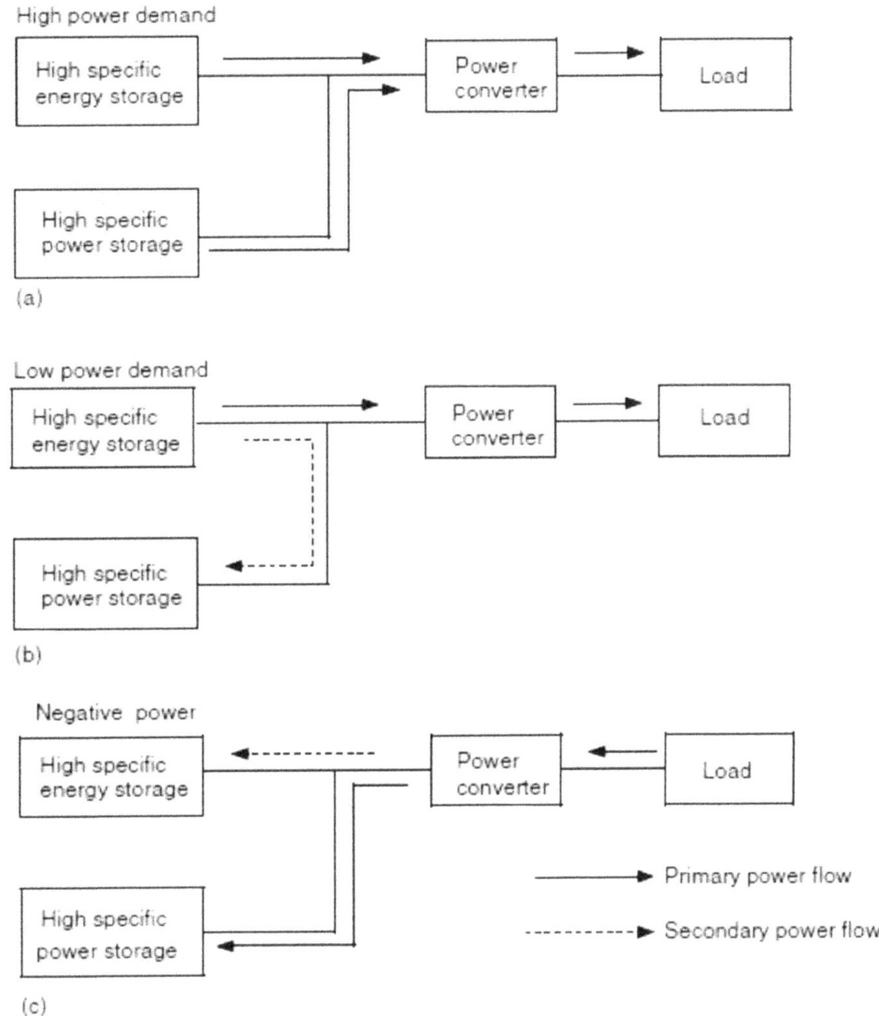

FIGURE 4.21. Concept of a hybrid energy storage operation

power storage, and only a limited part is absorbed by the high specific energy storage. In this way, the whole system would be much smaller in weight and size than if any one of them alone was the energy storage.

Based on the available technologies of various energy storages, there are several viable hybridization schemes for EVs and HEVs, typically, battery and battery hybrids, and battery and ultracapacitor hybrids. The latter is more natural since the ultracapacitor can offer much higher power than batteries, and it collaborates with various batteries to form the battery and ultracapacitor hybrids. During hybridization, the simplest way is to connect the ultracapacitors to the batteries directly and in parallel, as shown in Figure 4.22

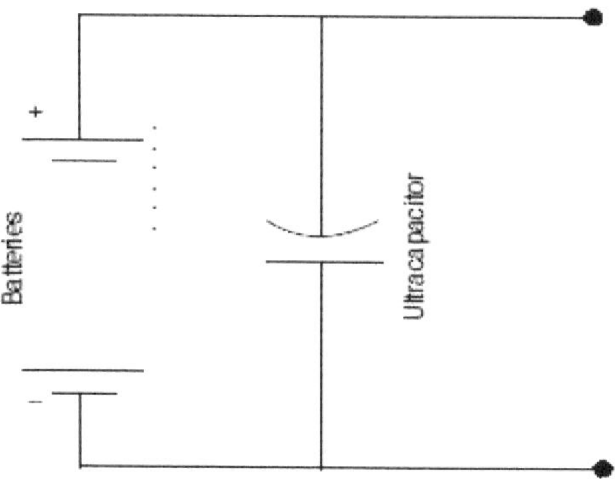

FIGURE 4.22. Direct and parallel connection of batteries and ultra capacitors

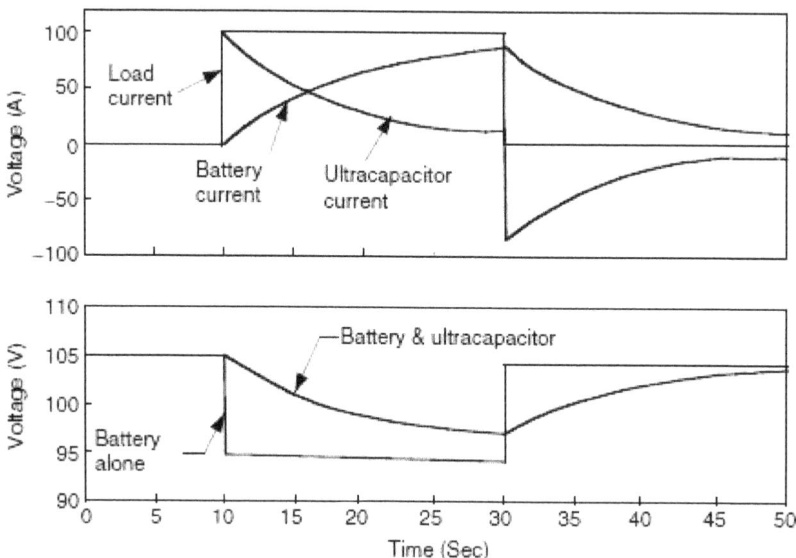

FIGURE 4.23. Variation of battery and ultra capacitor currents and voltages with a step current output change

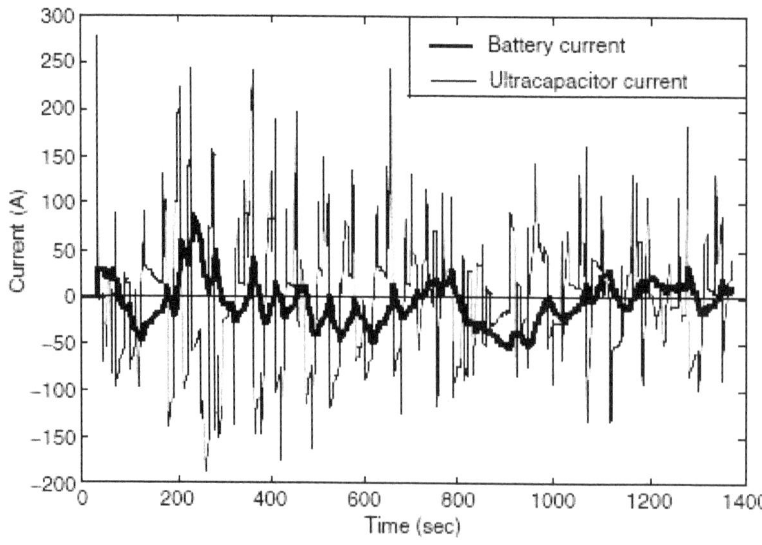

FIGURE4.24: Battery and ultra capacitor currents during operation of HEV in an FTP 75 urban

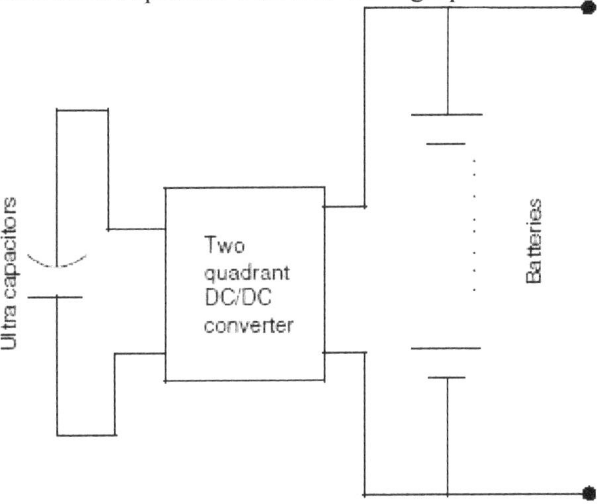

FIGURE 4.25. Actively controlled hybrid battery/ultracapacitor energy storage

In this configuration, the ultracapacitors simply act as a current filter, which can significantly level the peak current of the batteries and reduce the battery voltage drop as shown in Figure 10.20 and Figure 4.25. The major disadvantages of this configuration are that the power flow cannot be actively controlled andthe ultracapacitor energy cannot be fully used. Figure4.25 shows a configuration in which a two-quadrant DC/DC converter is placed between the batteries and ultracapacitors. This design allows the batteries and the ultracapacitors to have a different voltage, the power flow between them can be actively controlled, and the energy in the ultracapacitors can be fully used. In the long term, an ultrahigh-speed flywheel would replace the batteries in hybrid energy storage to obtain a highefficiency,compact, and long-life storage system for EVs and HEVs.

UNIT –V
ENERGY MANAGEMENT STRATEGIES

CLASSIFICATION OF HYBRID ECU:

The hybrid ECU is the heart of the control architecture of any HEV and it is also known energymanagement strategy (EMS). The EMS can be classified into following broad categories:

I. Rule based

II. Optimization based

The ***Rule Based*** strategies consist of following subcategories:

i. **Fuzzy based**: The fuzzy based control strategies are of three types

- Predictive,
- Adaptive
- Conventional

Deterministic Control: The deterministic controllers are subdivided into

- State Machine
- Power follower
- Thermostat Control

The Optimization based strategies are of following types:

i. **Global Optimization:** The global optimization methods are:

- Linear programming methods
- Dynamic Programming
- Stochastic Dynamic Programming
- Genetic Algorithms

ii. **Real time Optimization:** The real time optimization techniques are of following types:

- EFC minimization
- Robust control
- Model predictive

In **Figure 1** the classification tree of the various control techniques is shown. In the subsequent sections the Rule based control strategies will be discussed in detail.

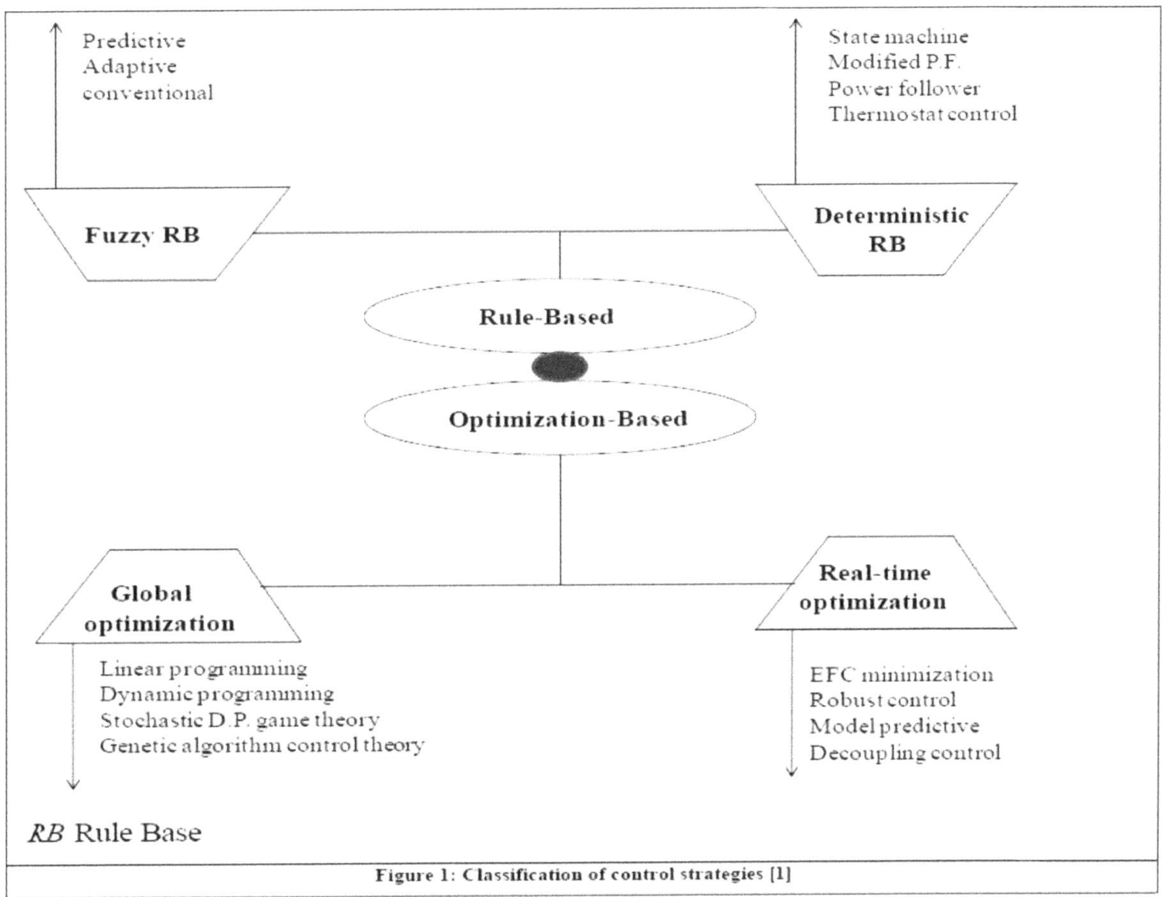

Figure 1: Classification of control strategies [1]

BASIC PRINCIPLES OF RULE BASED CONTROL METHODS:

Rule based control strategies can cope with the various operating modes of HEV. The rule-based strategies are developed using engineering insight and intuition, analysis of the ICE efficiency charts shown in **Figure 2** and the analysis of electrical component efficiency charts.

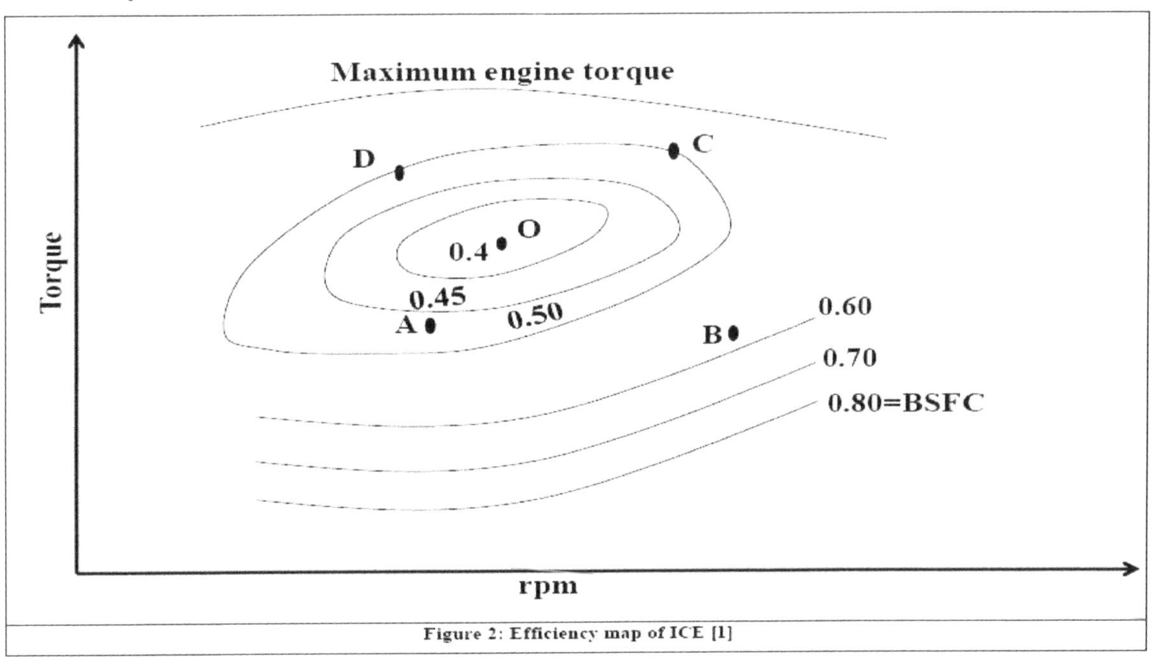

Figure 2: Efficiency map of ICE [1]

An example of developing rule-based strategy can be explained using the ICE efficiency map shown in **Figure 3**. The lines, which are drawn using engineering insight and intuition, divide the map into three regions: **A**, **B**, and **C**. The rules for operation of ICE in these three regions are:

- In the region **A** only, EM is used because in this region the fuel efficiency of the ICE is poor.
- In region **B** only ICE is used since this the region of high fuel efficiency.
- In region **C** both ICE and EM are used.

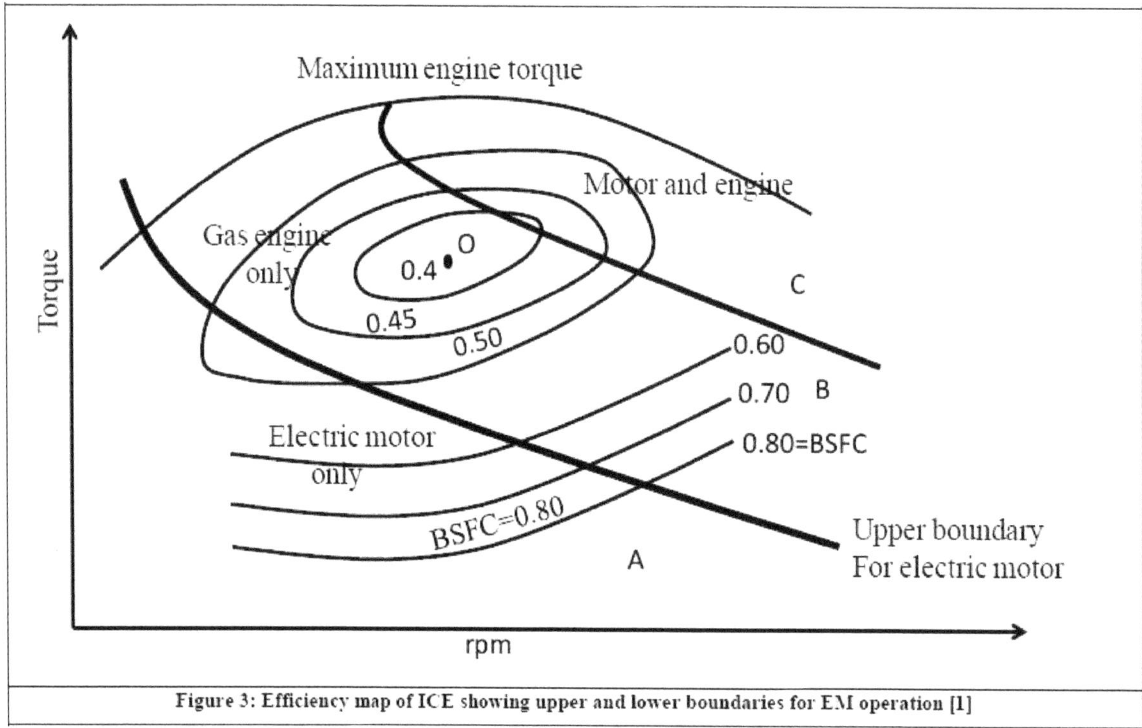

Figure 3: Efficiency map of ICE showing upper and lower boundaries for EM operation [1]

DETERMINISTIC RULE BASED STRATEGIES:

Heuristics based on analysis of power flow in HEV drivetrain, ICE efficiency map and human experiences are utilized to design deterministic rules. These rules are generally implemented using lookup tables to split requested power between the ICE and EM. The most commonly used strategies are:

- Thermostat (on/off) control
- Power follower control
- Modified power follower
- State Machine based controller

In the following sections the controllers marked in bold are explained. Power follower control In this strategy the ICE is the primary source of power and the EM is used to provide additional power when needed by the vehicle. Care is always taken to maintain the SOC of batteries within safe limits. The rule base that is generally used is:

- Below a certain minimum vehicle speed, only the EM is used.
- If the demanded power is greater than the maximum power that the ICE can produce at its operating speed, the EM is used to produce excess power.
- The EM charges the batteries by regenerative braking.

This is a very simple and effective strategy but the major disadvantage is that the efficiency of the entire drivetrain is not optimized

MODIFIED POWER FOLLOWER:

In order to improve the power follower controller a cost function is introduced. The role of this cost function is to strike a balance between fuel consumption and emissions at all operating points of HEV. The rule base for the proposed strategy is as follows: Define the range of operating points: The range ofoperating points (distribution of ICE and EM torques) is represented by the range of acceptable motor torques for the current torque request. The relation between the ICE, EM and requested torque is given by

$$T_{ice} = T_{request} - KT_{em}$$

where

$K =$ motor to ICE gear ratio

......................eq1

The greatest possible positive motor torque defines one extreme of the operating point range: This value is the minimum of three values:

- The driver's torque request
- The maximum rated positive torque of the motor at the current speed
- Maximum available positive torque from the EM, according to the limits imposed by the capability of the batteries

The greatest possible negative EM torque defines the other extreme of the operating point range. This value is the maximum of:

- The difference between the driver's torque request and the maximum positive torque available from the ICE
- The maximum rated negative torque of the EM at the current speed
- The maximum available negative torque from the EM, according to limits imposed by the capability of the battery.

For each candidate operating point, calculate the constituent factors for optimization:

The following steps are involved in this step:

Calculate the fuel energy that would be consumed by the ICE. The actual fuel energy consumed for a given ICE torque is affected by two things:

- Hot, steady state ICE fuel maps
- Temperature correction factors

For a given torque request and motor torque, **equation 1** sets the ICE torque. At this torque and given speed, the ICE map provides the fuel consumed by the ICE when it is hot (**Figure 4**). A cold ICE uses more fuel than a hot ICE. A cold ICE correspondingly produces more emissions than a hot ICE. The outputs of the ICE for cold and hot operation are given by

$$Cold\_use = Hot\_use\left(K_1 + \left(\frac{95 - Temp_{ice}}{75}\right)^{K_2}\right)$$

$$Fuel\_use = Fuel\_hot\left(K_1 + \left(\frac{95 - Temp_{ice}}{75}\right)^{3.1}\right)$$

$$Cold\_use = Hot\_use\left(K_1 + \left(\frac{95 - Temp_{ice}}{75}\right)^{K_2}\right)$$

$$Fuel\_use = Fuel\_hot\left(K_1 + \left(\frac{95 - Temp_{ice}}{75}\right)^{3.1}\right)$$

...........eq2

Calculate the effective fuel energy that would be consumed by EM for a time interval, for example 1 second using the following steps:

- Find fuel energy versus EM torque
- Find versus EM torque, accounting for gain due to regenerative braking SOC
- Combine the curves obtained in above steps
- Determine the equivalent energy by evaluating the curve from step3 at

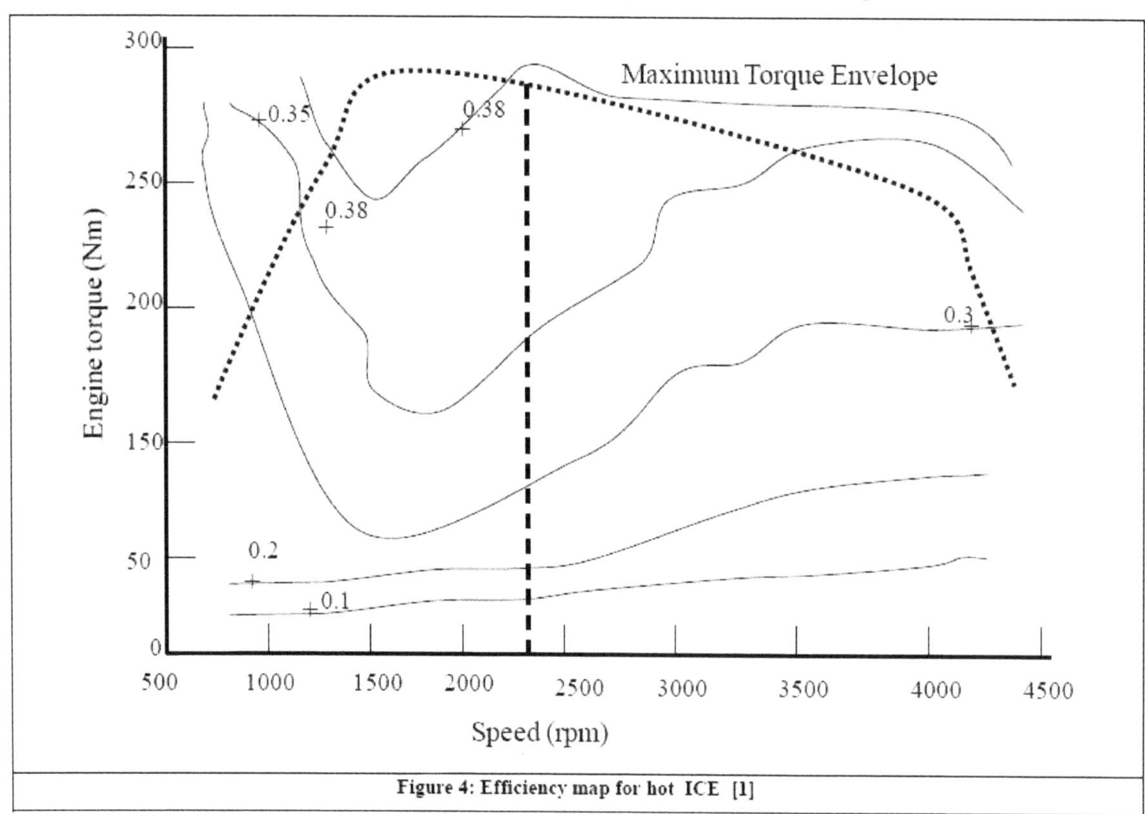

Figure 4: Efficiency map for hot ICE [1]

NORMALIZE THE CONSTITUENT FACTORS FOR EACH CANDIDATE OPERATING POINT:

The goals of minimizing energy and minimizing emissions can conflict with each other. The most efficient operating point will likely produce more pollution than less efficient operating points. Moreover, minimizing the amount of one pollutant can increase the amount of another. Hence, a second goal of the strategy is to allow prioritization of the relative importance of minimizing the fuel use and each of the pollutants. This prioritization is described in Steps 4 and 5 below. Apply user weighting to the results from step iii.: The relative importance of each of the normalized metrices is determined by two weighing factors. The first is a user weighing fore energy and the emissions. This is basically a Boolean switch for the user to toggle if he/she chooses to ignore certain emissions. User K

Apply target performance weighting: The target performance weighing factor is applied to result from step iv. The factor is given by t

$$K_{\text{target}} = \frac{\text{max of time averaged vehicle performance}}{\text{target performance}} \qquad \text{.............eq3}$$

Compute overall impact factor, which is a composite of results of **step iii** to **step v** for all operating points, that is

$$\text{Impact} = \frac{\sum\left(K^{*}_{user} K^{*}_{\text{target}} \text{normalized\_variables}\right)}{\sum\left(K^{*}_{user} K^{*}_{\text{target}}\right)} \qquad \text{..........eq4}$$

The flow chart of the control strategy is shown in **Figure 5**.

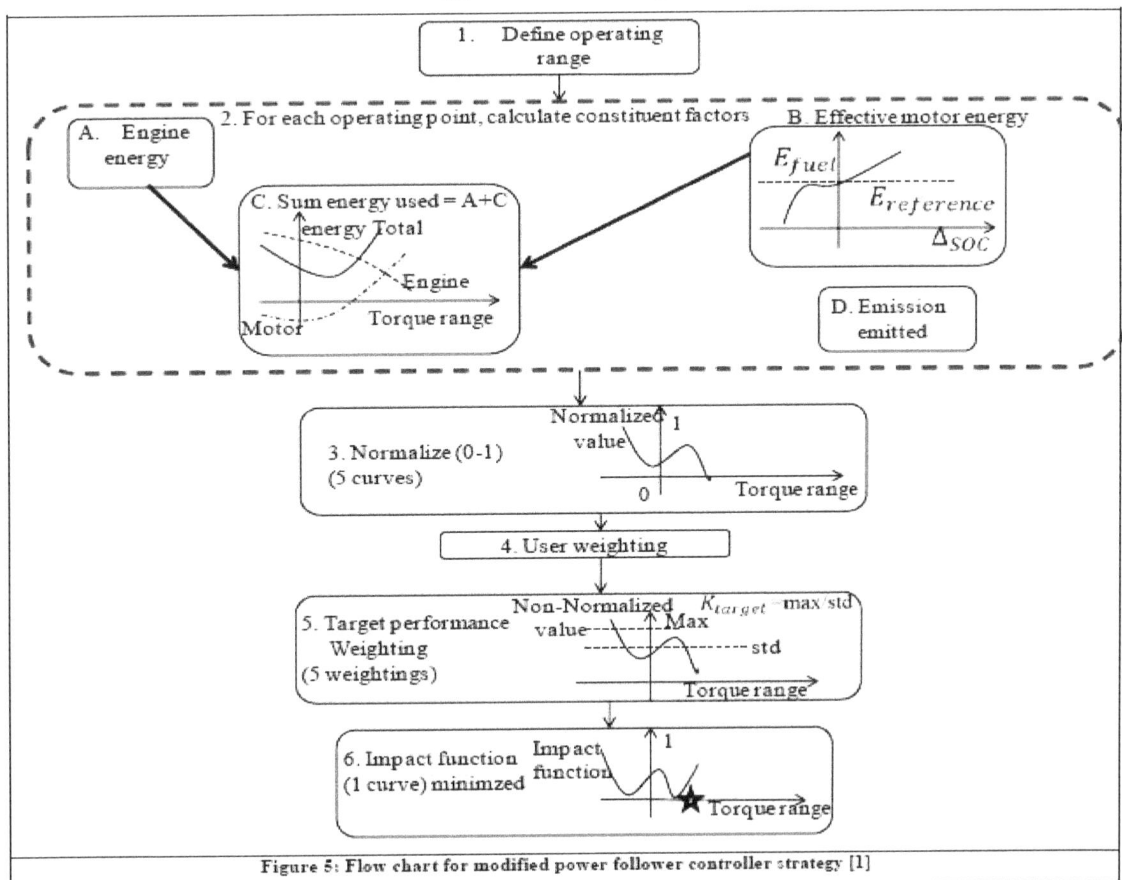

Figure 5: Flow chart for modified power follower controller strategy [1]

The final operating point is the operating point with the minimum impact factor. This strategyimproves the overall performance of the HEV drive train but is computationally expensive

State Machine Based :

The state machine dictates the operating mode of the HEV such:

- ENGINE (ICE propelling the vehicle)
- BOOSTING (both ICE and EM propelling the vehicle)
- CHARGING (ICE propelling the vehicle and charging the battery)

The transition between the operating modes is decided based on:

- the change in driver demand
- a change in vehicle operating condition
- a system or a subsystem fault.

The various states involved in the control strategy are listed in **Table 1**.

Table 1: States of an HEV

State	**ICE**	**Clutch**	**EM**	**Description**
Off	Off	Disengaged	Off	Vehicle off state
EM drive	Off	Disengaged	Motoring	EM propels the vehicle
Regeneration – Low velocity	Off	Disengaged	Generating	Regenerative Braking with ICE disconnected
Regeneration – High velocity	Off	Engaged	Generating	Regenerative Braking with ICE connected
ICE drive	On	Engaged	Off	ICE propelling the vehicle
Boost	On	Engaged	Motoring	ICE and EM propel the vehicle
Charging	On	Engaged	Generating	ICE propels the vehicle and charges the batteries
ICE Stop	Off	Disengaged	Motoring	Motor propelling the vehicle and ICE disconnected
ICE Start	On	Engaged	Motoring	Motor propelling the vehicle and starting the ICE
Bleed	On	Engaged	Motoring	ICE propelling the vehicle and motor discharging the battery

Implementation of a vehicle controller through state machines facilitates fault resilient supervisory control of the whole system.

www.ingramcontent.com/pod-product-compliance
Ingram Content Group UK Ltd.
Pitfield, Milton Keynes, MK11 3LW, UK
UKHW062008290726
14090UKWH00022B/1448